The Power Curse

The Power Curse

Influence and Illusion in World Politics

Giulio M. Gallarotti

Viva Books

New Delhi | Mumbai | Chennai | Kolkata | Bangalore | Hyderabad | Kochi | Guwahati

First Indian Edition 2011

VIVA BOOKS PRIVATE LIMITED

- 4737/23 Ansari Road, Daryaganj, New Delhi 110 002
  E-mail: vivadelhi@vivagroupindia.net, Tel. 42242200
- 76, Service Industries, Shirvane, Sector 1, Nerul, Navi Mumbai 400 706
  E-mail: vivamumbai@vivagroupindia.net, Tel. 27721273, 27721274
- Jamals Fazal Chambers, 26 Greams Road, Chennai 600 006
  E-mail: vivachennai@vivagroupindia.net, Tel. 28290304, 28294241
- B-103, Jindal Towers, 21/1A/3 Darga Road, Kolkata 700 017
  E-mail: vivakolkata@vivagroupindia.net, Tel. 22836381, 22816713
- 7, Sovereign Park Apartments, 56-58, K. R. Road, Basavanagudi, Bengaluru 560 004
  E-mail: vivabangalore@vivagroupindia.net, Tel. 26607409, 26607410
- 101-102 Mughal Marc Apartments, 3-4-637 to 641, Narayanguda, Hyderabad 500 029
  E-mail: vivahyderabad@vivagroupindia.net, Tel. 27564481, 27564482
- Beevi Towers, First Floor, SRM Road, Kaloor, Kochi 682 018, Kerala
  E-mail: vivakochi@vivagroupindia.net, Tel: 0484-2403055, 2403056
- 232, GNB Road, Beside UCO Bank, Silpukhuri, Guwahati 781 003
  E-mail: vivaguwahati@vivagroupindia.net, Tel: 0361-2666386

www.vivagroupindia.com

Published by arrangement with

Lynne Rienner Publishers, Inc.
1800 30th Street, Suite 314
Boulder, Colorado 80301
USA

ISBN : 978-81-309-1529-6

Published by Vinod Vasishtha for Viva Books Private Limited, 4737/23, Ansari Road, Daryaganj, New Delhi - 110 002. Printed and bound by Raj Press, R-3, Inderpuri, New Delhi - 110 012.

S0000 / S0800 / S0810

To Gem,
the source of my own power

Contents

Acknowledgments ix

1 Introduction 1

2 The Theory of the Power Curse 9

3 The Power Curse Across History 37

4 The Bush Doctrine and Power Illusion 99

5 In Lieu of Conclusions 153

References 183
Index 199
About the Book 207

Acknowledgments

THIS PROJECT essentially began with conversations about power with my friend and colleague Peter Rutland in the Public Affairs Center at Wesleyan University. After that inspiring day, ideas took shape and evolved to create this book.

Many individuals helped me on this journey; their generosity and insightfulness contributed immensely to the content of the book. I would especially like to thank David Baldwin, Philip Cerny, Michael Cox, Douglas Foyle, Richard Grossman, Robert Jervis, David Kearn, Joseph Nye, Nicholas Onuf, Lynne Rienner, Peter Rutland, Jack Snyder, and Alexander Wendt. I would also like to acknowledge the intellectual stimulation generated by my sons, Alessio and Giulio, whose youthful insights often led me to greater clarity in my thinking.

A special thanks goes to my wife, Gem, not only for being a constant intellectual inspiration with her precise and penetrating eye, but also for the innumerable ways she has filled my life with love and joy.

THE POWER CURSE

CHAPTER 1
Introduction

WRITING ABOUT power in politics recalls the unenviable task of writing about love in human relations: both phenomena are so intrinsic to their respective social environments that they may even define the very environments themselves. Felix Berenskoetter goes as far as to say that world politics itself is "held together by power relations" (2007, p. 1). But is there anything more to say on the subject? Or more appropriately, dare anyone say anything more? Silence in this case may be the better part of valor. However, closing the book entirely on debates about both love and power would make the world far less interesting, and in the case of power it would also be, from a scholarly and practical standpoint, wrong.

The case against rehashing the analysis of power centers paradoxically on both the pervasiveness of agreement and disagreement. After more than half a century following the inspirational works of Robert Dahl (1957) and Harold Lasswell and Abraham Kaplan (1950), scholars have yet to come up with a more definitive definition of power than Dahl's: of A causing B to do what B would otherwise not do (Barnett and Duvall 2005, p. 40). But concomitantly, after all this time, scholars have been unable to reach agreement on virtually every other aspect of power (Baldwin 2002, pp. 177, 188; Lukes 2007, p. 83). The purpose of this book is neither to trump the popular definition nor to settle age-old debates, but instead to challenge conventional wisdom by asking: Can the augmentation of power be a bad thing for nations?[1] The analysis in this book answers that question in the affirmative. Embracing the idea of a *power curse,* I argue that while the augmentation of power has obvious advantages and benefits, it also possesses inherent qualities that can weaken nations. And in the long run, these inherent weakening effects of power can generate the seeds of its own destruction. To the extent that nations fail to take account of, and correct for, these weakening effects, they are destined to become victims of *power illusion*—that is, in reality they become weaker and more vulnerable than they think. In this latter respect, it is unfortunately the case that the effects of the power curse are so ingrained and compelling that there is a strong tendency for such illusion to manifest itself even in the case of highly sensitized and enlightened national leaders. In other words, the power curse is hard to beat.

Understanding the power curse and power illusion is an especially important venture today. Aside from the need to better understand processes of power in international relations for scholarly and intellectual reasons, the world is at present in an especially tumultuous and sensitive period, and this situation promises to be with us into the future. Indeed, while the issue of power is at the very core of interactions among nations, the study of international power is still quite underdeveloped relative to its importance in international politics (Baldwin 2002; Berenskoetter 2007). Moreover, the traditional visions of power in international politics are poorly suited to understanding the modern world system: there is significant need for a more complex or "polymorphous" theory of power in world politics (Barnett and Duvall 2005, p. 40). The global system is in flux, while the power of nations continues to be the principal instrument for determining our collective fate as a planet. In terms of a historical timeline, there has been a greater transformation in the lives of humans in the past 100 years than in the preceding 12,000 (since the rise of farming communities). We are presently caught in this breakneck wave of change. In a sense, the modern world system has placed us in an environment where everything is coming harder and faster than ever before. And with this speed and magnitude of outcomes, we are faced with ever greater threats and opportunities.

Technology continues to evolve, bringing with it manifold dangers and opportunities. Weapons of mass destruction (WMD) continue to develop in ways that increase the speed and magnitude of threat. It may very well be the case that the level of national power and the capacity to use it appear to be outpacing the ability of nations to control it. The world politic demonstrates both processes of splintering (movements for independence) and processes of collectivization (regional and global integration). Shifting political boundaries and identities continue to present a potential source of instability between and within nations. Forces and processes that have heretofore been under the public and scholarly radar (environment, demographics, disease) have reared an ugly head and demonstrated that the dangers that face us in the twenty-first century are far more extensive and far more pernicious than we had perceived just several generations ago. New dangers from nonstate actors in the form of terrorism and their potential access to WMD have made it all the more difficult to assess, monitor, and manage threats to national security. Shifts in power among the great nations of the world promise a different hierarchy of influence in the future. Globalization and growing interdependence have continued to reshape relations among nations, resulting in both great opportunities as well as instability. The changing fates of democracy and capitalism have generated both points of convergence and points of conflict in world politics. The income gap has increased between rich and poor even after decades of concerted efforts on the part of nations and institutions to address such asymmetries. Indeed, Ulrich Beck (2005) has noted that the changes in the world have created a far more "hazy power space" than has heretofore been embraced by scholars and decisionmakers. Many of the manifestations of power have become transformed in ways that have made them difficult to gauge and consequently manage. Indeed, power itself has been transformed by the principal changes in world politics. This hazy power space requires new questions about power and its changing role in international politics.

In this dangerous new world, national power is the most influential means to shape international relations. Hence, leaders will be ever animated in pursuing national strength. In light of this power quest, the principal lessons of this book about power appear ever more relevant to the national interest. The problem of the power curse in the face of a dynamic world polity requires the utmost vigilance and perspicacity among national leaders. Indeed, the quest for power requires a far more enlightened and sophisticated vision of the process of power accumulation and the pervasive threats that inhere in the very process itself, one that matches the challenges of a complex and changing world. In attempting to compress this lesson into a simple message, for the sake of prescriptive elegance, perhaps we can remind national leaders of the old cliché: be careful what you wish for!

Theoretical Contributions

The theory of the power curse constitutes the principal theoretical contribution of this book. This theory represents the first systematic assessment of how the accumulation of power can diminish the influence of nations. I offer an expanded, integrated articulation of the idea of the paradoxes of power and apply it to a range of case studies. While other scholars have been attentive to such paradoxes, their articulations have tended to focus on more restricted sets of variables; there are also relatively few other case studies devoted to the phenomenon (see Maoz 1989; Baldwin 1989; Yarmolinsky and Foster 1983).

The logic of the theory presented in this book makes it applicable to the study not only of great powers (i.e., those that have reached or approximated primacy), but also of nations all the way down the power line. The logic of the power curse suggests a linear relationship between the processes of amassing power and the generation of weakening effects. In this respect, I propose another explanation of why great powers ultimately decline—by expanding the theoretical menu on hegemonic decline (Waltz 1979; Gilpin 1981; Keohane 1984; Kennedy 1987). But aside from bearing on the question of why primacy is so hard to maintain, I also address commonly scrutinized questions such as why primacy is so difficult to achieve and what obstacles confront nations on the road toward primacy. And the results of this inquiry suggest a number of pitfalls that nations should avoid if they wish to maximize their influence on the world stage (see Chapter 5).

I also explore the power curse within the context of a hard-soft power nexus. Integrating ideas of soft and hard power into a general theory of power facilitates possibilities for finding common ground in visions of power among paradigms of international relations heretofore seen as antithetical: realism versus neoliberalism and constructivism (Barnett and Duvall 2005; Digeser 1992). Such a synthesis would be built on a mutual acknowledgment of the need for a more sophisticated and complex understanding of the way international power relations unfold in the modern world.

In these respects the theoretical contributions of this book are intended to achieve the five principal goals of model building cited by Kevin Clarke and David Primo (2007): foundational, structural, generative, explicative, and predictive. The theory provides insights into a general class of problems: the problems associated with power accumulation (foundational). The theory is integrative in synthesizing disparate theoretical generalizations into a more general logic (structural). It produces nonobvious directions for further study: analyzing the negative consequences of power accumulation (generative). It explores causal mechanisms: the relationship between various types of power resources and the level of influence nations enjoy in the international system (explicative). And finally, the theory is capable of generating forecasts of events or hypotheses that can be tested (predictive).

Methodology

The methodology selected for assessing the explanatory value of the theory is principally that of the historical case study. Given the fact that such a methodology is often limited in its inferential power (representativeness) due to sampling constraints, the very best that a theory may aspire to is descriptive power, given the richness of detail in the analysis of the relationship between the principal variables—in other words, a theory illuminated by history. Moreover, the cases offer somewhat limited variation on the dependent variable, given that they all deal with states or actors facing a deterioration in their power positions (King, Keohane, and Verba 1994; Gerring

2004; George and Bennett 2005). But several things about the case studies in this book raise the inferential value of the analyses.

First, given that all of the five case studies—four in Chapter 3 and one on foreign policy under the George W. Bush administration in Chapter 4—involve either issue-specific primacy (domination of one issue) or general primacy (general supremacy in world affairs), the number of cases is not insignificant with respect to the universe of observations, since even issue-specific primacy in world affairs has not been common historically.[2] Because it is impossible to specify the number of universal observations, one cannot assess the relative size of the sample selected for study in this book. However, because it is reasonable to think that the universal set of observations is somewhat limited, a significant relative number of cases may indeed be represented.

Second, a variety of countries, encompassing a variety of issues and a variety of historical periods, have been selected. The historical continuum runs from Athenian imperialism in the fifth century B.C.E. to US foreign policy in the twenty-first century.[3] The specific issues covered are war, imperialism, foreign policy, monetary leadership, and monetary imperialism. Thus the sample has sufficient breadth to be at least compelling with respect to the inferential value of the findings it generates. More specifically, there are enough cross-unit reference points to at least diminish the inferential "boundedness" normally present in the case study method (Gerring 2004, p. 347; King, Keohane, and Verba 1994, p. 208).

Third, the events selected are important in the history of international politics and, as noted, the nations considered tended to either enjoy or approximate primacy at a general level or in respective issues. As such, the analysis concentrates on events that had a significant impact on international affairs in cases that are especially representative of the phenomena analyzed (i.e., involving very powerful nations). Thus the cases enjoy somewhat greater than usual descriptive and inferential value as a result of crucial-case properties (Eckstein 1975; Gerring 2004, p. 347; King, Keohane, and Verba 1994, pp. 209–212).[4]

Fourth, the processes that link the power curse and power illusion to a decline in influence are carefully traced in the case studies. This "process tracing" raises the inferential power of the theory given the careful comparative scrutiny of the modes of interaction among the principal variables (King, Keohane, and Verba 1994, pp. 85, 86; George and Bennett 2005, pp. 205–232).

Fifth, the analysis contains elements of a structured-focused comparison in evaluating the power curse and power illusion across two sets of cases: in Chapter 3, a different element of the power curse is scrutinized in each case study, while in Chapter 4, all of the elements are scrutinized in the case of US foreign policy under the Bush administration.[5] Such a congruence in the analysis across cases also enhances the inferential value of the case studies (George and McKeown 1985; George and Bennett 2005, pp. 181–204; Keohane, King, and Verba 1994, p. 45).

Finally, while the variation of the dependent variable is limited across cases, there are indeed visible variations of the relevant variables within the cases (i.e., longitudinal variation). Moreover, two further control cases are briefly presented in Chapter 5 in order to address this cross-sectional problem of selection on the dependent variable and to thus enhance the inferential value of the primary cases studied (Keohane, King, and Verba 1994, pp. 129–149). These control cases involve the monetary leadership of the Bank of France in the nineteenth century and British counterinsurgency in Malaya in the twentieth century.

Plan of the Book

Chapter 2 is the principal theoretical chapter of the book. Here I systematically develop the theory of the power curse and also consider the theory within a hard-soft power context.

Chapter 3 presents four case studies on the power curse and power illusion: one on each of the four elements of the power curse. Overstretch is analyzed in the context of Athenian imperialism in the Aegean and Asia Minor during the fifth century B.C.E. Moral hazard is analyzed in the context of the Bank of England and the British state as monetary leaders under the classical gold standard in the nineteenth century. The failure to adapt to complexity is analyzed in the context of the US war in Vietnam. And the vicious cycle of unilateralism is analyzed in the context of Great Britain's experience with the problem of depreciating silver during the late nineteenth and early twentieth centuries.

Chapter 4 analyzes all four elements of the power curse within the context of US foreign policy under the George W. Bush administration. Indeed, the analysis suggests that the policies of the Bush Doctrine were compelling manifestations of the power curse and ultimately led the administration to a state of power illusion. While it had been the intention of the Bush administration to enhance the power and standing of the United States in the world polity, its policies had the unfortunate effect of weakening the country and making it more vulnerable. Moreover, the actions dictated by the Bush Doctrine proved counterproductive in facilitating the administration's most treasured foreign policy goals: combating terrorism, limiting the spread of WMD, and promoting the spread of democracy.

Chapter 5 develops policy implications from the lessons generated by the theory and case studies. The implications are manifest in a set of policy prescriptions or strategies for dealing with the problems of the power curse. Indeed, these strategies underscore why decisionmakers are victimized by the power curse, and ultimately by power illusion, over and over again. The chapter also offers an analysis of control cases as foils for enhancing the inferential value of the principal cases. Finally, the chapter offers some ideas about a more integrated theory of power, one that synthesizes elements from the three leading paradigms of international relations: realism, neoliberalism, and constructivism. In searching for synthesis among these competing paradigms in the realm of power, the ideas offer building blocks for a more general theoretical integration of these three paradigms.

Notes

1. The idea that having more power (however conceived) is good for a nation tends in fact to unify the three main paradigms of international relations (realism, neoliberal institutionalism, and constructivism). Realists have most visibly embraced the utility of power, but neoliberal institutionalists and constructivists have also stressed the desirability of influence through ideas, rules, norms, and institutions (Hall 1997; Keohane 1984; Goldstein and Keohane 1993). Exceptions to this common wisdom are scholars who have analyzed the paradoxes of power (Maoz 1989; Baldwin 1989; Yarmolinsky and Foster 1983).

2. The term "primacy" is used instead of the term "hegemony." The latter has become a loaded term given the scholarly controversy over the subject, so much so that scholars increasingly use the former term. Robert Jervis defines primacy as a condition in which a state "is much more powerful than any other state" (1993, p. 52). I use the term simply to convey a dominant position at the global level, whether on a specific issue or across issues. See also Huntington 1993.

3. Adding an ancient case is especially important because case studies in international relations are commonly restricted to the modern and early modern periods.

4. In this particular manifestation of crucial-case methodology, they represent most-likely scenarios that are instrumental in evaluating theories with respect to falsification.

5. With respect to US foreign policy, the Bush Doctrine makes the case of US foreign policy under Bush an especially crucial historical laboratory for assessing the manifestations of the power curse and power illusion. The Bush Doctrine was oriented around the neoconservative belief that US primacy in the world must strongly dictate the course of US foreign policy—that is, this primacy imparted special roles, responsibilities, and privileges to the United States. Hence, foreign policy itself was grounded in perceptions of power. Moreover, since the doctrine embraced the use of hard power, it is an especially critical case for assessing how the power curse and power illusion manifest themselves within a hard-soft power nexus.

CHAPTER 2

The Theory of the Power Curse

WHILE THE literature on the paradoxes of power has suggested that the quest for power and even primacy can at times produce neutralizing and even counter-productive effects with respect to enhancing a nation's influence, there is yet to emerge a systematic attempt at building a theory of such processes. On a general level, the developments that lead nations to weaken themselves in attempting to augment their own power constitute the power curse. This process is both pernicious and pervasive. It inheres in the very processes that are meant to enhance national power. Hence the quest for power often creates the seeds of its own destruction. Nations that are not sensitized to the problems of the power curse, and hence make no compensatory adjustments in their strategies of power augmentation, invariably fall prey to power illusion. Unfortunately, it is in the nature of the power curse to generate power illusion, because processes that cause the power curse naturally drive nations to neglect or undervalue the weakening effects of the curse. Strategies to avoid power illusion would require leaders to perspicaciously think outside the box and carefully assess the accuracy of perceptions of national power and how they square with the consequences of the actual strategies of national empowerment (see Chapter 5 for prescriptions about confronting the power curse). In fact, the greater the power, the greater the manifestations of the power curse (i.e., the greater the weakening effects). Thus the power curse especially victimizes great powers. But it is clearly in the nature of processes of power augmentation to generate enervating effects for nations of all power classes; hence the power curse afflicts nations all the way down the power line.

The concepts of the power curse and power illusion are based on a more complex and sophisticated concept of power. Indeed, the concepts are based on a concern for net rather than nominal power optimization. Conventional views of power, especially those of realists, have traditionally espoused a vision of *nominal* power optimization—where influence is some linear outcome of the accumulation of hard-power resources—so that each new weapon system, or each new territorial acquisition, leads to a commensurate increase of influence over outcomes in the international system.[1] In a Robinson Crusoe world (where there are no reactions to one's initial actions), such might indeed be the case. But power is not such a phenomenon in a complex world, where each act to augment power generates reactions and consequences (feedback) that impact on the acts and the actors themselves. Sometimes the consequences promote a self-reinforcing process whereby the act generates increased influence: positive feedback (e.g., militarization generates perceptions of invincibility, which lead others to be more compliant with demands and threats). But in other cases, such acts generate countervailing effects that may neutralize attempts to increase influence, and even lead to a net loss in influence: negative feedback (e.g., processes creating countervailing actions that neutralize attempts at enhancing national influence). Hence the process of power optimization is a *net* rather than a *nominal* phenomenon. The traditional nominal view of power stems from a rather myopic view of power and an insensitivity to the context within which power is exercised. This myopia and insensitivity are the principal factors driving power illusion, and they stand in the way of fighting the deleterious effects of the power curse.[2] Those who suffer from power illusion see power as a static, nominal, and simple phenomenon that is not conditioned by the environment in which it is played out.

The power curse manifests itself in four fundamental ways: adapting to complex systems, overstretch, moral hazard, and a vicious cycle of unilateralism. For pedagogical purposes, a heuristic vehicle—the celebrated biblical tale of David and Goliath at the battle in the Valley of Elah as articulated in 1 Samuel 17—is employed to briefly demonstrate the general anatomy of the basic processes representing each of the elements of the power curse.[3] The story of David and Goliath is an especially illuminating device for demonstrating the mechanics of the power curse and power illusion, given that the weakening effects of power are quite glaring in the biblical account. The processes represented within each of the elements of the power curse are more extensively and historically analyzed in the case studies in Chapters 3 and 4.

Adapting to Complex Systems

Robert Jervis (1997) demonstrates that international politics is in fact a complex system. In such a system, relations among actors are never simple, nor are they intelligible through the use of explanatory models that fail to take into account the myriad and manifold interconnections that define interactive structures.[4] Jervis defines a complex system in terms of two prevailing characteristics: first, "a set of units or elements that are interconnected so that changes in some elements of their relations produce changes in other parts of their relations"; and second, "the entire system exhibits properties and behaviors that are different from those of its parts" (p. 6). Jervis goes on to note that the presence of complexity creates significant methodological difficulties in measuring and conceptualizing power (p. 74).[5] Indeed, system effects can turn the intuitive world that we understand and value on its head, often producing surprising results (i.e., powers of prediction in such environments often fall short).

A number of fundamental processes characterizing complexity are underscored in the literature. First, interconnections among actors are complicated in that they involve many factors (third parties and both direct and indirect effects that are not always obvious and are difficult to ascertain) that interact to produce specific outcomes. Because of this complexity, it is difficult to both fully foresee and even control one's fate. In such conditions, outcomes can be surprising and counterintuitive. Often, actions intended to bring about specific objectives can end up being counterproductive or self-defeating. Second, complexity is driven by feedback. Feedback represents reactions to and consequences of actions that affect the actions themselves in a way that may create outcomes that diverge from original expectations. Feedback is absolutely pervasive, because for every action there is some resulting reaction somewhere in the system that feeds back onto the original action and alters the impact of that action. When such feedback is pernicious or debilitating to nations, it is referred to as negative feedback. This recalls Dahl's concept (1957) of negative power: where actions on the part of some actors generate negative reactions from other actors. Finally, relationships are often nonlinear. This represents discontinuities in the relationships among actors. Often, small initiatives may have an enormous impact well beyond the scale of the initiatives. Conversely, very large initiatives may have very little impact on relations or outcomes in a system.

In a system such as international politics, where relationships and outcomes are complex and tightly coupled, stochastic and rarely linear, there are manifold possibilities for generating consequences that are self-defeating for nations pursuing strategies of power augmentation, whether within or across specific power resources (Jervis 1997). For instance, augmentation through excessive strategies targeted at hard power such as force and threat will alienate target nations and will incur the censure of third-party nations. This feedback will compromise the soft power of the perpetrating nations.

Over and above the self-punishment that emanates from interdependence, much political capital is eliminated in multilateral institutions that have traditionally empowered perpetrator nations. But even in the absence of force and threat, reliance on building up tangible resources without complementary soft actions—to make such resources less of a latent threat—may elicit reactions that are self-defeating. Without abating perceptions of latent threat, security dilemma outcomes may induce competing nations to undertake countervailing actions that neutralize attempts to obtain primacy or enhanced strength through tangible power resources, as in the case of an arms race or economic rivalry (Jervis 1997; Huntington 1993). However, even the supposedly innocuous "carrot" may generate some deleterious and unintended consequences for the donor. While foreign aid has been a mainstay of diplomacy in North-South relations, and transactions between nations have appeared to be mutually beneficial, few donor nations escape the backlash from both Northern and Southern societies: accusations of neoimperialism. Moreover, third-party actors have always looked at such attempts as bribery, and consequently the standing of donor nations has fallen even among actors not directly involved in the transactions.

Also, in an interdependent world, actions on the part of foreign populations and states have significant impacts on the interests of nations. Each nation faces a plethora of actors (states, transnational actors, individuals) in the world polity that can perpetrate actions either for or against its interests. So in some sense a condition of reciprocity exists in which there are actions and reactions in world politics among these actors. Favorable actions or policies on the part of nations toward other nations or actors may elicit reactions that are equally favorable with respect to particularistic goals; one may think of the reaction from a hostage population that has been liberated in war. Conversely, unfavorable actions may elicit reactions in kind; one may think of partisan groups fighting off an occupying force. To some extent this functions as an interactive network with very loosely specified expectations governing exchange (Gallarotti 1989). Economists have studied such arrangements in the context of loosely specified labor contracts. One of the issues studied has been the effects of such contracts on efficiency. Harvey Leibenstein (1966) coined the terms "x-efficiencies" and "x-inefficiencies" to describe differing levels of productivity that result from factors other than the structure and application of inputs (i.e., allocative efficiency). Even with similar input allocations, efficiency among firms may still vary greatly because of factors unrelated to the application of inputs (e.g., motivation, incentive schemes, differing managerial styles). In the international political system, as in the firm, these interactional networks may take a variety of forms that impact directly on the influence that nations may realize from their relations with other actors or nations. Hard power, for instance, may generate substantial x-inefficiencies (i.e., actions that cut against the interests of the perpetrating nations). When the activation of hard power takes a menacing form, naturally the perpetrating nations can expect adversarial reactions from target nations and populations. There is no clearer manifestation of this than some of the self-defeating elements in George W. Bush's policy to eradicate the threats of terrorism and weapons of mass destruction. Taking an aggressive and unilateralist approach to increasing the security of Americans by wiping out such threats generated reactions from target nations that have enhanced those threats all the more (see Chapter 4). In this respect, a number of scholars have proposed soft power as a preferable means of fighting terrorism (Lennon 2003).

Problems of complexity that confront nations are likely to grow in proportion with a nation's power. First, more powerful nations possess many more networks of latent and manifest interactions (i.e., things they are doing or could do around the world) within the international system, because of their growing resources (both hard and soft) and a growing presence in the system (see discussion on overstretch later in the chapter), thus increasing the complexity of their relations and challenging their capacity to understand and control the manifold consequences of this greater global network of interaction (Kennedy 1987). In short, more powerful nations have so much more to figure out and manage due to their increasing engagement within the international system. With this greater complexity facing them, greater powers are more likely to be victimized by the adverse consequences of this complexity. Second, the greater the power, the less vigilant that nations need to be in understanding and managing this complexity.[6] Analogously, very rich people simply need not worry about every turn in the investment environment that may adversely impact on their wealth. Marginal losses in influence become relatively smaller with growing power; hence stronger nations need not pay as much attention to such shifts and may consequently tend to mismanage their power relations. This would qualify as a complexity-specific manifestation of moral hazard. As nations become more powerful, and hence perceive themselves to be decreasingly vulnerable, they need not be as fastidious and perspicacious about managing risks. For weaker powers, because of their greater vulnerability, fewer risks are considered unimportant. But in a complex world, boundaries are extremely difficult to ascertain, as complex feedback loops may make what seem to be marginal questions actually more important questions (Jervis 1997). For example, whether gains and losses in bipolarization are central or marginal to great powers depends on whether or not the domino theory is correct (Jervis 1997; Waltz 1979).[7]

The story of David and Goliath starkly attests to the fact that Goliath and the Philistines were excessively victimized by their failure to adapt to complexity. Interactions among the Israelites and the Philistines were in fact never simple, fully predictable, nor fully understandable. Feedback loops colored all sets of their interactions, whether on or off the battlefield. While there is little evidence that the Israelites were any more enlightened than the Philistines in adapting to complexity, still the deficiencies of the Philistines were particularly glaring. To a large extent, moral hazard itself created a major disincentive to adapt to complexity. After all, superior power, collectively in their army and in their great champion Goliath, made them less perspicacious about keeping up with changes in weaponry and its battlefield applications. Hence the sling used by a shepherd boy became all the more dangerous, because the Philistines did not fully analyze and anticipate the manifold ways in which a projectile might penetrate the defenses of their champion. A better-adapted plan might have featured a helmet with a lower forehead plate, or an alteration in any or all of the tactical deficiencies demonstrated by Goliath and his people. Complexity generates change and consequently new challenges in military adaptation, and in this respect the Philistines were deficient in adjusting. David appears to have adapted much better to the tactical imperatives given the choice of Goliath's weapons. While David's refusal to don armor and use conventional weapons may seem irrational and may feed well into the religious significance of the story (i.e., the giant was no match for the defenseless boy while God was on the side of David), still one could interpret this from a military perspective as maximizing the destructive force of the chosen weapon. The sling required maximum physical freedom, as its effectiveness was based on speed and agility. A sword and armor would have just slowed David down.

In a related vein, the outcome of the battle attests to the presence of what complexity theorists refer to as nonlinearities and counterintuitive or unexpected outcomes (Jervis 1997). More specifically, changes in outcomes often do not change as expected in an incremental fashion in response to incremental changes in the underlying conditions. If one were doing a relative assessment of the value of each incremental addition to the weaponry and battlefield experience of the two protagonists, it would surely reflect an incremental advantage developing in favor of the giant. Both Goliath's experience and weaponry painted a relatively imposing picture. But in fact, and counterintuitively, the relative advantages of Goliath in experience and weaponry worked against him. Given the bulkiness of the armor and his knowledge of conventional battlefield tactics, he placed himself in the most vulnerable position. Unfortunately for Goliath, with respect to this particular battle scenario, his experience led him to do all of the wrong things (Rofe 1987, p. 117). David's inexperience, on the other hand, worked in his favor. He had never taken part in battle and had no experience in contemporary battlefield tactics. A more experienced and knowledgeable soldier may have indeed tried to take on Goliath on the giant's own terms, which would have been disastrous for the challenger. But surely the courage would have been difficult to stir up in a warrior who was well versed in what the giant could do in battle; hence a conventional challenge may never have materialized. Indeed, no Israelite soldier ever emerged (until David) to challenge Goliath after forty days of taunting.

These deficiencies with respect to complacency regarding military research and development and the counterintuitive outcomes with respect to weapons and tactics were compounded by the Philistine choice of goading the Israelites into battle at Elah. The strategy of having their champion taunt the Israelites and mock their God (twice a day for forty days) caused significant anger on the part of the Israelites: "shall ye be our servants" and "I do taunt the armies of Israel today" (1 Samuel 17:9–10). This generated a greater countervailing posture on the part of the targeted Israelites and thus created even greater hostility toward Goliath and the Philistines: extensive negative feedback. Samuel's account attributes David's acceptance of the challenge to the great anger that Goliath's irreverence generated in the young man: "Who is this uncircumcised Philistine, that he should have taunted the armies of the living God?" (1 Samuel 17:26).[8] This anger was instrumental in causing the young David to take his leap of faith. The anger was all the more compounded when Goliath actually mocked David on the battlefield: "The Philistine cursed David by his God" (1 Samuel 17:43). In this respect, the negative feedback that proved detrimental to the giant was manifest in the heightened countervailing force delivered by David as a result of the latter's anger. In war, as well as in any competition, one never wants to make their opponents angrier, as such vituperation will make opponents more fierce in their opposition. Speculating from the account of Samuel, it appears that without the anger that was generated by the giant's taunting and insults, it would have been difficult for David to do several of the things that ultimately led to the death of the giant: first, to summon the courage to challenge Goliath and stay the course of battle; second, to summon the strength to cast a projectile at a speed that actually penetrated the giant's skull; and third, to summon the incredible strength needed to lift Goliath's massive sword and perpetrate a sufficiently vigorous blow to sever the giant's head. It would appear that the physiological manifestation of anger with respect to the release of adrenalin made an angry David far braver and stronger than the perceived persona, and hence gave him the capability of defeating a giant who appeared far less animated about fighting a shepherd boy.

Overstretch

In addition to the effects of complexity, the augmentation of power generates another deleterious consequence in the form of overstretch. In their analysis of great powers, Paul Kennedy (1987), Robert Gilpin (1981), and Jack Snyder (1991) have perhaps best highlighted the problem of overstretch. They underscore the effects of different levels of analysis in promoting this tendency. Snyder analyzes expansion as a process driven by the domestic political interests that benefit from such expansion. Kennedy sees overstretch as a structural pathology of economic growth leading to expansion, but this greater global presence becomes increasingly difficult to support in a world of greater competition when nations are faced with inherent economic decline. Gilpin underscores the interplay of internal and external factors leading to overextension. He posits that great powers will be overextended in maintaining their international position as a result of a tendency to overinvest in the provision of public goods and a concomitant tendency for the costs of maintaining an international presence to rise. This greater burden will continually outpace the capacity of the internal military-economic system, which itself is in decline, to support that position. For all three scholars, the possibilities of overstretch are an occupational hazard of the quest for power. This is the case because expansion and the quest for power are self-feeding processes: the more that is bitten off, the greater the appetite must become to accommodate increasing nourishment. This will occur for three reasons.

First, the expanding quest for influence breeds mission creep. A growing presence in the international system is self-reinforcing because the maintenance costs of involvement in foreign affairs grow along with the size of the stake in the system (Kennedy 1987; Jervis 2003a).[9] Empires are the best example of such a process. The growth in empires has been traditionally shaped by the need to protect trade routes in the colonial network, which has called for more bases and more soldiers (Bartlett 1969; Galbraith 1960). Attempts at domination or primacy have historically shown a tendency toward mission creep. John Galbraith (1960) underscores the compelling nature of this process in the expansion of British empire in the nineteenth century: expansion was reinforced by what he refers to as "turbulent frontiers." Robert Jervis (2003a) avers that dominant nations are especially prone to develop pockets of negative feedback that adversely affect their standing in the international system because of mission creep: a growing global presence leads to many points of involvement that generate international hostility toward the dominant nation.

Second, nations can experience a process of growing dependence on their expanded domains. Much of this is a normal function of being increasingly endowed with external sources of influence like tribute, colonies, bases, markets, resources, and allies (Kennedy 1987, p. xxiii).[10] But above and beyond this normal dependence, nations may become overly dependent on these external sources of power because of moral hazard: nations can be lax about developing internal resources to achieve self-sufficiency when they have an expanded domain that provides many benefits with minimal internal adjustment costs. For example, both dependence and overdependence plagued the ancient Roman and Athenian empires (the latter is discussed in Chapter 3). In both cases the domestic economies grew increasingly unable to evolve in ways that were able to meet the costs of supporting a large empire (French 1964).

Finally, both mission creep and growing dependence are driven by domestic political effects that reinforce this expansion. Expansion often creates new interest groups and energizes old interest groups in the domestic political game that benefit from such expansion, and hence use their political influence to promote expansionist policies. Jack Snyder (1991) has argued that such domestic interests become politically dominant in influencing state policies when they can form greater coalitions among themselves and others (through logrolling).[11] Snyder goes on to show the impact of this process in numerous case studies of empire on the part of industrialized states over the past two centuries. Fred Block (1977) demonstrates how the growing internationalism of US foreign policy after World War II was strongly driven by US business interests that benefited from foreign investment and trade. But while Block and Snyder chronicle domestic reinforcement of expansion in pluralistic-democratic systems, domestic factors are nonetheless important in more autocratic systems where the actions and interests of smaller elite groups and autocrats themselves provide the domestic political stimulus for expansionist policies.

One of the most salient and pernicious manifestations of this process in the context of soft and hard power occurs as a result of popular domestic reactions to such expansion, both in the expansionist nation and in the target nation. Very often the domestic economic and social burdens of such overstretch undermine the domestic popular support that is necessary to maintain it.[12] This could have manifold consequences for the policy of expansion. One of the most pernicious is the fact that it could create political shockwaves at home that severely undermine the position of the ruling regime or administration, thus leaving it in turmoil. This may enervate the international influence of that nation for a variety of reasons owing to the fact that the nation is politically incapable of effectively managing its foreign relations in a state of political weakness. In this case, erstwhile enemies may take more liberties against it geostrategically, nations (whether hostile or friendly) may be less influenced by its demands and requests, and it will be incapable of pursuing compelling opportunities in the international system. But also enervating in this context is the soft power compromised on the part of target populations and other nations. Even when not overtly imperialistic, a growing international presence causes disturbances among the people of target nations. They may be x-inefficient in attending to the interest of the expansionist nation, and they may be x-efficient in undermining the foreign presence. Either way, such a posture generates substantial weakening effects for the expansionist nation because it increases the burden of expansion. In terms of third-party nations (not targets of expansion), the expansion itself may compromise their goodwill and potential support, such that the expansionist nation is left with fewer venues of assistance in maintaining its international presence (i.e., more potential adversaries and fewer allies).

With respect to the David and Goliath story, Samuel tells us little about the characteristics of the Philistines as warriors and imperialists. We do know from Samuel that the Israelites and Philistines fought a number of destructive wars, with the Philistines having their way with the Israelites early on and the Israelites turning the tide under Saul and David. Actually, the historical texts tell us more about such things and so in this respect the biblical account will be augmented by history. The Philistines originated as a sea-faring people with possible connections to the island of Crete. Their empire and settlements were at first constricted to coastal areas, where they emerged as a powerful political and commercial force in the region (Erlich 1996, p. 23). Their own imperial ambitions to expand inland were compounded by a regional power vacuum in the late Bronze Age and early Iron Age that was created by the decline of Egypt and Assyria (Erlich 1996, p. 24; Gray 1962, p. 124). As they expanded inland with an increasing number of cities and possessions, and the problem of mission creep augmented the burden of expansion, the empire's weight became exceedingly difficult to bear. This was mainly a function of a people who were more advantaged on the seas and less equipped to maintain an empire on land. But the expansion set in motion countervailing forces that compounded the difficulty and led the Philistine imperial machine further into overstretch (Gray 1962, p. 126).

As we see from Samuel, the ongoing Philistine assaults and convincing victories over the combined tribes of Israel in the period of the Judges led to great cooperation among the divisive tribes (negative feedback). The battle at Elah, as noted, was the first initiative of a monarchy that was largely established (under Saul) to create greater political unification as a means of fielding strong armies against Philistine assaults. Indeed that battle was won by the Israelites, but the campaigns that followed showed the Philistines often crumbling in the face of the heroic David and his unified armies forged from the disparate tribes. Moreover, the power vacuum, while it limited confrontation from heretofore hegemonic powers in the region, also allowed the rise of a number of smaller states to a greater power status, and these states became ever more menacing to the Philistines. Among those states that were especially menacing were Judah, Moab, Ammon, Edom, Damascus, Hammath, the Aramaean states, and of course the Israelites themselves (Gray 1962, p. 124). Indeed, the Philistines were cursed with great enough power to overexpand significantly inland, and create adversaries of numerous states, which in the end compounded their demise.

Moral Hazard

Perceptions of limited vulnerability, due to the possession of insurance or significant power over conditions that may affect actors, generally have a tendency to lead those actors either toward complacency about developing alternative means of staving off adverse outcomes or toward more reckless behavior. All such behavioral consequences may in effect lead actors to become even more vulnerable than would otherwise be the case in the absence of such insurance or power. Social scientists have commonly referred to such tendencies as moral hazard.[13] The examples in everyday life are numerous: seatbelts and vehicles with four-wheel drive encourage drivers to speed and drive less defensively. Similarly, the level of insurance that actors purchase has pronounced effects on generating hazardous behavior. The phenomenon is especially visible in financial markets with the 2008–2009 subprime crisis and subsequent financial meltdown: possibilities to diversify and transfer risk have led to extremely risky lending on the part of banks and other financial intermediaries.

Since reckless behavior and complacency will rise with perceptions of limited vulnerability, it stands to reason that as nations become more powerful they will also more likely become victimized by moral hazard. In this case, well-endowed nations may be delinquent in fully appreciating and developing a full range of resources that could serve them in facing the challenges emanating from the world system. As noted, a tendency to be complacent in the face of complexity is one manifestation of moral hazard, but the consequences of moral hazard are more extensive and manifold. They embrace numerous modes of reckless and complacent tendencies that enervate or place nations at greater risk. Robert Gilpin (1996, p. 413), for example, observes that with respect to the power structure among national economies, primacy generates moral hazard effects in the form of a tendency toward stasis (i.e., avoiding change). Societies that have enjoyed the fruits of economic primacy have an incentive toward complacency when assessing opportunities for alterations in economic institutions and policies. In this respect, nations that have enjoyed primacy have faced a natural tendency toward economic decline because they are less vigilant than rising powers in instituting changes that would keep them at the head of the power hierarchy (i.e., a "fat cat" syndrome). Building on a Schumpeterian theory of economic decline (i.e., that the success of capitalism undermines risk-taking among entrepreneurs), Gilpin applies this logic at a more general political-economic level by citing the domestic effects of primacy. He observes that in a nation that enjoys political-economic primacy, "society becomes conservative, less innovative and less willing to run risks" (1981, p. 154). In becoming more concerned with preserving the gains that have come with such primacy, society is less animated in pushing leaders to stay ahead of the power curve in terms of innovation and resources. In a similar vein, John Mearsheimer (2001, p. 34) locates a tendency toward complacency at the highest levels of power accumulation (hegemony), and this complacency will diminish actions geared toward the accumulation of power (stasis) and primacy.

In the story of David and Goliath, Goliath and the Philistines fell victim to moral hazard in a number of ways. And paradoxically, as a result, their great strength, both as an army of warriors and in the person of their champion, actually brought about their undoing. Specifically with respect to the battle between the two champions, Goliath's great physical advantage over what he perceived to be a harmless shepherd made him easy prey for what ended up being in actuality a highly skilled warrior. Samuel's account is ripe with manifestations of the giant's overconfidence. The detail of the size of the giant and of his armor and weapons, in contrast to the modest armaments of the boy (staff, sling, five stones), underscores the relative imbalance between the warriors (1 Samuel 17:4–7, 40).[14] The relative asymmetry is all the more romanticized in Samuel's account when Saul implores the "youth" not to attempt battle with a "man," and also when David refuses to don armor and carry a sword into battle, preferring his simple shepherd's gear (1 Samuel 17:33, 38–39). The overconfidence that left Goliath easy prey to the deadly aim of the shepherd boy is aptly chronicled. The giant approached the boy with "disdain," seeing that he was "but a youth, and ruddy, and withal of a fair countenance" (1 Samuel 17:42). Both curiosity and overconfidence brought the giant "nearer and nearer unto David" (1 Samuel 17:41).[15] The epic story of David's inspired actions that follows is familiar to everyone, irrespective of culture and faith. But there may be an untold story of Goliath's demise that sheds greater light on the incident. It is apparent that both the Philistines and Goliath were at fault. Complacency and overconfidence led them to deadly actions.

Goliath was, in effect, muscle-bound both physically and militarily. Success in conventional battle tactics gave an edge to unusually large warriors with especially bulky armor in such one-on-one confrontations. But great size and heavy armor create vulnerabilities against more unusual weapons, such as the sling, that require speed and quickness. In actuality, the sling has historically been a deadly battlefield weapon whose use has been chronicled back to the Bronze Age (Rosenthal and Mozeson 1990, p. 62).[16] The fact that it was being used by a shepherd boy made it all the more dangerous as shepherds of the period used slings as a weapon against animals that preyed on their herds. It is far harder to hit an animal of prey from a distance than a large and immobile target up close. In fact, Samuel's account pays just such respect to David's skill with a sling in the boy's reply to Saul's pleas not to fight: "Thy servant kept his father's sheep; and when there came a lion, or a bear. . . . I went out after him, and smote him" (1 Samuel 17:34–35). Surely a more perspicacious warrior and tribe, who were less blinded by the moral hazard of superior physical power in conventional battlefield armaments, would have been more vigilant against the use of slings and leery of the skills of shepherds with such instruments. Goliath instead might as well have painted a bull's-eye on his forehead, and the Philistines let him.

But aside from poor consultation and preparation for their champion, the story of David suggests that the Philistines may have collectively fallen prey to moral hazard in other ways. The place selected for battle, the Valley of Elah, was anything but a perfect strategic location for a battle with the Israelites (Rofe 1987, p. 123). Both armies, as Samuel recounts, stood on opposing mountain sides of the valley (1 Samuel 17:3). First, such a battle theater gives no one the incentive to attack, as the attacker would be launching an assault uphill against an entrenched army: a suicidal scenario even in the face of inferior weapons and manpower. It is no surprise that Goliath came out for forty consecutive days to challenge the Israelites to send forth a champion, given the military stalemate. Moreover, the Israelites knew their terrain well, and history tells us that in their actual wars, the Israelites were skilled tacticians especially gifted at exploiting geographic opportunities in theaters of battle (Rosenthal and Mozeson 1990, pp. 14, 22). The Philistines had compelling reasons for falling victim to moral hazard and consequently to power illusion. They had convincingly defeated the Israelites in numerous battles before, as is duly recounted in the earlier chapters of the Book of Samuel, with the most stunning defeat causing the Israelites to lose the famous Arc of the Covenant (1 Samuel 4–5).[17] Second, it was the first major military exercise for Israel under the new monarchy (which was born as a result of this battle), and Saul (the new king and commander) had exhibited neither the military skill of his successor David nor the political skill of David in reining in the divisive tribal culture among the Israelites. His bouts with depression certainly didn't enhance his skills as commander and chief (Erlich 1996, p. 24; Gray 1962, p. 128). Third, the

Israelite army was a militia force generally composed of peasants who were simply defending their homelands (Erlich 1996, p. 23; Finkelstein and Silberman 2006, p. 1). Fourth, both biblical and archeological accounts suggest that the Philistines were ahead of the Israelites in the military adaptation of iron (Gray 1962, p. 124; 1 Samuel 12:19–22). Finally, Goliath was considered unbeatable. All of these made a suboptimal theater of battle supportable. The victimization from moral hazard manifest itself in the general outcome of the battle, an outcome that revealed the neutralization of all of the Philistines' military advantages. Upon the giant's collapse, they retreated from a poorly unified militia army that was attacking them uphill. So unprepared were the Philistines for the course of events that took place, that the Israelites were able to advance as far as the Philistine camp and destroy it as well (1 Samuel 17:53).[18] It is clear that the moral hazard that plagued the Philistines, notwithstanding their military superiority, discouraged them from contemplating a "plan B."[19]

Vicious Cycle of Unilateralism

Finally, the power curse is compounded by the emergence of a vicious cycle of unilateralism. The consequences of moral hazard with respect to international regimes and organizations may generate an unfortunate consequence for nations pursuing power outside of a collective context. As greater power is accumulated, nations become increasingly self-reliant. The moral hazard effect comes in the fact that greater power leads nations to be less perspicacious about investing in alternative power resources that could be called upon when unilateral primacy fails to deliver the goods. In this respect, powerful nations are not as dependent as less powerful nations on international institutions. Self-reliance also may increase the capacity to defend oneself in an anarchic environment (Mearsheimer 2001, pp. 30–33). Nations can attend to their specific needs with extensive freedom. But even where the level of threat is not extreme, pursuing goals outside of the constraints of multilateral commitments minimizes impediments to action and maximizes flexibility. Hence, the greater the power a nation possesses, the more able it is to indulge in independent action. As the tendency toward self-reliance becomes more extensive with the growth of unilateral power and capabilities, it is likely to introduce a vicious cycle of unilateralism. That is to say, as nations pursue their goals in an increasingly unilateral context that is insensitive to their prior commitments in international regimes and organizations, they may compromise their positions in such institutions and consequently no longer be able to rely on them as a source of power. Hence they will have to increasingly rely on their own unilateral power as opportunities to pursue national interests in other venues are closed off. In this case, the old cliché of "using it or losing it" is apropos.

But such intransigent unilateralism may create a self-reinforcing problem for another reason. If the unilateralist nation is a very powerful nation, its unwillingness to cooperate in regimes and institutions may increasingly doom possibilities for the emergence or maintenance of such regimes and institutions. This is because existing regimes and institutions have come to rely heavily on the contributions and participation (i.e., finances and political power) of such powerful nations. Without such ongoing support, the very influence of these regimes and institutions may be compromised. And even more deleterious for the unilateralist is the possibility that beyond "losing them" as sources of power, potential alienation might create enemies out of what once were erstwhile supporters. In this case, attempts at unilateral primacy create a kind of balance-of-power process, with international institutions filling the role of countervailing coalitions. In such a case, the vicious cycle of unilateralism will be compounded not by the fact that these institutions are undersupplied, but because alienation of the rank and file will create a more recalcitrant membership. Consequently, the unilateralist nation will find that these institutions do not function as desirably in its interests, thus giving such a nation greater incentives to indulge in unilateral actions, which then compound the vicious cycle process (Gallarotti 2004).

But losing multilateral support networks in interdependent environments confronts unilateralist nations with perhaps the most debilitating consequence of the vicious cycle itself: the fact that unilateral actions are in fact often inferior to multilateral actions in addressing the principal needs of even the most powerful nations. In an interdependent and globalized environment, as presently exists in the international system, many foreign policy goals and problems cannot be effectively addressed outside of a multilateral framework simply because they are multilateral in nature and hence require the cooperation of other nations in order to be effectively dealt with. Moreover, powerful nations may prefer the route of coercing compliance when they require specific actions on the part of other nations. But realistically, no nation (no matter how powerful) could adopt a decision-rule to simply extract compliance from other nations, on whose actions they rely, through coercion on every important matter. In the present international system, such tyrannical impunity is unthinkable. Hence the vicious cycle of unilateralism can produce deleterious consequences even for the most powerful nations.

The fact that great or dominant powers tend to invest heavily in building regimes and international organizations suggests that indeed such levers of influence are important to these nations (Keohane 1984, p. 31). The idea of the vicious cycle does not propose that such institutions will wither, but only that even if they do exist, dominant nations will often find it tempting to act outside of their parameters, and this will have an impact on both the organizations and the unilateralist nations. The fact that such institutions are supported by nations that are endowed with greater independence suggests that they still serve a variety of purposes in the interest of dominant nations, such as legitimacy, reputation, a hedge against unilateral bottlenecks, and market facilitators (Alt, Calvert, and Humes 1988; Cox 1980; Gallarotti 1991; Keohane 1984). Moreover, because of the fact that these institutions are largely built and supported by powerful nations, they often serve complementary roles in the interests of the powerful nations themselves (Cox 1980; Keohane 1984).[20] But as the institutions take on a more multilateral power structure in their governance (i.e., democratic momentum in the evolution of governance), a disjuncture will often occur such that the functions of these institutions may diverge from the interests of the powerful nations that originally built them (Cox 1987). This gives powerful nations incentives to contemplate greater actions outside these institutions.

Choices between unilateralism and multilateralism closely conform to choices between hard and soft power, respectively. Since a fundamental component of soft power is cooperation, and since unilateral actions are generally perpetrated with a nation's own (hard) resources, choices that lead to vicious cycles of unilateralism represent an overinvestment in hard power at the expense of soft power. In this respect the problem of a vicious cycle has a manifold bearing on weakening effects that emanate across the hard-soft power nexus.

With respect to the story of David and Goliath, we can see the manifestations of such a vicious cycle among the Philistines at two levels: the collective and individual military levels. Collectively, it appears that their expansion led the Philistines into pervasive conflict with numerous states in the region. And while conflict among these states themselves was also extensive, the Philistines had a special skill for alienating more states than did the other growing states in the region. To some extent they took the place of the dreaded Assyrians and Egyptians as those military powers declined and climbed into the role of principal imperialistic state in the region, and hence became a salient target of all the states. Disdaining cooperation in order to expand, the Philistines placed themselves in an unenviable position in the region. And since hatred of the Philistines often trumped hatred for each other, the other states in the region found great incentives to work collectively against the Philistines, while the Philistines found fewer opportunities for such alliances and consequently found themselves increasingly isolated.[21] It is clear that alliances and associations would have reinforced the territorial ambitions of the Philistines. In this respect, acting alone was an inferior strategy for attaining and maintaining empire.

At the individual level, there is much in the selection of the giant as a champion by the Philistines that manifests the elements of a vicious cycle of unilateral dependence. In this particular case, relying on one champion, especially a giant, promised to be inferior to reliance on an entire army. In general, giants are plagued by various inherent physical flaws (i.e., the inherent flaws of gigantism). They are more likely to suffer from arterial fibrillation, which is an abnormal quivering of the heart's upper chambers. The reason for this is that they tend to have enlarged left atriums. They are also more likely to develop left ventricular dysfunction. This tends to reduce their physical strength and life-span. Furthermore, they are prone to a genetic disorder called Marfan syndrome (symptoms being lightheadedness and chest pain), which can sometimes prove fatal. Moreover, they are generally plagued by abnormalities in their vision: most commonly, flawed peripheral vision. Finally, even if physically imposing, such champions are human, and humans can perform poorly on any given day for a variety of reasons.

Specifically in the case of Goliath, the extensive physical burden of donning his armor and walking out under the massive weight to challenge the Israelites twice daily for forty days would have been anything but beneficial given the likelihood of heart disease.[22] But his giant stature limited him on the battlefield as well, as his vision may have been suspect and like most giants he was prone to lightheadedness. David may have been able to maneuver easily outside of Goliath's effective field of vision, or he may have picked a fortuitous moment of lightheadedness to hurl the famous stone. But even as physically imposing a champion as Goliath was, the Philistines might have been better served by developing a plan in which their army would take the initiative in the battle. As noted, the fact that they ran off after Goliath fell suggests that advanced planning regarding the risks of relying on giant champions was sorely lacking (1 Samuel 17:51).

* * *

Some of the interaction effects among these four elements have already been mentioned. Indeed, the interaction effects run deep and are varied. Moral hazard essentially can affect all other three by making nations more likely to act independently, expand beyond their effective limits, and adapt less perspicaciously to complexity. Feedback can also occur across all of these elements. Greater expansion may lead nations to heightened perceptions of safety and thus promote greater moral hazard. Complexity may make independent action more desirable as multilateral relations grow increasingly difficult to manage. Independence may make further expansion necessary as nations substitute a greater international presence for allies and supporters. But for the purpose of greater theoretical simplicity and a clearer assessment of the individual effects of each process, I have chosen to analyze the manifestations of the power curse within distinct weakening processes rather than one integrated model of weakening effects. This allows us to view and trace the process of the power curse in a less convoluted theoretical structure.

The Power Curse in the Context of Hard and Soft Power

The power curse and power illusion often manifest themselves in the context of soft and hard power. This section analyzes hard and soft power and considers how the power curse and power illusion apply specifically across this hard-soft power nexus.

Soft vs. Hard Power

In his recent work, Joseph Nye underscores the importance of "soft power" in maintaining national influence in world politics. Soft power is largely portrayed as the influence that a nation enjoys as a result of a positive image among the community of nations (i.e., being admired). This is differentiated from the more conventional tangible resources, or "hard power," that a nation may employ to change the behavior of other nations.[23] Nye refers to soft power as "co-optive power" in that it leads others to "want what you want," while hard power is called "command or control power" in that it impels or compels others to change through use of inducement or coercion (carrots or sticks). In the hard-power context, interests are opposed, while in the soft-power context, there is generally less conflict of interest.

Modern realists have tended to espouse a hard concept of power.[24] For John Mearsheimer "power is based on the particular material capabilities that a state possesses." These material capabilities are essentially "tangible assets" that determine a nation's "military" strength. He divides state power into two kinds: "latent" and "military." The latter is determined by the strength of its military forces, while the former is conceived of as "the socio-economic ingredients that go into building military power." The assets that constitute latent power derive principally from population and wealth. As Mearsheimer states, "Great powers need money, technology, and personnel to build military forces and to fight wars, and a state's latent power refers to the raw potential it can draw on when competing with rival states" (2001, p. 55). The emphasis falls on the tangible power lexicon that determines a nation's capacities to employ force and wealth in pursuit of its goals. Kenneth Waltz shows a similar "hard" disposition in defining power: "size of population and territory, resource endowment, economic capability, military strength, political stability and competence" (1979, p. 131).[25] Similarly, Robert Gilpin defines power as "the military, economic, and technological capabilities of states" (1981, p. 13). Hence, for realists, national influence essentially depends on the ability to use coercion (force and threats) and wealth (bribery). Ultimately, "muscle" and "riches" fundamentally determine a nation's power: these material resources constitute the *ultima ratio* in anarchy (Hall 1997, p. 592).

Soft power has become somewhat misunderstood. It has become all too common to equate the concept with influence emanating from the seductive cultural values created by movies, television, radio, and fashion (Fraser 2003). Soft power is much more. For Nye, the admiration and emulation that compose soft power come from two fundamental sources: domestic political culture and policies, and foreign policy.

Under international sources of soft power (i.e., foreign policy), we can include the following (see Table 2.1 for a systematic categorization of soft power). First, nations must adopt a multilateral rather than unilateral posture in the promotion of their foreign policies. Nye's work (2002) on US foreign policy is most engaged in this issue of multilateralism versus unilateralism. In this vein, respect for international treaties and alliance commitments is central to the creation of soft power. Forsaking erstwhile allies and international commitments in favor of unilateral solutions produces a "maverick" image that comprises traditional sources of power embedded in multilateral support networks. Second, nations must show a willingness

Table 2.1 Sources of Soft Power

International Sources	Domestic Sources
• Reliance on multilateral cooperation	Culture
• Respect for international law and conventions	• Social cohesion
• Respect for international treaties and alliance commitments	• Quality of life
• Willingness to sacrifice short-term national interests	• Liberalism
• Economic openness	• Opportunity
	• Tolerance
	• "Vital life force"
	Political institutions
	• Democracy
	• Constitutionalism
	• Liberalism
	• Pluralism
	• Functional government bureaucracy

to sacrifice short-term national interest in order to contribute toward substantive collaborative schemes that address important multilateral problems. Finally, a nation must pursue policies of economic openness. This dictates a foreign economic policy orientation that relies on liberal tenets. Hence, with respect to the international basis of soft power, nations must demonstrate a fundamental respect for international law, regimes, and institutions. This respect can easily be compromised when nations pursue their self-interest and unilateralism in opposition to such venues of cooperation.

Nye also underscores the importance of domestic culture and politics as sources of soft power. As he notes, "How America behaves at home can enhance its image and perceived legitimacy, and that in turn can help advance its foreign policy objectives" (2004b, pp. 56–57). Culturally, soft power is enhanced by social cohesion (limited social cleavages), quality of life, liberalism, opportunity, tolerance, and the intoxicating characteristics of a culture that generate both admiration and emulation—its "vital life force" (Nye 2002, pp. 113–114, 119, 141). Politically, institutions must reflect broad principals of democratic enfranchisement; the system must represent a set of rules that delivers constitutionalism, liberalism, pluralism, and a functional bureaucracy.

The Growing Importance of Soft Power in Modern World Politics

Changes in world politics in the modern age have elevated the importance of soft power relative to hard power for nations seeking to maximize and maintain their influence. In this transformed international system, soft power will be a crucial element in enhancing influence over international outcomes, because it has become more difficult to impel and compel nations and nonstate actors through bribery and coercion. The world stage has become less amenable to Hobbesian brutes, but more amenable to actors that are well apprised of the soft opportunities and constraints imposed by the new global system. In fact, nations that comport themselves in a manner that disregards the growing importance of soft power risk much. Even gargantuan efforts to increase influence may be rendered self-defeating if they rely exclusively on hard power. In this case, the strength or influence a nation acquires through such hard initiatives may in fact be illusory. The changes in world politics that have raised the importance of soft power relative to hard power have been pervasive and compelling.

First, with the advent of nuclear power, the costs of using or even threatening force have skyrocketed. Robert Keohane and Joseph Nye (1989) have long averred the diminished utility of coercion in a world where such force could impose far greater costs on societies than they are willing to bear. Indeed, the neoliberal catechism has concluded that such diminution has broken down the former hierarchy of issues that traditionally preserved the status of security atop the hierarchy of international salience. Robert Jervis (1993, 1988, 2002) has proclaimed a new age of the "security community," meaning that war between major powers is almost unthinkable because the costs of war have become too high. John Mueller (1988) modifies the nuclear deterrent argument somewhat by maintaining that even conventional war itself, which can be nearly as devastating in an age of advanced technology, is a deterrent. In short, the utility of respect, admiration, and cooperation (i.e., soft power) has increased relative to the utility of coercion in statecraft. Moreover, the dangers that the hard resources of military technology have produced require an ever-increasing commitment to the instruments of soft power in order for humans to achieve sustainable security.

This diminishing utility of hard power also functions within a specific political, social, and economic context marshaled by modernization: the context of interdependence (Herz 1957; Osgood and Tucker 1967; Keohane and Nye 1989; Nye 2004a). Using sticks, of whatever kind (whether manifest or latent), generates considerable costs among interdependent actors. Indeed, in a world of social and economic interpenetration, to punish or threaten another nation is to some extent tantamount to self-punishment, given that surely some of a perpetrating nation's interests will be compromised (e.g., its own companies and citizens may suffer from punitive acts intended to harm a target nation).[26] In such an environment, strategies for optimizing national wealth and power have shifted from war and competition to cooperation. But even more elusive than the quest to contain damage to the sender nation is the quest to impose specific outcomes upon the target nation. In a globalized world, targeted actors have much room to maneuver and many possibilities of escape. Transnational actors can avoid being compelled by carrots and sticks because of their access to the international political economy. They can merely escape buy-offs and coercion by taking refuge in their many international havens. This modern day "economic feudalism" is shifting the nexus of power from the territorial state to transnational networks (Nye 2002, p. 75). In such an environment, transnational actors have become ever more elusive (multinational corporations) and ever more dangerous (terrorists). The ineffectiveness of sanctions is also a testament to how easily targeted regimes can avoid the deleterious consequences of punitive actions by taking advantage of the international marketplace, both above ground and below. Neither economic nor military strength can any longer guarantee the capacity to compel or deter. Instead, favorable outcomes can be delivered through cooperation and the respect and admiration garnered from soft power.

Compounding the increasing utility of soft power relative to hard power are four other factors: democratization, globalization, the rise of the guardian state, and the growth of international organizations and regimes. The growth and consolidation of democracy compounds the disutility of coercion, as the actors bearing the greatest burden of such coercion (the people) have political power over decisionmakers. The democratic peace phenomenon, for example, has shifted the power equation considerably (Doyle 1997; Russett and Oneal 2001; Ray 1995). As people become more empowered, they consolidate strong political impediments to the use of force and threat. Furthermore, democratic culture naturally drives national leaders toward soft power, which is grounded in respect for the democratic process at both the national and international levels. Hence, national leaders are much more constrained to work within acceptable policy boundaries, boundaries that increasingly discourage force, threat, and bribery. Rather, outcomes are engineered through policies that are more consistent with democratic legitimacy.

Globalization has compounded the effects of interdependence by enhancing the process of social and economic interpenetration among nations. The information age has given civil societies the capacity to receive and transmit information across nations in a manifold and speedy way. Greater links allow for enhanced networking among transnational actors. As the international stakes of these actors grow, so do their incentives to expend political capital within their own domestic political systems to reinforce the economic ties between their nations (Milner 1988). Other technological manifestations of globalization magnify and solidify these links, such that transnational networks are pervasive forces in world politics. This access to foreign governments and citizens also compounds the effects of democratization in creating political impediments to the use of hard power.[27] These forces have both diminished possibilities of political conflict and shifted the nexus of competition away from force, threat, and bribery (Rosecrance 1999). As Nye puts is, these networks "will have soft power of their own as they attract citizens into coalitions that cut across national boundaries. Politics in part then becomes a competition for attractiveness, legitimacy, and credibility" (2004b, p. 31).

The rise and consolidation of the guardian state in the twentieth century have worked through the political vehicle of democracy to further diminish the utility of hard power relative to soft power. Social and political changes have made modern populations more sensitive to their economic fates and less enamored of a "warrior ethic" (Nye 2004b, p. 19). With the rise of this welfare and economic orientation and the consolidation of democracy, political leaders have been driven more by economic imperative and less by foreign adventurism as a source of political survival (Gallarotti 2000; Ruggie 1983). This has shifted not only domestic but also foreign policy orientations. This economic welfare concern has put a premium on cooperation that can deliver economic prosperity and stability, and worked against hard-power policies that might compromise these goals. The guardian mentality has served to socialize national leaders to a greater extent (making them more docile and more respectful of legitimate means of statecraft) as compared to their nineteenth-century predecessors, and consequently has reduced incentives to extract compliance through force, threat, and bribery. For Jervis (2002), this diminution of the "warrior ethic" is a fundamental change in values that has consolidated the new security community.[28] Moreover, Jervis underscores how these new economic imperatives have augmented the benefits of peace, another crucial factor contributing to the rise of the security community.

Finally, the growth of international organizations and regimes since 1945 has essentially cast nations more firmly within networks of cooperation (Krasner 1983; Keohane and Nye 1989). As these networks have grown in size and stature, so too has the power of the norms and laws they represent. More precisely, with the growth and consolidation of these cooperative networks, unilateral actions that disregard such institutions are becoming more costly. In a sense, these networks have, to some extent, ratcheted up the minimum level of civil behavior in international politics, and consequently raised the importance of soft power dramatically. Expectations have gravitated more toward the sanctity of such institutions; hence, actions that cut against these expectations generate greater fallout than they would in an environment where no such institutional superstructure existed. In short, the spread of cooperative networks has made coercion and bribery less lucrative. But beyond international regimes and institutions as constraining agents, their growth and strength have made them desirable because of the opportunities they provide. As Keohane and Nye note, the "ability to choose the organizational forum for an issue and to mobilize votes will be an important political resource" in such an environment (1989, p. 37).

The Power Curse and Power Illusion in a Hard-Soft Power Context

One of the principal themes of the scholarship on soft power is that nations have continued to compromise their influence by continuing to rely on hard power at the exclusion of soft power. Indeed, the case studies in this book strongly vindicate this theme by demonstrating it to be a compelling manifestation of the power curse and power illusion. Excesses in pursuing hard power often generate weakening effects by crowding out or diminishing soft-power resources. One of the most pernicious effects of the power curse in the context of a soft-hard power nexus lies in the possibility that using hard-power resources can actually undermine a nation's soft power, and hence lead to considerable net-losses in national influence. Hence the strength that a nation may perceive as resulting from vigorous reliance on hard power is often illusory. The elements of the power curse all demonstrate prospects for such counterproductive outcomes within the hard-soft power nexus. Excessive reliance on coercion or force may create a backlash of vituperation that increases countervailing threats and responses (negative feedback in complex systems). Excessive reliance on unilateral solutions to pressing problems may undermine a nation's access to multilateral support networks whose assistance is necessary for effectively confronting such problems. This may lead the nation down an enervating path if it falls into a vicious cycle of unilateralism. Furthermore, significant endowments of hard-power resources may undermine incentives for nations to perspicaciously develop complementary soft-power resources (i.e., the moral hazard of hard power). Moreover, the compelling needs generated by overstretch (i.e., dependence and mission creep) may create significant pressures to rely on hard power in the form of direct methods of command and control, but such methods may generate points of tension that make command and control ever more elusive objectives.

But within this hard-soft power nexus, overreliance on soft power might also generate negative consequences for a nation's influence. Certainly in complex systems, cooperation or actions based on respect for international law may lead to detrimental consequences in a variety of ways in this context. For example, a nation's exclusive reliance on diplomacy in the face of aggressive actions may convey a lack of resolve, which in turn might lead that nation to compromise its ability to maintain important resources from alliance partners in the face of threats (i.e., nations will not support allies that are reluctant to honor their alliance commitments). In the context of other elements of the power curse, overstretch could occur in the form of cooperation as well. For example, nations that take on too many commitments in multilateral schemes may find that this strategy generates a deleterious drain on important resources. Furthermore, moral hazard may occur in the form of a false sense of security from the admiration garnered through soft power, thus leading nations not to prepare for aggressive acts (i.e., a suboptimal military capacity).

In this respect, disregarding the merits of hard power in an anarchical world presents significant dangers as well. Nations that pursue the saintly route at the exclusion of muscle may also fall into the trap of the power curse and power illusion. Influence based on goodwill alone is fragile. Nations may lack the muscle to defend themselves against force or coercion, or they may be unable to secure outcomes that are beneficial. Hence the logic that identifies ways in which reliance on hard power alone can be self-defeating could be relevant to a strategy that is overreliant on soft power as well, although the self-defeating processes would manifest themselves in different forms. Optimal strategies for power acquisition will require some diversification between muscle and goodwill (i.e., between hard and soft power). To recall a quote made famous by Al Capone: "You can get further with a kind word and a gun, than with a kind word alone."

But the pervasiveness of soft-hard power effects aside, it should be emphasized that manifestations across the hard-soft power divide are only a subset of a far greater constellation of the effects of the power curse and power illusion. In fact, the effects of the power curse and power illusion appear within the specific hard- and soft-power resources themselves (and not just across these two types of resources). Excessive pursuit of one hard-power resource may compromise other hard-power resources, thus weakening the victimized nations in net terms. For example, overreliance on military solutions may diminish the availability of economic aid. Similarly, excessive development of some soft-power resources may come at the expense of other soft resources. For example, excessively courting friendship and alliance with one set of nations may turn their competitors against the suitor, thus compromising the suitor's soft power with those latter nations.

In sum, the effects of the power curse and power illusion manifest themselves over all types of power resources. While their manifestations across the hard-soft power nexus represent only a subset of their effects, it is nonetheless important to explore their theoretical implications, especially given the changes in world politics that have raised the importance of soft power relative to hard power.

Notes

1. Realists have tended to espouse such a view, even though they have indeed acknowledged the existence of countervailing reactions to attempts at primacy or power augmentation. See especially the definitions of power in Waltz 1979 (pp. 113, 131), Gilpin 1981 (p. 13), and Mearsheimer 2001 (p. 55).

2. Power illusion is not strictly dependent on assumptions about styles of decisionmaking. It may be a function of rational decisionmaking, such as elites engaging in overstretch due to domestic interest-group pressure—in this case an adverse outcome would result from what is considered domestic political rationality by elites. But in some cases, power illusion may be brought on by tendencies that cut against rational behavior. For example, elites may engage in counterproductive policies that in fact weaken their nations because they do not acquire the necessary information to adapt to complexity. This is a testament to the pervasiveness and pernicious character of power illusion: it can result from a variety of decision orientations.

3. While the biblical account of the battle and the historical knowledge of the period are rich in detail, I augment the theory with some speculation of my own for pedagogical purposes. Like in the story of David and Goliath, there are numerous historical cases of weaker powers winning contests between asymmetrical forces

(the American Revolutionary War, the Vietnam War, the Soviet campaign in Afghanistan). Analyzing these historical cases in the context of the power curse (as with the case of Vietnam in this book) could be equally revealing. Quotes from the Book of Samuel are taken from http://www.hareidi.org/bible/1_samuel17.htm#1.

4. The reference to complexity includes both the formal mathematical work done in the area of chaos as well as the work done by social scientists, biologists, and ecologists. This literature is far too extensive to cite here, but an impressive compilation is found in Jervis 1997, an application of complexity theory to international politics that draws on the full array of all these strands of scholarship. In addition, extremely helpful and fairly celebrated introductions to the study of complexity that are intelligible to nonscientists include Gleick 1988, Gould 1989, Lewin 1992, Kellert 1993, and Ruelle 1991. On systems in international politics, see also Kaplan 1957, Waltz 1979, Gilpin 1981, and Snyder and Jervis 1993.

5. David Baldwin (2002, pp. 179–181) also attests to difficulties of measurement and conceptualization when more complex understandings of power relations are sought.

6. This recalls Karl Deutsch's idea of pathological learning by the powerful (1966, p. 248). In short, powerful actors are sufficiently resilient to the environments around them, such that they do not have to learn as effectively about (and consequently adapt to) the changes within these environments vis-à-vis less powerful (and hence more vulnerable) actors.

7. Kenneth Waltz (1979, pp. 171–191) suggests that multipolar and unipolar systems are likely to generate more moral hazard than a bipolar system. Waltz posits that in a bipolar structure, there is in fact a tendency for competition between superpowers to lead them to overreact to events in the periphery rather than becoming dangerously complacent. But he qualifies the argument by noting that events in the periphery of a bipolar structure do become "relatively inconsequential," and that superpowers that indeed perceive this face a tendency to desensitize themselves to marginal gains and losses (i.e., develop a complacency generated by the moral hazard of great relative power). This argument is developed in Waltz's discussion of why a superpower may "tolerate" changes in the periphery of the system (pp. 190–191). Moreover, the duopolistic nature of a bipolar system creates greater stability among superpower relations, thus somewhat damping the competition that drives superpowers to overreact. Hence, for Waltz, all structures have the capacity to generate some moral hazard owing to the strength of great powers.

8. Biblical scholars disagree over the nature of David's incentives. Those who have embraced the brash and opportunist character of the David of the Bible underscore the temptation of Saul's bounty for the head of the giant: riches, marriage to Saul's daughter, and honor among the Israelites (1 Samuel 17:25). It is clear in the next passage, however, that David is more concerned with the giant's effrontery and irreverence in taunting the "armies of the living God" (1 Samuel 17:26; see Isser 2003, p. 125).

9. The literature on hegemony differs on the motivations for this growing presence. Benevolent strands of the theory posit a more altruistic motivation that produces a commitment to provide the necessary public goods to stabilize an international system or issue. More coercive strands posit a more particularistic self-interest as motivating a kind of management that brings the lion's share of the gains from a system or issue to the hegemon. On these competing visions of hegemonic engagement, see Snidal 1985.

10. Kennedy (1987, p. xvi) sees the relationship between foreign expansion and wealth as reciprocal: acquiring a larger international presence requires great wealth, but such a presence is instrumental in sustaining that wealth.

11. Snyder (1991) portrays a process of policymaking in which the energized coalition reinforces (through the state apparatus) a belief in power and security through expansion: the myth of empire.

12. Notwithstanding the special-interest coalitions that benefit from the expansion that supports such a policy, when the burdens become excessive for their societies, even their influence will fall short of being able to sustain such policies in the face of mass discontent.

13. This conceptualization of "moral hazard" takes a broader view of risk-encouraging behavior than the more restricted use of the term, which is often equated with the risk-encouraging consequences of owning insurance against specific disasters. This conceptualization encompasses characteristics or factors that actually insulate actors from risk in the broadest sense, hence diminishing the incentives against acting recklessly. An actor may be insulated from risk for reasons other than insurance. For instance, having excessive physical strength might encourage an individual to get into more fights. Or, having an extremely large vehicle with elaborate safety features might encourage an individual to drive faster than he or she normally would, or may encourage him or her to drive under more hazardous conditions. In this respect, this broad conceptualization of moral hazard encompasses numerous processes characterized by overconfidence and complacency in the face of risk.

14. Historical and literary analysis suggests the integration of Greek heroic elements into the story, as Goliath was clad in gear more appropriate to a late–Iron Age Greek hoplite than an early–Iron Age Philistine warrior (Finkelstein and Silberman 2006, pp. 196–198; Rofe 1987, p. 133). The height of Goliath ("six cubits and a span") has generated much debate among biblical scholars and historians alike. Estimates vary, from six feet, six inches tall as derived from the Dead Sea Scrolls version, to nine feet, six inches tall as derived from the Masoretic text.

15. Goliath's complacency led him to violate common battle tactics of the period. In addition to a sword, he was armed with a spear and javelin (1 Samuel 17:6–7). Normally, at least one of those should be hurled at the opponent before engaging them at close quarters with a sword (Finkelstein and Silberman 2006, pp. 1–2).

16. Monroe Rosenthal and Isaac Mozeson (1990, p. 14) note that the Israelites of the period were especially receptive to adopting the military weapons and tactics of their enemies. It may very well be that slings figured prominently in the outcomes of some of the actual battles between the Israelites and the Philistines. And this may have in fact generated the seed of the epic story.

17. Historical accounts portray the Philistines emerging as a strong political and commercial power in the region at the turn of the first millennium B.C.E. (Erlich 1996, p. 23).

18. In this case, the conventions of trial by champions may have limited the Philistines' flexibility to respond to Goliath's defeat.

19. Reading ahead in the Book of Samuel reveals an interesting event that may testify to the pervasive influence of moral hazard. In this case, David himself may have fallen victim after his victory. When fleeing from Saul after the battle, David traveled and stopped at Nob for food with neither a military escort nor a

sword. The priest who greeted him appeared disconcerted at his lack of caution, given that David was being pursued not only by Saul, but also by Philistine sympathizers. While Samuel gives little explanation of this perceived recklessness, it is logically consistent with the expectation of moral hazard: David's victory with a sling (possibly supported by his faith as a chosen soldier of God) may have emboldened him to act with impunity. In fact, this tendency accords well with the roguish behavior attributed to David in biblical accounts that chronicle his adventures after the battle at Elah (1 Samuel 21:1–10; Isser 2003, pp. 34, 39).

20. This explains why so many of the functions performed by regimes and organizations are considered "redundant," in that these functions are also performed (or could be performed) by individual nations (Gallarotti 1991).

21. While biblical accounts portray such a picture, and this is not surprising given that the Philistines were perhaps the leading antagonists of the Israelites, there is sufficient evidence of such outcomes in the historical accounts of the period (Gray 1962; Erlich 1996).

22. Was David the beneficiary of a lucky break in the form of a stroke felling the giant? This would make the story far less inspirational from a religious standpoint.

23. Nye introduced the concept of soft power in 1990 and began further applying and developing it a decade later (see Nye 1990a, 1990b, 2002, 2003, 2004a, 2004b, 2007). On soft power from both supportive and critical perspectives, see especially a recent collection of essays in Berenskoetter and Williams 2007. See also Baldwin 2002, Gallarotti 2004, Lennon 2003, Ferguson 2003, Fraser 2003, and Meade 2004. As well, Alastair Johnston's work on socialization (2008) introduces categories that reflect processes of soft power.

24. Michael Barnett and Raymond Duvall (2005, p. 40), as well as Brian Schmidt (2007, p. 61), aver that the common realist visions of power are oriented around the idea of nations using "material resources" to influence other nations, whether through force or bribery.

25. Waltz never clarifies the meaning of "competence," but one might infer sound management of the tangible assets through leadership, policy, and decision-making.

26. Moreover, these "multilayered," "multilevel," and "multinodal" manifestations of power have caused scholars to question traditional conceptions of power as processes of leverage monopolized by the state (Cerny, forthcoming).

27. Barbara Haskel (1980) highlights the importance of access to societies as a means of power in the interpenetrated political economy of the modern world.

28. William McNeil (1982, p. 307) notes how the martial "cult of heroism" became especially strong in the late nineteenth century, fueled by an educational system that underscored patriotism and study of the classics.

CHAPTER 3

The Power Curse Across History

THE FOUR case studies explored in this chapter represent historical manifestations of the power curse and power illusion in environments of issue-specific primacy and general global primacy; the first three cases are of the former, while the fourth case is of the latter. While they have not been selected randomly, they are sufficiently broad, both substantively and historically, and sufficiently salient historically, to deliver compelling if not definitive conclusions about how the power curse and power illusion can victimize powerful nations. Furthermore, as cases involving primacy, they carry a crucial-case relevance with respect to scrutinizing events in most-likely cases, thereby facilitating a falsification analysis.

Each case study explores one of the four elements of the power curse. Overstretch is analyzed in the context of Athenian imperialism in the Aegean and Asia Minor during the fifth century B.C.E. Moral hazard is analyzed in the context of the Bank of England and the British state as monetary leaders under the classical gold standard in the nineteenth century. The vicious cycle of unilateralism is analyzed in the context of Great Britain's experience with the problem of depreciating silver during the late nineteenth and early twentieth centuries. And finally, the failure to adapt to complexity is analyzed in the context of the US war in Vietnam in the 1960s and 1970s.

Athenian Imperialism and Overstretch: The Delian League

The weakening effects of the power curse with respect to the tendency toward overstretch manifested themselves clearly in the case of ancient Athens and the Delian League. The Delian League (477 B.C.E.) began as an alliance among Athens and a number of other Greek city-states after the failure of the Persian invasion of mainland Greece in 480 B.C.E. The purpose of the league was to punish and gain some recompense from the Persians for having invaded the mainland several times in the 490s and 480s, as well as to liberate Greek states that were still under the yoke of Persian imperial rule, mainly on the coast of Asia Minor and the neighboring islands. Hence the nature of the league itself began as an expansionist enterprise that sought to extract the spoils of war and to free Greek states (Wilcoxon 1979, p. 145; McGregor 1987, p. 32; Souza 2002, p. 11). It was called "Delian" because it was consecrated on the island of Delos, the site of its first treasury. Athens became the de jure leader of the league after the Greek allies that had fought off the Persian invasion of 480 found the continuation of Spartan military leadership, in the person of Pausanius, who was considered excessively autocratic, untenable. The departure of Pausanius and the Spartans from the league was important because they took their traditional allies (mainly neighboring states on the Peloponnesus—referred to as the Peloponnesian League) with them, thus creating two alliance blocs in the Greek world (McGregor 1987, pp. 31–32).

As time went on the Delian League grew and came to be dominated by Athens as an empire rather than an alliance. The imperialist grip of Athens grew concomitantly with Athenian dependence on the league and mission creep. The interaction of these three factors—growing dependence, mission creep, and imperial grip (fueled by domestic political support)—led to a process of self-feeding expansion that would eventually destroy Athens as a dominant military and commercial power. Crucial to this debilitating process of overstretch was the role that hard and soft power played. The need to overexpand led Athens to compromise almost all of its soft power, which it had earned as leader of the earlier league against Persian aggression. The loss of this soft power was central to the unraveling of the empire and the eventual demise of Athens as a great power in the Aegean. Hence the great power that Athenians perceived (and that was so eloquently proclaimed by Athenian leaders like Pericles) as deriving from the possession of an ever-expanding empire was, in the long-run, only illusory. In reality the empire ended up carrying the seeds of Athenian decline.

Athens was actually predisposed to become a great imperial presence. Within its province, Attica, it was a natural nodal center for clearing trade in foodstuffs. In the greater geographic arena of the Aegean and beyond, Attica was endowed with great strategic characteristics. It had a very long coastline, with lots of natural harbors, and it was conveniently located on important trade routes between Italy, Sicily, and Asia Minor. The natural highway of expansion was the sea, as land travel across the Balkans was far more difficult. The economy of Athens and Attica compounded the natural endowments of Athens by creating important push effects. While Attica was one of the most fertile regions in Greece, and therefore produced a lion's share of Greek grains, it was always a net food importer, given Greece's relative inferiority as a grain-producing environment (being far more arid than other states around southern Italy, Asia Minor, and the Hellespont). Moreover, the environment was also poor for producing another important good: timber. However, Attica was far more prolific at producing other goods that were in high demand throughout the ancient world: olive oil; wine; and metals such as zinc, lead, and silver.[1] This led to a natural disposition on the part of Athens to become a naval and commercial power, which it finally became in the sixth century with the expansion of trade. The Athenians were also learning from the great sea peoples of the region that wealth and power could best be facilitated by maintaining a secure trading network of states, whether through imperialism or trade agreements (French 1964, pp. 2–8; McGregor 1987, p. 50).

This natural inclination toward commercial primacy was enhanced by political initiatives in the sixth century that facilitated greater economic activity. Solon (elected archon in 594), who was famous for his political reforms that paved the way for democracy under Cleisthenes a century later, enacted a number of reforms that enhanced economic and commercial activity in Athens. Under his reforms, Athens developed a more vigorous urban economy, with the growth of Athens' first significant urban class, and a greater interstate presence.[2] The economic power that Solon baptized was further confirmed and consolidated under the famous tyrant Peisistratus (archon from 541 to 527). It was under Peisistratus's rule that Athens achieved economic primacy in the Greek world. Peisistratus further encouraged the evolution of an urban economy by attracting subsistence farmers to the city, through changes in the debt laws that made it harder for farmers to borrow. It was under his rule that a large urban population first appeared in Athens, changing both the economic and the political landscape—a boon to the evolution of democracy as populist politics became a force. Hence the stage for imperial Athens was set: a state with a natural capacity to trade, blessed with strategic gifts as a sea power, and a diversified economy with a large urban population that was extremely dependent on imports. The Delian League would become the vehicle through which these growing inclinations and structural endowments would manifest themselves (French 1964, pp. 16–33).

While Athens was structurally predisposed to expand commercially, the precise form and timing of expansion were driven by proximate causes that developed at the turn of the sixth century. The Persian invasions of the 490s and 480s were costly for the Greeks, but they also forced the Greek states to work together as never before under leading states such as Sparta and Athens. They also pushed economic growth and encouraged the development of greater military capacities in Sparta and Athens.[3] This leadership led to the development of the bipolar structure of power in the Greek world, with Athens and Sparta rising above the rest. Moreover, the patterns of alliance formation around the two poles later developed into power blocs, with the Spartans leading the Peloponnesian League and the Athenians leading the northern and coastal Greek states. But in fighting the Persians, two things became apparent to the Greeks. First, winning battles and securing territories in war could be a lucrative enterprise; successful campaigns could be self-financing as a result of the spoils of war (booty, tribute, slaves, war reparations). And second, for the same reasons, an empire could be quite lucrative. The Greek states in Ionia (coastal Asia Minor) and the Hellespont that had fallen under the yoke of Persian imperialism were generating great economic and strategic benefits for the Persians. Ironically, Athens would end up falling into the same trap as did the Persians, a trap that created the Delian League in the first place (McGregor 1987, pp. 15–29).[4]

These lessons became more glaring as the Delian League began its business of liberating Ionian Greek states from the yoke of Persian imperialism and incorporating non-Greek territories. And as the expansion continued, the prizes and strategic benefits became all the more compelling. Early campaigns that liberated and took Serstus and Byzantium proved extremely lucrative, and these were followed by a series of campaigns throughout the Aegean in the 470s that were aimed at generating great wealth and strategically vital allies and colonies. There was a distinct difference in the functioning of the early versus the late league. Early-league relations were significantly better than they would become later on, due to the fact that Athenian policy had not yet tipped away from a soft-power base to a more tyrannical policy founded predominantly on hard power (coercion) and exploitation. And even though the lion's share of benefits from trade and military campaigns would fall to Athens even early on, league relations were still carried on in the wake of its enlightened leadership against the Persians. The Delian League was conceived as a democratic association, with a treasury maintained on neutral Delos and a synod in which decisions were to be made collectively (McGregor 1987, pp. 39–42).

As time went on the Delian League became more of an empire, with members becoming de facto subjects. As the empire grew and Athens entered into larger military campaigns during the (first) Peloponnesian War of the 450s and 440s, Athens's management of the league shifted increasingly away from a soft-power policy and toward a hard-power predilection.[5] Athenians came to dominate decisions, and as leaders of the military campaigns they determined how the prizes of war would be used. Athens also determined the use of money and military goods (men and ships) contributed by league members. Athens came to employ contributions and spoils of war, with cold disregard to its oath on Delos, as its own private stash. In fact, the treasury was moved from Delos to Athens in 454 and the synod became only a symbolic institution. By the mid–fifth century, Athens was a full-blown imperial state on an ever-increasing quest for greater power through greater expansion. The quest for empire manifested itself across the fifth century as a self-reinforcing process of growth, one that fed upon itself. As the empire grew, so grew the need for further expansion. This process of self-reinforcement was driven by a natural tendency toward mission creep as well as a vicious cycle of dependence. That such processes could continue even to the point of self-destructive or debilitating policies is in great part attributable to the domestic political support for expansion that existed in Athens throughout the century (Souza 2002, pp. 12–13; McGregor 1987, pp. 32–42).[6]

The evolution of the Athenian economy placed it on a road toward excessive dependence on commercial and military expansion (D. Kagan 2003, p. 8; Romilly 1963, p. 71). Athens's natural proclivity for sea and military power, coupled with its development as a money economy and commercial center, created a voracious imperial appetite. The reforms of Solon and Peisistratus deviated the Athenian population away from the land and toward the city. The transformation of Athenian agriculture followed as small landholders sought urban employment and left their land to be consolidated into greater agricultural estates. Since Attican grains were far less abundant and inferior to those of other grain-producing centers of the ancient world (such as Sicily, southern Italy, and Asia Minor), and a growing capacity to trade made it possible to acquire those superior grains, Athens became ever more anxious to import them and less anxious to produce its own. Instead, the larger landed estates shifted to cash crops, which better fit the terrain in Attica, thus pulling over much of the agricultural capital devoted to grain production. This evolving trade structure based on comparative advantage made Athens ever more dependent on trade for its basic foodstuffs (French 1964, p. 65). From an economic standpoint this development may be seen as a more efficient outcome, but from a policy standpoint it showed an element of moral hazard: Athenian leaders became lax in preserving food self-sufficiency when it was far easier to import grain than force farmers to grind out shallow wheat yields on land better suited to cash crops. Indeed, Athenians frequently lamented and debated the question of such a declining self-sufficiency, even through the golden years of Athenian history (French 1964, pp. 64, 88). Moreover, the growing wealth and economy of Athens produced a manufacturing sector that grew far greater than the size of its domestic market, and hence manufacturers (primarily artisans and craftsmen) became dependent on foreign markets for their survival. And with their growing wealth came the means and need to import an ever-increasing number of goods, both for their businesses as well as for their own private consumption. This interaction of economic and commercial growth was a major factor in producing a vicious cycle of imperial expansion for Athens (French 1964, pp. 41–44).

Aside from the commercial dependence generated by a growing empire, and which in turn encouraged ever more growth, the Delian League itself provided a number of essential benefits upon which Athens became quite dependent. Originally, each member was required to contribute money or military assets—essentially tributes rather than contributions. These went to a treasury, which was essentially used for the greater good of Athens.[7] One especially important use for tributes was to finance public service jobs that relieved the problem of urban unemployment in a city-state that was transitioning out of agriculture and toward a manufacturing economy (Romilly 1963, pp. 74–75). A great many Athenian citizens—soldiers, sailors, builders, and artisans--were deriving a livelihood from the high level of public spending made possible by the economic and imperial success of Athens. As these groups grew and their political importance rose with the advent of democracy, there was an ongoing need to earn enough money to keep everyone gainfully employed and supported (Wilcoxon 1979, p. 146; French 1964, pp. 40–44, 148–153).[8] But even in military campaigns that served the purpose of the collective security of the Delian League, it was Athens that was benefiting, because of its control of military and commercial activity within the league's geographic domain. The league gave Athens the money and means to expand its empire, and with the growing empire came more money and resources that could be used to further expand, hence the vicious cycle of expansion that eventually led to overstretch.

The expansion was also valuable in several other ways besides tributes and military assets. Acquiring new territories and liberating Greek states provided Athens with strategic outlets and bases from which to maintain their military and commercial ventures. New colonial territories and new league members were especially important in connecting the Athenian commercial and military network, given the small size of ships (and hence limited capacity to carry supplies) and the slow speed of travel. Trade and military networks could only function in chainlike structures, and only where travel distances were small and bases or ports were sufficiently endowed to supply provisions for ships in need. The further out these links could be forged, the greater incentive to extend the networks all the more, hence another manifestation of the vicious cycle of expansion that set the stage for overstretch.

Moreover, acquiring territories for colonists was a crucial means of solving the problems of urban unemployment. When shortfalls in employment did hit Athens, or indeed when rural groups found the transition to the city or commercial agriculture difficult, colonies proved to be effective ways of sopping up the excess population and keeping the Athenian citizenry content. Colonies had been serving such economic relief purposes as far back as Peisistratus's rule in the sixth century B.C.E. (Wilcoxon 1979, p. 146; French 1964, p. 48).[9] Finally, foreign acquisitions provided another wealth-generating asset of the ancient world: slaves. Campaigns against non-Greek territories yielded a hoard of people who could be traded as slaves. Athens, in fact, became the very center of the slave trade in the Aegean in this period, and slaves became some of its most valuable imports and reexports. Moreover, slaves served important functions back in Athens in providing services to keep the military and economic machine running smoothly (French 1964, p. 50).

But the empire, as it expanded, became all the more costly to maintain, which elicited greater expansion in order to cover these costs. In this development we see one of the most deleterious weakening effects of Athenian empire in the fifth century. It became far easier to fund the expansion by further expansion because that was less painful than making fundamental changes back in Athens (restructuring economic practices, relocating unemployed groups, fiscal caution). In this respect, the ease of funding expansion with further expansion generated moral hazard for Athenian policymakers with respect to developing indigenous capacity to control a great empire (French 1964, pp. 44–48; McGregor 1987, p. 53). The weakening effects of this moral hazard were numerous and manifold: in terms of economic and military development, the easy money of empire alleviated the need for more painful polices that forced Athens to grow and diversify in ways that made it independent of imperial resources.[10] To some extent, the old adage "it is easier to steal than work" made a compelling impression on imperial Athens. Moreover, such an incentive structure encouraged war (to obtain spoils). Even though its allies were providing a lion's share of the resources, wars were exceptionally costly for Athens: commerce suffered, fiscal demands rose, and in the larger wars Athenian agriculture was severely affected (McGregor 1987, p. 142). However, as long as there were no major shocks to the system that would indeed test the independent strength of Athens to hold its empire, the expansion could persist. But in fact, as an independent power that could effectively control its commercial and imperial network, the relative power of Athens was weakening. It would ultimately take the famous (second) Peloponnesian War of 431–404 B.C.E., together with the Sicilian campaign (the high point of Athenian greed, discussed later), to demonstrate the dangers of this debilitating process.[11]

Mission creep played an especially important role in driving the overexpansion of the empire. As noted, the military and commercial technology at the time precluded long military campaigns and commercial ventures without a train of "staging points" or networks. Hence a growing empire, for both economic and strategic reasons, generated a need for a military presence that was geographically conterminous. Commercial voyages needed to be protected, trade routes needed to be secured, and the administration of colonies and allies generated significant public expenses. In fact, both military and commercial ventures were never really independent under ancient imperial practices. Military campaigns were accompanied by large commercial flotillas that supplied the needs of war and addressed its business aspects (trade for slaves, commerce with foreign populations). Hence it is no surprise the geographic structure of the Delian League came to conform closely with the sea paths and inland passages that composed the dominant trade routes through the Greek world. But as time progressed and the empire grew, Athens became increasingly burdened with securing such a network, especially at peripheries where Athenian growth intruded into the spheres of other powerful states (Romilly 1963, pp. 66–67; French 1964, pp. 46–48, 109–116; McGregor 1987, pp. 94, 108–109).

Political support for empire at home, which fueled expansion all the more, was clearly a manifestation of the Athenian dependence on empire, as dominant political groups in Athens all had vested interests in growth. As noted, the shift from agriculture to manufacture and commerce in Athens increased the number of people who had a vested interest in empire, requiring more jobs for urban groups and greater commercial opportunities for landed estates and merchant classes. It is no coincidence that democracy could flourish under an imperial regime, as a growing empire made it possible to placate urban and rural groups with greater economic benefits (Wilcoxon 1979, p. 173). With the growth of commercial power in Athens in the sixth century B.C.E. under Peisistratus, the pattern of imperial populism was set, and Athens would be compelled to follow this pattern into the Periclean age of the fifth century. In becoming a commercial economy, Athens needed money—the key to political control of its population. And there was no greater means of generating money than through imperial expansion (French 1964, pp. 41–47).[12]

Interestingly, there was a logistical bias in Athenian democracy that favored the maintenance of empire. Decisions on important issues were made by votes in the Ecclesia (the entire citizen body). But given the difficulty of travel, the citizens who tended to attend such votes were urban dwellers and wealthy rural residents such as estate holders (McGregor 1987, pp. 114–115). Both these groups were especially rewarded by the possession of an empire and thus sought to support it in their voting decisions. Furthermore, in terms of coalition building, urban interests had an advantage over the politically fractured petty Attican dynasts (many of whom did not support imperialism) in acting collectively. This gave urban interests, whose fates were more intimately caught up in imperial Athens, an advantage in political mobilization (French 1964, pp. 60–67). Moreover, the empire became an asset even for the disgruntled Athenians who might have created problems for the policy agendas of Athenian leaders: if things deteriorated at home, these Athenians could be resettled in areas that enhanced their economic opportunities. So for a multitude of reasons, the empire was propelled by Athenian democracy (Thucydides 1985, VI:24; Wilcoxon 1979, p. 146).

Athenian imperial tyranny would prove to be a crucial factor affecting the geostrategic fate of Athens throughout the fifth century. And it would be one of the most important causes of the ultimate demise of the empire, and of Athens itself as an Aegean power. The Athenian imperial style was severe: demanding significant tributes, often imposing governments onto Delian League members, confiscating land (cleruchs), and severely punishing states that either revolted or refused to join the league. Cities might be sacked, entire male populations might be exterminated, and women and children would be abducted (McGregor 1987, pp. 170–174). Thucydides makes ongoing references to this tyranny throughout his *History of the Peloponnesian War.*[13] Athenians felt that expansion necessitated such severe methods and financial demands as their ever-increasing empire became more difficult to maintain.[14] But such methods also made the Delian states more recalcitrant, and their ongoing rebellions required increasingly greater resources to suppress and stabilize (i.e., occupation through garrisons), which led to a vicious cycle of Athenian tyranny (Forde 2000, p. 166).[15] All of the soft power that made a league under Athenian leadership possible during the Persian wars was compromised with the advent of this more tyrannical style of imperial policy. While this style may have enhanced the derivation of hard-power resources from the empire, it jeopardized the very legitimacy that made a great empire sustainable. Hence, Athens fell into the classic trap of power illusion as it pertains to power curse effects across the hard-soft power nexus.

But this burden of tyranny was sustainable as long as crucial events did not cause the system to buckle under its own inherent flaws. In this respect, the weakening effects of overstretch for the Athenians were never glaring in the short run of expansion, as each small burden could be supported by a large superstructure. However, the process was debilitating in the long run. When the tyranny of small burdens became unbearable, the debilitating consequences came rapidly and in the form of great shocks.[16]

Although colonial recalcitrance was a continuous drain on Athenian power, it served as an especially detrimental strategic factor during the Peloponnesian War of 431 to 404 B.C.E., which led to the ultimate defeat of Athens. The costs of keeping Delian League members in the alliance were considerable given the nature and length of ancient military campaigns, even when great powers faced smaller states. The war itself carried the ultimate shocks that revealed the latent weakening effects of Athenian expansion and greed. And in keeping with the fundamental inspiration for Athenian expansion, the war too was a result of Athens's own quest to increase its empire and even extend its sphere of influence beyond the Greek world. In both the great Peloponnesian War and its antecedents in the 450s and 440s, Athens incited Spartan action by expanding into Spartan spheres of influence. In this respect, we see one of the most dangerous consequences of overstretch: with an expanding presence in any international system, the likelihood of violating other spheres of influence, and consequently eliciting countervailing responses, increases with the level of expansion (Souza 2002, pp. 13–18, 28–31; McGregor 1987, p. 167).

The Peloponnesian War, throughout its course, was debilitating for Athens and its allies. The empire's ever-expanding demands on its allies increasingly aggravated these states; their discontent, in turn, required Athens to increase the severity of its imperialism, provoking rebellious upheavals that hampered its war effort (Souza 2002, p. 16; McGregor 1987, pp. 134–136).[17] Athens itself began facing fiscal strains and agricultural decimation that it had never faced in the course of the conflict-ridden years prior to the great war (French 1964, p. 169). But even after a torturous first decade, with both a weary Spartan League and an equally weary Athenian alliance instituting the so-called Peace of Nicias from 421 to 415, the Athenian appetite for empire never withered (McGregor 1987, p. 153). Even under the peace, Athens continued to expand its sphere. Eventually, this expansionism culminated in a campaign to capture Sicily in 414 and 413. It was this quest for Sicily that brought the ultimate and tragic consequences of imperial expansion crashing down upon Athens.

Sicily was long a desired prize for imperial Athens. It was one of the great producers of grain of the ancient world, an entrepôt at the crossroads of the major ancient trade routes, and a strategic platform to southern Europe. With its incorporation, it gave the Athenian empire a springboard to expand well beyond the Greek world. Upon resumption of the Peloponnesian War after the Peace of Nicias, Athens fixed its sights squarely on Sicily. In his *History,* Thucydides chronicles the Athenian decision to take the bold step of extending the war to a second front, in southern Italy. A speech by Alcibiades, one of history's most fascinating rogues, was featured as manifesting the rationale for such a bold quest. Alcibiades alluded to the great successes of the Athenian forefathers in building a great state and empire, and he urged the Athenians to continue their expansionist legacy into Sicily for the greater prosperity and glory of the empire: that which stops growing begins to rot (Thucydides 1985, VI:16–18).[18] But for Thucydides, it was this hubris of Alcibiades, and that of the Athenians whom Alcibiades convinced, that ultimately proved disastrous for Athens. Thucydides indeed cited this lack of moderation in conducting the war as the death knell for Athenian greatness. He noted how Athens could have averted disaster "if she avoided adding to her empire during the course of the war, and if she did nothing to risk the safety of the city itself." Athens did neither, with the biggest "mistake" being the expedition against Sicily (Thucydides 1985, II:65). Indeed, the quest for Sicily was the final act of overstretch that would break Athens's back: it was a far more challenging prize than Athens could conquer and maintain (Williams 1998, p. 215; Thucydides 1985, IV:55).

The crushing defeat of the entire Athenian expeditionary force in Sicily in 413 B.C.E. marked a crucial turning point in the war from which Athens's position quickly deteriorated. First, with the Athenian military decimated, and consequently its ability to punish rebellious alliance members compromised, disgruntled Delian states defected in droves to the Spartan side. Second, noncommitted states quickly joined the Spartan side once the course of the war became more predictable.[19] Third, with the Athenians decimated and Sparta gaining more allies, the psychological and strategic momentum shifted toward the Peloponnesians, and an emboldened Sparta adopted a more aggressive military strategy geared toward ultimate victory. Finally, the Persians, smelling blood and a possible means of redominating the Ionian Greek states that the Delian League had taken from them, joined into an alliance with Sparta against Athens. The tide had turned and the death knell sounded. It was here that overdependence on the empire became most glaring. Athens, having depended excessively on the empire for both the financial and the military resources to carry on its war effort, was left without sources for rebuilding its military power, and void of allies and bases. It had insufficient resources of its own due to years of failing to develop its own indigenous capabilities in the pursuit of easy money and resources from the empire. The Athenians, thanks to pure attrition, the inferior level of communication and transportation technology, and the seasonal character of ancient warfare, hung on for a number of years after their defeat at Sicily. But the fatal blow had been struck in 413. It was only a matter of time until the great empire, along with its great city, would fall in 404 B.C.E. (Souza 2002, p. 82; Thucydides 1985, VIII:2; McGregor 1987, p. 160).

In his *History,* Thucydides himself drew a distinction between the kind of policy that Athens used to acquire leadership in the Delian League and under which Athens prospered (i.e., Athens's soft power made it a respected and desired leader), and the later imperial policy that was used to maintain and augment the league, a far more tyrannical policy grounded in the use of hard power (Thucydides 1985, II:65; Connor 1984, p. 161; Crane 1998, p. 17; Garst 1989, p. 11). The great sphere of influence that the Athenians began forging with their enlightened leadership in the Persian wars was eventually compromised by greed and the need to ruthlessly acquire more wealth and resources. But in making itself materially stronger, Athens compromised a crucial source of its influence in the Greek world: its soft power. Athens's overexpansion was a function of its growing dependence on empire, whose increasing riches augmented its appetite. This was compounded by the expansive bias in mission creep and domestic politics. But in failing to develop its own independent capacity to survive without imperial resources, it became overly dependent on empire, and consequently had to manage its allies harshly in order to feed its increasing needs. In the end, as a result of its loss of soft power, Athens became a tragic victim of the power curse: its own structurally driven appetite for power (overstretch) turned its empire against it. In the long run, the great glory and power that Athenians attributed to their imperial presence was only illusory. In a culture that honored the golden mean of moderation in life, Athens had destroyed itself through excess. Perhaps Thucydides best summed up Athenian victimization by the power curse and power illusion: in its quest to "enslave" others, Athens ended up enslaving itself (1985, VII:72).

Moral Hazard in Nineteenth-Century British Finance

Both the British state and the Bank of England, Britain's central bank, fell prey to the power curse in the nineteenth century. Britain's financial primacy in the global economy afflicted both the state and the bank with financial moral hazard. This moral hazard manifested itself most visibly in an overly complacent posture toward financial conditions both in the British financial system as well as in the global financial system. More specifically, in terms of governmental intervention and regulation (the British state) and central banking duties (the Bank of England), primacy led to numerous deficiencies on the part of both entities with respect to financial oversight and management. The moral hazard manifested itself across the hard-soft power nexus as well as within the composition of hard-power resources specifically. Enormous financial hard power led to deficiencies in the development of both soft and hard managerial resources that would have made the state and the bank better managers of the gold standard, both in Britain and internationally. The moral hazard of financial primacy led the state and the bank to become muscle-bound as financial managers. The great power over capital they enjoyed led them to neglect developing other, more flexible tools to manage capital flows and financial systems. The lack of these other tools comprised both hard- and soft-power instruments.

Early industrialization and primacy in global commerce brought Britain significant gains in global finance. As the first great economic power and the world's greatest trading nation, Britain assumed financial primacy in the global economy. Much has been said about this primacy, but a revealing testament can be gleaned from comparing British finance in the nineteenth century with that of the second leading financial power at that time: France.[20] Britain had a central bank 106 years before France. The British fiscal revolution took place about a century before that of France. Banknote use also became widespread in Britain about a century before it did in France. Bills of exchange came into widespread use in Britain more than two centuries before they did in France. Insurance services were introduced in Britain more than a century before they were in France. The London clearinghouse also predated the French clearinghouse by about a century. Finally, as late as 1863, only about a quarter of France had access to banking. Compare this with the fact that in 1855, Wales and England had 409 banks with 1,185 banking offices, thus creating extensive access to banking in Britain (Kindleberger 1984, pp. 114–115). This primacy made Britain, and London specifically, the very centers of global finance. Most of world trade and investment was cleared through the London market, and sterling became the principal vehicle currency in the global economy. As the century progressed, Britain's gold standard spread and gold became the principal metallic money, thus enhancing Britain's primacy (Gallarotti 1993, 1995a; Bordo and Rockoff 1996).

This primacy manifested itself in unmatched power over the flow of capital (Lindert 1969). Hence, Britain and London enjoyed unrivaled hard financial power over global capital.[21] London became the conduit through which global finance flowed, and its position strengthened as the century progressed due to growth of the world economy and increasing adoption of the gold standard. The London market was the largest and most diversified in the world by far. Sterling and gold became the principal global currencies (both for hard and soft reasons), the result being that British financial houses came to manage a lion's share of global commerce and investment. Notwithstanding the greater use of fiduciary reserves (i.e., nonmetallic) across the century, we see that even upon the eve of World War I, official reserves among the central banks of the leading thirty-five nations were still dominated by gold (about 68 percent of official reserves). With respect to sterling, no other currency came close to its role as a reserve currency. Even with the significant growth of the other two leading European currencies—francs and marks—over the latter half of the nineteenth century, sterling still reigned supreme. Among the official reserves of the thirty-five leading nations, sterling reserves were about equal to francs and marks combined (Lindert 1969).

The financial pulling power of London was compounded by its role as the leading gold market in the world. As gold came into greater use across the century, this pulling power increased. London's ascension as a gold market derived from all of the factors that gave it primacy as a financial market in general, especially domination of trade and early industrialization. But London was all the more central in the global gold market because it was the freest gold market in the world. No other market had fewer impediments in the exchange and shipment of gold. The entrance and exit costs of gold shipments through London were the lowest in the world. As with the primacy of financial intermediaries, gold brokers and complementary financial services in metal dealings were the most experienced and abundant in the world (Gallarotti 1995a, p. 197; US Senate 1910, p. 112).

At the very core of the powerful British financial machine was the Bank of England. The bank itself was the major player in the British financial market. It originated in 1694 as the official bank of the British government and developed unrivaled size and power among British joint-stock banks. Its bank rate was perceived as the most influential single financial mechanism in world finance. It was often said during the nineteenth century that the right bank rate could "draw gold from the moon." As the central bank in the most powerful financial market of the period (London), the bank had the power to shape the flow of capital both nationally and internationally. Hence it was widely regarded as having the capacity to control Britain's and London's economic fates.

This financial primacy led to extreme confidence on the part of the directors of the Bank of England as well as the British government in the ability of the bank to maintain financial stability in Britain. The view presented in testimonies by the directors of the bank attests to a sense of supreme confidence in the belief that the bank could attract whatever gold and capital it desired by simply manipulating its bank rate: "experience seems to prove that the raising of the bank rate . . . never fails to attract gold" (US Senate 1910, p. 26). In the minds of political leaders and monetary authorities, this effectively made the British financial system impervious to prolonged financial crises. In the public mind as well as elite minds, the system was bulletproof. Such perceptions led to an extreme (and in fact false) sense of invulnerability. In turn, this confidence led to a type of financial moral hazard that rendered both the Bank of England and the British government more deficient as money managers than they otherwise would have been if perceptions had assessed British financial power to be more limited.[22]

As for the British government, financial moral hazard produced an inferior track record of financial oversight compared to other governments of leading financial markets. In general, governments of leading nations were far less involved in financial oversight than their successors would be in the period after World War I. This was a function of the prevalence of the market society of the nineteenth century (Polanyi 1957). Governments were not significantly involved in economic regulation in general, and even less so with respect to finance. Bank regulation and scrutiny by governments were in their infancy in the nineteenth century, and this was true across leading nations. Governments imposed few regulations on banks and other financial intermediaries. What regulations did exist tended to be restricted to rules governing requirements for the issue of banknotes. These regulations tended to assign some level of acceptable backing (whether specie or fiduciary reserves) when banks were printing money. Aside from regulations about the backing of banknotes, banking regulations were fairly synonymous with company law. Such laws regulated corporate governance and general business operations rather than specific banking practices.

But even at this lower level of general scrutiny and financial regulation, the track record of the British state was still demonstrably inferior to that of the governments of other leading financial powers. The British government had actually intervened more frequently in financial crises before 1825 through the use of exchequer bills (i.e., enhancing liquidity in crises by issuing more government securities). The year 1825 became a watermark for the government's separation from any role as lender of last resort. The famous Tory leader George Canning manifested the new norm in a letter to Lord Liverpool saying that given the Bank of England's "power to lend on goods," it was the bank's duty to relieve the British government of crisis lending and assume sole responsibility for lending in last resort. Interestingly, as the bank became financially stronger, the government itself slipped into the background as a financial guarantor (Kindleberger 1984, p. 91; Fetter 1965, p. 119).[23]

Historically, banking was the least-supervised and least-regulated industry in Britain.[24] Aside from regulations on procedures for backing the issue of banknotes, more general rules for handling banking transactions (deposits, lending, reserve requirements, discounting, accounting, branching) hardly existed in Britain, though such rules were more visible elsewhere in Europe. A prominent British banker of the period testified that British joint-stock banks were under "no supervision or examination" from the government (US Senate 1910, p. 34). Conversely, outside Britain there was much more direct government supervision and management of banking. In France, for example, the minister of finance could at any time inquire into the actions of the central bank, and in Germany the Reichsbank was principally run by government representatives. In both France and Germany, there were regulations about procedures for central bank discounting, requirements for holding government securities, as well as rules about the creation of regional branches of the central banks. In both nations, governments granted more of a monopoly over note issue to their central banks. Moreover, cooperation with and oversight of private banking was much more vigorous outside Britain (US Senate 1910, pp. 9, 11, 206, 209, 335).

Specifically in relation to its central bank, the British government was far more removed from bank operations compared to other European governments. The British government treated the Bank of England as it did other joint-stock banks in terms of supervision and regulation. We see a consistency in testimonies from Bank of England directors from the time of the Bank Charter Hearings in 1832 to the inception of the National Monetary Commission in 1910: the bank had little to do with the government outside of its business as repository for the government's accounts. The bank did depend on the government for periodic renewal of its charter, but there is no evidence that such a position of power was ever turned into direct influence over policy. In terms of government influence, the bank functioned as an island (Gallarotti 1995a, p. 95; US Senate 1910, pp. 8, 11).

Indeed, differing financial conditions in Britain versus elsewhere gave the respective European states differing incentives over the level of public involvement in banking. The British government was faced with greater moral hazard because its financial system was the largest and deepest in the world. Hence it was far more self-sufficient in crises than were other systems. Aside from being financially more bulletproof, the power to attract capital both on the part of the Bank of England and the London market more generally provided more built-in shock absorbers than were enjoyed in other leading financial markets. Finally, as an early industrializer, the British state had been less intimately involved with the course and evolution of banking. This was not the case with later industrializers outside Britain, which found governmental involvement necessary to foster the scale of economic activity necessary to catch up with the early industrializers (Gerschenkron 1962).[25]

Moral hazard on the part of the British government also manifested itself at the international level. The Foreign Office adhered to the same laissez-faire orientation subscribed to by other parts of the British government. There is an especially stark contrast with other European states in this respect, especially France and Germany. In fact, in Britain, economic matters were given the lowest priority among foreign officers. And it is not clear that the Foreign Office itself had any coherent policy on economic affairs. Britain's foreign financial ventures were already well established and robust by the time outside competition came onto the scene—another manifestation of the early industrializer effect (Wilkins 2003). Other governments had to play a greater role in promoting the causes of their investors (as latecomers) in order to break through British financial primacy. Britain was enjoying the benefits of the imperialism of private investment, and hence intervention was not as crucial. This in turn gave the British Foreign Office far less incentive to intervene in foreign markets (Gallagher and Robinson 1953). But in this case, the financial power of the home financial market compounded the moral hazard of the Foreign Office, as the lure of sterling made British ventures that much less vulnerable (Platt 1968, p. 10; Feis 1930, p. 87).

Having a more active interventionist presence would have laid more robust foundations for the British financial system. Opting out of having an economic presence left the system essentially to itself and the Bank of England. While the system was large and robust, and the Bank of England a powerful financial actor, still the system was prone to various destabilizing outcomes throughout the century, such as liquidity crises. More vigorous government involvement, as was visible in other financial markets, whether through hard power (direct regulation) or soft power (facilitating cooperation among banks), would have allowed the British system to better ride the waves of financial instability. While crises were never fatal to the system (i.e., never caused a suspension of gold convertibility), the system was cursed with a long line of shocks that were either poorly managed or excessively prolonged (Gallarotti 1995a, pp. 129–131).

Like the British government, the Bank of England also fell prey to financial moral hazard. In fact, it is fairly safe to say that the bank exhibited one of the poorest records of central banking among leading industrial powers during the nineteenth century. Even the United States, which had no central bank, showed better public financial management. In the US case, it was the treasury that effectively filled the role of lender of last resort (Bagehot [1873] 1921). While a great deal of this emanated from a common problem among central banks at the time—their function, largely, as profit-making joint-stock companies—it was the power of both the British market and the Bank of England's rate itself to attract capital in times of liquidity crunches that led to what essentially amounted to an underdevelopment of central banking functions on the part of the bank.[26] This power allowed the bank the luxury of indulging more on the profit side of its dual, public-private mandate but at the cost of adverse consequences for the British financial system.

One of the ways in which moral hazard manifested itself in the functions of the Bank of England was in the fact that the power of the rate to "draw gold from the moon" led to the underdevelopment of its other central banking functions, functions in which central banks in other leading markets were better endowed. In this respect, reliance on one instrument of central banking rendered the Bank of England muscle-bound.[27] First, as noted, the bank was relatively weak in terms of its supervision and regulation of private banking in Britain. Other central banks were far more vigorous in regulating and supervising the private sector (US Senate 1910). Above and beyond official links to the banking sector, the Bank of England fell short in cultivating even informal links (i.e., soft financial power). As one prominent banker testified in the late nineteenth century: "There is no official way of communicating, no regular meeting between the [British] banks and the Bank of England" (US Senate 1910, p. 51). This was in stark contrast to the practice of central banks elsewhere in Europe. For example, Georges Brincard of Credit Lyonnais underscored how relations between the Bank of France and other French banks were "intimate" (US Senate 1910, p. 243). Second, the Bank of England carried on very few open-market operations as a means of influencing financial conditions in Britain.[28] In fact, the government issued no requirements that even obligated the bank to hold government securities. The Bank of France, in contrast, had to hold a sizable portfolio of government securities (US Senate 1910, p. 194). Third, management of the money supply, in general, showed relatively glaring deficiencies in Britain. Unlike in most other leading nations, there was no monopoly of note issue in Britain in the nineteenth century: private banks could print money as well. Monetary experts at the time underscored the potential financial risk that competitive issue carried. This owed to the fact that competitive issue reduced the direct influence that central banks had over the respective national money supplies, and in Britain this was all the more tenuous due to the limited soft power of the Bank of England (i.e., its minimal cooperation with private banks).[29] Fourth, the ability of the Bank of England to influence regional credit markets was restricted relative to central banks outside Britain given the comparatively fewer number of branches it possessed. In 1910 it had 11 branches, compared to the 188 branches of the Bank of France and the 493 branches of the Reichsbank (US Senate 1910, pp. 10, 191, 338).

Fifth, common central-banking devices to manage the gold reserves were the most underdeveloped in Britain. All central banks at the time used instruments called "gold devices" to manage their gold reserves.[30] Gold reserves in central banks were the very foundation upon which the private financial systems of gold-standard nations rested. These standards required that financial institutions be able to convert fiduciary assets into gold on demand. Since private banks wanted to maximize profits and hence hold as few gold reserves as possible (because gold holdings generated no interest), the gold holdings in central banks became the ultimate reserve for the entire banking systems, as private banks would use these reserves in times of need. Because the pulling power of the Bank of England's rate was so vigorous, the bank felt less compelled to develop more clever and effective gold devices to manage the gold reserve. In this sense, it was relatively weaker than other banks, such as the Reichsbank and the Bank of France, which proved masterful in the development of effective gold devices (Gallarotti 1995a, p. 48). Moreover, in terms of being a facilitator of financial clearing among banks—an especially important role in allowing private banks to stay liquid—the Bank of England was far inferior to banks outside Britain. The Bank of France and the Reichsbank were prolific in this function, as bankers of the period underscored. The Giro Konto of the Reichsbank was hailed as a model for systems of interbank clearing. The Bank of England did not even clear payments between its own branches for private banks and was not even a full member of London's clearinghouse (US Senate 1910, pp. 24, 204, 345, 386).

Finally, perhaps the Bank of England's biggest deficiency was in its role as lender of last resort.[31] It was in this respect, even with its own great pulling power, and that of the London market, that the bank's "thin film" of gold reserves was most criticized. After all, Britain had faced some severe financial crises in the first half of the century and some milder ones in the second half. While the bank and London could draw capital from the far reaches of the globe, the system was still prone to lingering liquidity crunches. Moreover, given that sterling was the leading currency in the world, the meager reserves of the Bank of England had to support the international liabilities of Britain in addition to the domestic liabilities of British finance. This was a very large pool of liabilities to be buttressed on so small a pedestal of gold. In terms of convertibility, any short-run liquidations of any size would quickly deplete the bank's reserves. This great international burden made the banking community in Britain even more nervous about the stability of the British financial system.[32] Other leading nations held far greater gold reserves in their central banks and held far fewer domestic and international liabilities. The Bank of France, for example, became famous during the period as the very best central bank with respect to managing a gold reserve. The French golden "hoard" was often held up as the antithesis of British financial irresponsibility (Patron 1910; Gallarotti 2005). Moreover, the other central banks had an advantage over the Bank of England in protecting their gold reserves because they maintained the option of converting notes into silver when gold was scarce. The Bank of England's convertibility was based almost entirely on gold alone (US Senate 1910, p. 216).[33]

Beyond Walter Bagehot's scathing critiques ([1873] 1921), this relative insecurity among British financiers compared to their counterparts in other nations was poignantly clear from official banking testimonies of the late nineteenth century (US Senate 1910, pp. 58, 111, 196). According to these testimonies, financiers and central bankers in other nations demonstrated a supreme confidence in the ability of their central banks to make metallic conversions in periods of need, and also in the willingness of central banks to lend liberally in such times.[34] In Britain, financiers exhibited skepticism on both counts (US Senate 1910, p. 111). Unlike directors of other central banks, the directors of the Bank of England never assuaged such fears with definitive statements about their obligations to lend in last resort.

The actual behavior of the Bank of England surrounding British financial crises in the nineteenth century (when its powers to lend in last resort were most required) reflects actions and attitudes that were consistent with this relatively deficient central-banking posture. Although the power of the British capital market and the Bank of England imparted a strong measure of stability to British finance, the vulnerabilities of the bank as a result of financial moral hazard became clearly evident when financial conditions did deteriorate.[35] The bank's track record of "imprudent behavior" during financial crises casts doubt upon its role as a stabilizing force in British finance (Andreades 1909, p. 332). When looking especially at the famous crises of 1847, 1857, 1866, and 1906–1907, a pattern of less-than-stellar central banking emerges. The bank's own investments often fueled excessive speculation that led to financial bubbles in British finance; it coterminously allowed its reserves to fall to excessively low levels, thus fueling panic (which the bank initially was unable to abate, and in the post-crisis period often responded by too harshly raising its discount rate); and it proved to be overly restrictive in lending in last resort (Gallarotti 1995a, pp. 129–130; Fetter 1965, pp. 14–15, 60, 113–114, 165; Kindleberger 1984, p. 91; Andreades 1909, pp. 250–253; Bagehot [1873] 1921, pp. 111, 170).

But the one ongoing and destabilizing consequence of the bank's financial moral hazard that emanated from its power curse was its excessive reliance on manipulating its discount rate in order to manage its reserves. Since the rate had proved influential, and this influence had discouraged the bank from developing other tools of central banking, it was faced with a vicious cycle of dependence on its rate to achieve its financial goals. In the crises mentioned above, it would have been better if the bank had managed them without excessively raising its discount rate, which made liquidity crunches all the more severe. But the rate had essentially become the principal tool and hence drew the greatest use. More generally, excessive reliance on the rate to manage gold reserves, combined with significantly low reserves, forced the bank to alter the rate all too often. In contrast, central banks outside Britain held significantly larger gold reserves and hence were able to maintain more stable rates. The relatively more unstable rate in Britain produced a far less desirable environment within which to conduct financial and commercial transactions. The erratic bank rate became a prime target for criticism in the British business community. In fact, consortia of private banks proposed a number of initiatives (which ultimately failed) to pool their resources in order to form a more stable alternative to the bank's own instruments in influencing credit conditions in British finance (Wood 1939, p. 148; De Cecco 1974, p. 193; Gallarotti 1995a, p. 128).

This relative deficiency of the Bank of England as a central banker became even more pernicious relative to other nations. Central banks outside Britain were much less competitive with private banks in their financial markets. The directors of these central banks, and the private banking communities in their nations, attested strongly to the fact that the public functions of the central banks trumped their private mandate. These banks were more restricted in the financial transactions they were allowed to engage in, and their central bank discount rates were kept at a level that gave private banks an advantage in discounting and principal banking services. The Bank of England was not as restricted in its business practices, nor was it perceived to be such a guardian public institution. Its own discount rate often followed the market very closely, especially in fair-weather conditions when its public functions were less crucial. In fact, it was perceived as, and acted like, a fierce competitor among British financial houses. Its business practices directly competed with those of private banks in all areas of financial intermediation. This created a far more unstable financial environment in Britain relative to other financial markets: in the case of the Bank of England, there was a strong incentive for it to allow major joint-stock banks to fail (US Senate 1910, pp. 24, 199, 211, 343, 353, 390; Fetter 1965, p. 259; King 1936, p. 159; Gallarotti 1995a, p. 116).

At the international level, we can also see manifestations of the Bank of England's power curse. Given its great power over international capital flows, the bank plodded through the nineteenth century as anything but a vigilant overseer of international financial conditions. Indeed, it should have embraced such a role given the fact that London was a principal target of demand for liquidity in the case of international financial crises. Shocks would always be felt at the core, and hence the bank should have been more mindful of the state of international financial conditions. Evidence overwhelmingly shows that it was even more complacent about international financial conditions than it was about national conditions. Interestingly, it was the Bank of France that played the most pronounced role as international central banker during the second half of the century. Also interesting was the relative weakness of Paris vis-à-vis London as a financial market that drove the Bank of France to be more vigilant in intervening in international markets when crises occurred or were imminent.[36]

Indeed, a greater incentive on the parts of the British government and Bank of England to develop both hard and soft financial power would have benefited the British financial system and the international system significantly. In this respect, the moral hazard emanating from the financial power curse left British finance worse off. Developing softer power capacities specifically would have generated significant stabilizing benefits. A glaring testament to this was the case of the 1890 Barings financial crisis in Britain. This crisis was resolved by the perspicacity of the governor of the Bank of England at the time (William Lidderdale), who at his own individual initiative thought it prudent to solicit the cooperation of various private banks and the Russian government in creating a lending consortium to aid Barings. There was in fact much demand among private bankers in Britain for more extensive cooperation among major players in British finance, but leadership on the part of the Bank of England (which could have forged many more systematic institutions to guard British finance) was not forthcoming. Consequently, the bank squandered numerous opportunities for enhancing the financial stability of Britain through such soft financial power. Certainly, the Bank of France forged such cooperative initiatives to stave off major international financial crises. Indeed, it was the informal international financial networks (i.e., the soft financial power elements of interbank cooperation) that the Bank of France made principal use of in managing international crises in this period (Gallarotti 2005).

In sum, the great financial power of the British economy and of the Bank of England specifically proved in many ways to be a curse for both the British government and the bank itself with respect to their roles as financial guardians. The moral hazard generated by preponderant power over international capital markets made both the state and the bank complacent as financial managers, at both the domestic and international levels. This complacency actually retarded the development of more extensive and robust hard and soft financial mechanisms that could have been employed to stabilize and protect British finance from internal and external shocks. In this sense, moral hazard made both the British state and the Bank of England muscle-bound as financial managers. This was most evident in periods surrounding financial crises, when lack of monitoring, intervention, and central-banking tools resulted in a deterioration of the British financial system, especially during crises that were too large for the bank to effectively abate through rate adjustment. Fortunately for British finance and global finance in the nineteenth century, the well-functioning greater political economy of the period resulted in few exogenous shocks that severely tested Britain and its central bank. Hence the track record of financial stability in Britain and the developed world in the nineteenth century emerged despite British central banking rather than as a direct result of it.[37]

The Vicious Cycle of Unilateralism and Britain's Silver Problem

The depreciation of silver in the late nineteenth century and its consequences for the economic interests of Great Britain represent another manifestation of the power curse. In this case, the power curse manifested itself in a vicious cycle of unilateralism that cut against British colonial and economic interests. As the silver depreciation created greater problems and concern for British trade and finance, Britain continually shied away from optimal solutions for arresting the depreciation (in this case it was a multilateral arrangement to support the price of silver—a soft-power solution to the problem), in large part because it perceived itself as possessing the unilateral muscle to both withstand the consequences of the problem as well as manage it.[38] As prospects for a multilateral solution to the problem became ever more remote because of British intransigence, Britain was forced to rely more on its own unilateral perspicacity (primarily its hard economic resources) to deal with the consequences of the depreciation. In the end, the harder unilateral solutions proved much inferior to the softer multilateral options in dealing with the silver problem.

From the mid-1870s to the end of the century, silver lost approximately one-third of its value. This decline was driven by a number of secular processes, most notably that nations were becoming increasingly enamored with the gold standard. In fact, Britain's own soft power as a role model drove developed nations toward a gold standard. The reversion to gold was compounded by a greater need for a high-value currency with which to conduct the higher-value transactions that were occurring in wealthy societies (since silver was about one-fifteenth the value of gold, it would have been inconvenient to carry a mass of silver coins to make such large transactions). Once the depreciation began, the shifting political balance between gold and silver users (which favored stable money groups over inflationists) gave gold greater backing in national governments. As more nations began demonetizing silver, a chain-gang effect resulted, with other nations becoming increasingly anxious to move from silver to a gold standard.[39] With the significant increase in worldwide production of silver, coupled with the increased monetary use of gold, supply increasingly superseded demand, hence the depreciation in the market value of silver (Gallarotti 1993, 1995a).

The consequences of the depreciation for Great Britain were widely perceived as grave. In fact, three major government-sponsored commissions were organized in this period to analyze the economic consequences of the fall in the value of silver and to suggest solutions.[40] It is interesting that all three commissions underscored a multilateral solution (i.e., the soft solution) as being the very best means of abating the fall of silver, but in the absence of such prospects, each drew up varying suggestions for unilateral responses to the problem.[41] The inquiries all demonstrated extensive and pervasive concerns among the British people about the consequences of the depreciation. All three commissions agreed that the British government should vigorously address the situation as an economic priority.

Concerns for the consequences of the silver problem all involved fundamental sources of British wealth and economic power, with India being cast at the very center of the issue. Britain faced the problem of trading with nations still officially on silver or bimetal standards in a period when their currencies were depreciating vis-à-vis sterling (Bagchi 1989, p. 69). This generated the threat that trade balances with these nations, which had been strong historically, might deteriorate to the detriment of Britain: depreciation of other currencies would make foreign goods cheaper relative to British goods, hence creating an advantage for the former. While many nations were gravitating toward gold, some of them did not make the official change until well after the 1870s—for example, Austria did not adopt the gold standard until 1892, the United States not until 1900, nor did India, which kept a silver standard until 1893.[42] This was an especially crucial period for British trade, as British industries were trying to adjust to greater competition from new industries in the developed world as well as to competition from textiles in the undeveloped world. In addition to these threats to Britain's commercial primacy, a loss in competitiveness from currency depreciation in silver-standard nations compounded the problem all the more. All three of Britain's monetary commissions allocated significant attention to the problem of trading prospects in the face of silver depreciation (Great Britain 1888, 1893, 1899). And while they tried to assuage fears about the extent of this trade effect, they never definitively dispelled the belief that British trade would be adversely affected by the silver problem.[43] But irrespective of their views on the size of the trade problem, all three commissions resolutely affirmed that the concerns in British society were grave and pervasive, and that those concerns themselves were reason enough for the British government to resolutely devise a solution to the silver problem.[44]

The most important trade consequence of the depreciation of silver involved India, whose currency (the rupee) was silver. Hence the depreciation of silver caused a concomitant depreciation of the rupee. India was the very lynchpin of Britain's commercial strength, especially in the crucial period of industrial decline after 1850. India came to occupy a critically important role in the rising multilateral trade networks that arose after 1850. In virtually all of the trading networks that it anchored, it tended to run up large trade surpluses with other nations, while running up large deficits with Britain. India was also Britain's largest trading partner. Hence, India was the key factor in maintaining Britain's strong trade position through these crucial years (Saul 1960; De Cecco 1974; Bagchi 1989; Roy 2000). The strong colonial association kept the demand for British imports very high, even though many of the goods (especially textiles) were also produced in India itself. While other nations were shifting out of silver to gold, the British government entertained no such serious prospects for India until the 1890s. Hence, Britain faced the possibility of continuing to trade with its largest trading partner under conditions of currency depreciation: as the rupee depreciated, it would make it harder for Britain to export goods to India and would also increase British imports from India.[45] This prospect was compounded by an already-increasing competitiveness in Indian industries that were replicating British know-how and technology as a result of large British foreign direct investment in Indian manufacturing after 1850 (Southgate 1969, p. 166). Furthermore, India was an important source of capital for London. Colonial ties made Indian capital very sensitive to demand for investment in London in times of need. Stable finance in India was essential for it to continue being an important source of capital for London (De Cecco 1974, p. 62). Moreover, the unstable rupee was a nightmare for British investors who were trading in rupee-denominated investments at a lower value (Great Britain 1888, p. 144; Great Britain 1893, p. 21; Keynes [1913] 1971, p. 2).

Even more threatening to British economic interests were the effects of silver depreciation on the finances of India. As the jewel of Britain's imperial system, a healthy India was crucial to the economic well-being of Britain, and not just in the area of trade (Great Britain 1888, pp. 207–208; Southgate 1969, p. 155). Britain essentially relied on India as a colony for what amounted to tribute (although the economic transfers were always manifest in the exchange of goods and services, as opposed to direct tribute). Britain was compensated for various services that provided public goods to India (infrastructures, defense). These "home charges" were extensive and provided both the British government and British citizens with significant earnings (De Cecco 1974, p. 63). In this panoply of colonial dealings were tens of thousands of resident British ex-patriots and British industries that derived their livelihoods in India. The home-charges problem was perhaps the most underscored in the official documents and analyses of the silver problem with respect to India. The home charges were in effect denominated and paid in gold, while the Indian government of course raised its revenues in silver (collecting taxes in rupees). With the depreciation of the silver rupee vis-à-vis British sterling, the Indian government had to shoulder an increasing burden in covering the home charges. Britain's various monetary commissions spent a great deal of time on the problem of paying the home charges (Great Britain 1888, 1893, 1899). This placed a great strain on Indian finance, as the Indian government found it necessary either to continue to struggle or to resort to increased taxation. Tax increases caused widespread discontent and made the colonial position of Britain all the more precarious (Great Britain 1893, p. 23; De Cecco 1974, p. 66). This was the case because taxes were already historically high in India (a vestige of colonial policy) and India was prone to problems of recession and famine (especially in the 1890s). Taxing an already burdened population in periods of deprivation seriously threatened Britain's hold over its colonial jewel, a colony that by all accounts "could not be given up" (Southgate 1969, pp. 155, 165).

Donald Southgate (1969, p. 170) sees strong seeds of anticolonialism arising in the 1890s as a result of these converging crises. This is a clear manifestation of power illusion, as great financial strength in Britain made the British often insensitive and "callous" in the face of India's problems (and insensitive also to its own economic consequences). This callousness was all the more reprehensible given continuing pleas on the part of Indian officials to the British government to do something about these problems (Bagchi 1989, p. 78).

But just as menacing for British economic interests were the effects on British ex-patriots living and working in India. These British citizens sent wages earned in India back to their families living in Britain. With the declining value of the rupee (with which they were paid), the value of the remittances to Britain (after being converted into gold) fell. In effect, a large population of British citizens faced the problem of a secular decline in their wages. The three monetary commissions placed this problem alongside home charges as one of the most devastating effects of the silver problem in India. And while the statistical evidence produced by the commissions did not confirm an actual trade impact of the depreciating rupee, the statistical findings regarding both home charges and remittances were definitively alarming (Great Britain 1888, 1893, 1899).

Moreover, India, aside from serving a crucial economic role for Britain, also played a key strategic role for the British in the East. India was a platform from which Britain secured many of its trade routes to the East and also for launching military operations in southern and central Asia. Indeed, the Indian army was carefully modernized and maintained as a possible means of deflecting a possible attack from Russia on British territories (Bartlett 1969, p. 182).

The British government had three crucial opportunities to facilitate a multilateral solution to the silver problem. A multilateral solution was the only effective solution because a stable global price of silver could only be maintained by a large number of nations agreeing to maintain the demand for silver by keeping their mints open to silver coinage (Bagchi 1989, p. 86; Great Britain 1899, p. 465; Gallarotti 1995a, pp. 66–78). No nation had the power to unilaterally support the price of silver, as the level of silver stocks far outstripped the size of any single financial system (a fact about which Britain remained skeptical until the 1890s). This of course did not necessarily mean unlimited coinage of silver, but a viable solution could be achieved by nations agreeing to maintain some minimum level of silver coinage. As silver continued to decline in the 1870s, and nations moved to restrict silver coinage in preparation for shifting to gold standards, nations became more reluctant to consider multilateral plans for maintaining silver purchases at their mints. The situation devolved more and more into a Prisoner's Dilemma, with nations reluctant to make the first cooperative move in buying silver, as this opened them up to exploitation: other nations would dump depreciating silver on them, and of course the holders of silver would get stuck with a worthless metal (Bagchi 1989, p. 89; Gallarotti 1995a, pp. 66–78).

The three opportunities came in the form of three international monetary conferences (1878, 1881, and 1892) organized by both the United States and France, whose bimetallist past gave them extensive incentives to try to maintain the price of silver. Having had a long tradition in the use of silver, both nations were pervaded by extensive economic interests that had a stake in the value of silver. France and the United States attempted a reestablishment of bimetallism in one form or another in the first two conferences, while the United States was the main force in the third conference, which was oriented more around a plan for supporting the price of silver through limited silver-minting commitments on the part of participant nations. On the whole, developed nations were willing to cooperate with a number of proposals launched at the conferences, with the exception of Germany at the conference of 1878. They were especially agreeable to limited buying-commitments for silver, as underscored in the conference of 1892. The real lynchpin to the success of the negotiations was Britain. As the leading market for precious metals, Britain was to bear an important responsibility. Without Britain, nations were reluctant to commit, as any plan to stabilize the price of precious metals depended on its own willingness to commit to buying silver. Without Britain, such plans were risky, and hence nations would be stuck buying lots of silver that might eventually lose its value (Gallarotti 1995a, pp. 66–78).

Britain was exceedingly reluctant to cooperate in any of these schemes. British reluctance derived from several factors, all intricately related to the power curse, which drove Britain to prefer unilateral solutions to the depreciation of silver. Interestingly, one important factor derived from its own soft power as a role model. First, the British government was reluctant to make any changes, even the most minor alterations to its domestic financial system, which was seen by many Brits as having helped deliver economic primacy to the country in the nineteenth century. Britain's own financial power was perceived as a function of its historical financial unilateralism, and hence it was merely sticking with a strategy that had always delivered in the past.[46] Second, India had historically been the largest market for silver in the world throughout the nineteenth century. So extensive was the use of silver in India, both monetary and commercial, that in the 1850s and 1860s the net imports of silver into India actually surpassed the global production of silver in those years (Gallarotti 1995a, p. 163). In this sense, many Brits believed they could solve the silver problem by employing Britain's own colonial sphere, and thus maintaining a unilateral posture. There was no convincing evidence in the opinion of many Brits that India could not unilaterally support the price of silver just by continuing its past level of silver importation (Great Britain 1893, p. 21). And, while Indian net silver imports did indeed decline after 1870, many Brits continued to hope for a revival of Indian silver imports.

Third, British moral hazard emanating from commercial and financial primacy compounded the role-model disposition against significant financial change. And as the leading financial and commercial power in the world, Britain was equipped to absorb the shocks of silver depreciation far more than any other nation (a fact that showed up in the differing diplomatic positions at the conferences). Furthermore, Britain could always use commercial policies to keep the Indian market open to British goods even if the rupee depreciated. In the final analysis, perceptions of Britain's limited economic vulnerability made the perceived costs of avoiding changes in their sacred financial orthodoxy appear tolerable. Moreover, the depreciation of silver in the last third of the nineteenth century, while secularly significant, occurred in an incremental and smooth, rather than lumpy, fashion, aside from some sharp depreciations in the 1880s and 1890s and the subsequent depreciation of the Indian rupee (Bagchi 1989, p. 68; Gallarotti 1995a, p. 166).[47] Fourth, there remained some hope among Brits that the French and more probably the Americans would undertake unilateral actions (or possibly effect bilateral or multilateral solutions) to keep silver from depreciating. In this respect, Britain acted as a free-rider (a unilateral posture of malign neglect) on the actions of France and the United States that impressed Britain enough that it hoped other nations would form a bimetallist union at the various conferences (Bagchi 1989, p. 89). Beyond and above this leadership, the United States passed two bills (stimulated by the political agitation of silver interests) that called for unilateral measures to guarantee the public purchase of silver for the purpose of coinage: the Bland Act of 1878 and the Sherman Act of 1892. Finally, there was an obvious preference for a unilateral solution over multilateral solutions, all things being equal. This would allow Britain to avoid any entangling monetary commitments that might dictate undesirable changes in its policies and practices (Great Britain 1888, p. 200).

British intransigence fundamentally doomed prospects for multilateral solutions to the problem of depreciating silver, and this reflects a fundamental property of the power curse as manifest in a vicious cycle of unilateralism. British intransigence essentially made other nations less resolute in cooperating because without Britain, as noted, little could be accomplished. This declining commitment on the part of other nations showed up in a declining resolve to try to resuscitate bimetallism across nations, as the conference of 1892 only aspired to a price-support scheme for silver rather than an international bimetallist solution (which was proposed at the conferences of 1878 and 1881). And after 1892, nations gave up. In effect, Britain's unilateral posture became more necessary as its unwillingness to build multilateral solutions stripped nations of the resolve to do so. Diminishing resolve meant fewer attempts by other nations to catalyze such solutions and hence fewer opportunities for Britain to take advantage of them. Therefore, we see the emergence of a vicious cycle of unilateralism: Britain undermined multilateral efforts to solve its problems and had to rely ever more frequently on its own unilateral resources. The timing of the three monetary commissions reflects this vicious cycle well: all came after attempts to institute an international bimetallist solution had failed. The commissions reflect the fact that Britain was in a unilateral bind. And even though they hailed a multilateral solution as the most effective means of maintaining a stable price of silver, it was also clear from the work of the commissions that Britain had to focus on unilateral plans to solve the India problem.

In the 1890s, Britain finally took some action to arrest the depreciation of the rupee. This is consistent with power curse effects in that it took several decades of adverse consequences to stimulate action on the part of a great power: Britain realized it was being nicked to death. Interestingly, it was only after the failure of the third conference (1892) to carve a multilateral solution that Britain finally took the plunge and called for the limitation of silver coinage in India in 1893. Since silver could no longer be minted into rupees in unlimited quantities, it was now possible to stabilize the value of the rupee, and avoid all the problems that emanated from a depreciation of the Indian currency relative to sterling. But the road ahead for Indian finance was not very clear in the 1890s, a fact that was quite evident in the many options that British financial experts were proposing, and that were extensively chronicled in the reports of the three commissions (1888, 1893, and 1899). The question was whether India should adopt a gold standard, a full or limited gold-exchange standard, or keep a silver standard with limited silver coinage. All the plans had their merits, but each was a unilateral response to the silver problem and appeared far inferior to the system that existed when the price of silver did not deteriorate, a solution that could have been brought about had Britain been willing to support a multilateral agreement. And, as noted, it was clear from the findings of the three monetary commissions that a unilateral fix to the rupee problem was indeed only a second-best solution (Great Britain 1888, 1893, 1899). But in keeping with the vicious cycle effect, Britain no longer had any options outside of unilateral solutions to the Indian problem, and even those were fraught with major problems.

A full gold standard called for exclusive use of gold as a store of value and unit of account, and also called for extensive circulation of gold coin. A full gold-exchange standard was fundamentally the same, but economized on the use of gold by limiting its circulation. Yet under a full gold-exchange standard, as opposed to a limited gold-exchange standard, banks were obliged to convert notes, checks, and other fiduciary assets into gold on demand. Under a limited exchange standard, the conversion into gold was discretionary. A silver standard with limits on the minting of silver was in effect the system instituted in 1893 when Britain suspended the free minting of silver. Ultimately, the regime progressed to a limited gold-exchange standard when laws were passed to make sterling legal tender in India and to convert notes and rupees into gold in a discretionary manner. And despite attempts to largely replace the use of silver with the use of gold and paper currency by Indian and British officials (i.e., attempts to make India function more like the British system), the financial system essentially muddled through the rest of the prewar period as a limited gold-exchange standard. The grand designs to rationalize Indian finance along British models, a solution that each of the silver commissions proposed, all failed.

There was much support for instituting a full gold standard like Britain's, as demonstrated in the reports of the three monetary commissions. This would have meant introducing a substantial circulation of gold coin in India. John Maynard Keynes ([1913] 1971) himself was adamant about the folly of a British gold standard in India, as India was poorly suited for such a regime. India had never coined gold, although British sovereigns did circulate in limited fashion. India was culturally tied to the use of silver, as both a medium of exchange and a commercial asset (jewelry). Indian families collected silver for personal use, but it also served as a financial reserve in times of crisis. Furthermore, transactions in India were small and hence better suited to the low-value silver coins that circulated (De Cecco 1974, p. 68; Great Britain 1893, pp. 36–37). The use of paper notes and checks was crucial to a full gold standard system, as gold was insufficient to meet all transactions, yet paper and checks were little-used in India. In fact, British experiments to introduce gold circulation and universal notes along British lines—by making sterling legal tender and calling for the printing of small notes with legal tender in all of India—failed. Since notes had traditionally been issued in seven regions and had legal tender only within those respective regions, people never trusted the universal note. Under restricted use of notes and checks, it would be extremely difficult to keep enough gold in the Indian economy to cover both circulation and reserve needs (Great Britain 1893, p. 29; Bagchi 1989, p. 69; Keynes [1913] 1971, p. 13). Moreover, interbank clearing between coin and notes would be costly in such a large nation where transport costs of metal would be high. When introduced, gold never stayed in circulation, as it was either hoarded or sold to bullion dealers who exported it out of the country. In reality, Indians could never be dislodged from a traditional dependence on silver money (Keynes [1913] 1971, pp. 13, 27–32, 51–53; Great Britain 1888, p. 98; Roy 2000, p. 226). Finally, it was underscored by monetary experts that with new coinage systems, India could expect significant problems involving counterfeiting (Great Britain 1893, p. 37).

A full gold-exchange standard, which relied heavily on gold as the major reserve currency, was also fraught with many problems for India, given that it shared most of the properties of a full gold standard (without the circulation). Such a regime required that banks commit to converting paper notes and silver into gold on demand. While the British government enacted laws calling for such conversions, the laws were never more than discretionary, which meant that banks did not have to comply if gold was scarce. It was never certain that India could retain enough gold to support mandatory conversion. With the tendency to either hoard gold or export it, gold flows appeared to be more directed outwardly than inwardly. In fact, the power of India to attract gold was limited by several factors. The first was the lack of a central bank. The second was a very underdeveloped capital market; hence its attractiveness as a target for gold investments was limited. Third, given its close colonial relationship to Britain and British finance, the Indian economy was vulnerable to destabilizing gold drains to London when gold was in high demand there (Keynes [1913] 1971, pp. 41–42).[48] Finally, because the Bank of England, aside from holding some of the Indian government's gold, had no real paternalistic relationship with Indian finance (i.e., it was not a lender of last resort), it could not create enough confidence to stimulate more gold flows to India (Keynes [1913] 1971, pp. 5–6, 111).

While the Indian system from 1893 to 1914 muddled through as a de jure limited gold-exchange standard, in reality the failures of Britain's attempts to more vigorously encourage the use of gold made the system work more closely to a silver standard with limited silver coinage. However, after silver minting was limited in 1893, the management of the monetary system passed on to the Indian and British governments.[49] Before the limitation of silver coinage, the system had in the past been largely self-maintaining, with very limited management regarding reserve requirements and other banking laws. Since coins were freely minted, the demand for silver coin was met by a natural forthcoming supply of silver. Moreover, the value of the rupee was determined by the market. As long as the price of silver did not deteriorate, as was the case until 1875, this system of free minting delivered stable outcomes for the Indian financial system. Now that free minting was suspended, officials had to defend the value of the rupee by determining just how many rupees should be coined. But in this case, officials had little idea about how to effectively manage the supply of currency through regulated minting (Great Britain 1893, p. 27). Moreover, the attempt to bring a gold-exchange standard to India now forced the governing officials to make more extensive managerial arrangements—through laws and regulations—to ensure a sufficient level of gold reserves in order to meet the demand for gold. Officials were neither well-qualified to undertake, nor comfortable accepting, these responsibilities. The difficulty of now managing a system that was previously self-sustaining elicited more than limited sentiments for the good old days of a self-regulating system. In fact, the Herschell Committee cited widespread discontent with the idea of putting the government in charge of managing money in India and also underscored how desirable it would be to return Indian finance to the more automatic system that existed before mints were closed, as that had proved effective in delivering stability in financial markets (Great Britain 1893, pp. 38, 45).[50] But of course, the automatic system could only be reinstituted with a stable price of silver, as it called for free minting of the metal into rupees. And to do this after 1875, a multilateral solution to the silver problem was needed. Such a multilateral solution would have made possible a return to a more automatic system in India.

The inferiority of the unilateral solution to the problem of the rupee was evident both in the structure of financial and monetary governance in India as well as in the eventual track record in the management of India's financial and monetary systems. The structure of monetary and financial regulation in India in the nineteenth century reflected a system of unilateral management that was poorly suited to attend to the rupee problem. First, as noted, there was no central bank, nor even a state bank, in India. The government had commissioned several president banks that were responsible for note creation and dealing with government accounts, but none took any responsibility for the entire Indian economy. The banks functioned only regionally and were severely limited in their operations, they were few (only three), and India was a very large nation (Keynes [1913] 1971, pp. 142–143).[51] The only real candidate for lender of last resort was the Indian government, which could theoretically draw on the state treasury in need, but this was never a systematic role of the government.

Second, in this very large country, the Indian financial market was quite underdeveloped, poorly integrated, and chaotic, given its historically unregulated condition.[52] Now that the government had to manage the system more vigorously, this meant creating laws and institutions where few had existed before, and ensuring that these levers of control were operating effectively over large expanses of territory in a chaotic financial market. As hard as this was, it was even more difficult to integrate the Indian financial market. As a result of the size of India and the low level of transportation and communication technology, the financial market had always functioned on a regional basis, with seven major financial regions having evolved (each having its own power to issue paper money). But even within the regions, there was a high level of local parochialism in banking and finance. Past British attempts to unify and rationalize the market had failed miserably. Financial integration and rationalization under such conditions required Herculean efforts at the least (Keynes [1913] 1971, p. 40).

Third, the financial bureaucracy in India appeared poorly qualified to undertake such management. Keynes ([1913] 1971, p. 167) himself was exceptionally scathing in his diatribes against the qualifications of these bureaucrats. He called Indian financial officials "amateurs," noting that high government financial officials in India never made finance their careers. This was a function of the fluidity of the Indian government: bureaucrats moved from office to office throughout their careers, never specializing in one issue. Keynes noted how, typically, finance was overseen by mid-level officials who only learned about finance through on-the-job training, but would leave after five years to assume offices overseeing what were considered to be higher-level matters. Hence, to add to the problem of inexperienced bureaucrats, finance was not accorded a significant status in colonial affairs. Furthermore, the bureaucrats now had to manage money with central-banking instruments that had been little used in India when credit conditions unfolded more automatically: open-market operations and managing gold reserves.

And finally, Indian monetary and financial policy was fractured across three jurisdictions: London, Calcutta, and the provinces. With a fractious structure of competing jurisdictions, which worked little in concert, it was difficult to promote an effective system of governance (Roy 2000, pp. 234–247).

It appears that Keynes's penetrating insights were on the mark when we look at the record of monetary and financial management on the part of these officials: a record that revealed a far more chaotic state than had occurred in India when the silver-standard system was functioning without extensive management. The transitional period of introducing a new system in the 1890s played havoc with monetary and fiscal policies, of course (Keynes [1913] 1971, p. 1; Bagchi 1989, pp. 92–93). But monetary policy never adapted to the unique conditions in the Indian economy. The need for currency varied significantly and seasonally, with great demand being generated during periods of harvest when farmers were selling their crops. The off-season demand was far less pressing. The levers for monetary policy were weak, since there was no state or central bank with the power to issue currency (Roy 2000, p. 238). The president banks had limited issue and their notes were never much used outside their regional boundaries (Keynes [1913] 1971, pp. 30–32). Attempts on the part of the government to issue universal notes failed, as people had little confidence in the new notes. Moreover, accommodations in the coinage of rupees were not sufficient to balance the market for currency. The use of minting to stabilize credit conditions was limited by the need to protect the value of the rupee. Since Britain suspended the free coinage of silver for the purpose of halting the depreciation of silver, the management of coinage ended up bearing a major burden for supporting the rupee; hence it did not have the flexibility to be used to stabilize the monetary system. The result was a very unstable cycle of circulation and credit across the year.[53] In times of harvest and high demand, credit conditions were tight and currency was scarce, while other periods saw looser credit conditions and an excess of currency. This produced sharp variations in economic activity throughout the year in the business cycle. Under the former system (before Britain imposed a unilateral solution), the supply of currency and credit had been perfectly free to accommodate seasonal demands, because India was practicing free coinage, and hence the seasonal credit and business cycles were more stable.

But even over longer periods, unilateral management proved destabilizing. Monetary officials never enjoyed much success in evening out the seasonal variations in credit conditions in the long term under the unilateral solution to the Indian problem. This was evident in the wide seasonal swing in interest rates, which under the old system had been more stable; free minting had been sufficient to meet the high demand for silver, but this now had to occur through discount rates that depressed economic activity (Keynes [1913] 1971, pp. 172–174). From the time the mints in India were closed to the adoption of free silver minting in 1893, monetary officials made it a principal goal to raise the value of the rupee vis-à-vis sterling. And indeed the value of the rupee was incrementally raised during the 1890s until it was stabilized in the early years of the twentieth century, and it was managed so as to maintain a stable value until World War I in 1914. Unfortunately, the management of the value of the rupee was often insensitive to prevailing conditions in India, and this left some significant economic scars that actually fueled the rise of anticolonialism. Credit conditions had to be kept abnormally tight throughout the 1890s, as such conditions were needed to revive the value of the rupee (Great Britain 1899, p. 475; Bagchi 1989, p. 105). The 1890s saw some tumultuous events in India in the form of severe economic downturns and famines. These crises were not well managed, in that the need to stabilize the rupee was never seriously compromised so as to accommodate the events that transpired. If anything, Britain had an incentive to err on the side of a strong rupee, as that gave British traders an edge and kept remittances from India to Britain at a high value. As a result, there seemed a secular tendency in the 1890s to keep rupees scarce for the purpose of maintaining their value (Roy 2000, pp. 234–237; Keynes [1913] 1971, p. 1). But afterward, credit conditions became unstable as periods of tight credit alternated with periods of significant inflation: a testament to the poor monetary management on the part of the government. This was a function of the fairly inelastic supply of money—owing to a need to keep the value of the rupee stable—in the face of significant swings in the demand for money (Great Britain 1893, p. 22; Bagchi 1989, p. 93; Great Britain 1899, pp. 468, 474; Roy 2000, pp. 238–242).

Moreover, the management of bank reserves was also quite poor—no surprise since the lack of a central bank precluded the use of a pervasive discount rate (which was so effective in Britain) to manage reserve levels (Keynes [1913] 1971, p. 169). First of all, the gold reserves in India never amounted to very much, a grave failure in itself considering the British goal of injecting more gold into the Indian system (Keynes [1913] 1971, p. 34). But having never had to defend the rupee with metallic and foreign reserves, monetary officials were never quite sure about the optimal mix and levels of reserves for ensuring sufficient circulation and defending the value of the rupee. Officials were never quite clear on the relation between reserve money and circulation money, and often invested far too many of their assets in London as opposed to keeping them in India (Keynes [1913] 1971, pp. 7–9). The unstable cycle that afflicted Indian reserves from 1905 to 1908 is testament to this poor management. A large agricultural output from 1905 to 1907 raised the demand for rupees, leading Indian officials to scramble to augment the silver reserves, but as these silver reserves became excessive as a result of selling sterling to obtain them, gold reserves naturally ran low. This occurred in the context of a global financial crisis in 1907 that pulled additional gold out of India, leaving gold reserves excessively low. But this had a significant impact on the value of the rupee, which declined because India did not have enough gold to sell in order to maintain its value. So low did reserves fall, that the rupee's value had to be restored by selling securities. This episode in the mismanagement of reserves was more commonly visible in frequently alternating shortages between gold and silver reserves. A fundamental problem that plagued Indian officials throughout this period of a unilateral solution was that the two fundamental monetary goals of Indian officials—stabilizing credit markets in India and stabilizing the value of the rupee—were frequently incompatible. It was often the case that one had to be sacrificed for the other, usually in favor of the latter (Keynes [1913] 1971, pp. 92–100, 111–126).

Over the period from 1893 to 1914, a lack of central-banking mechanisms, an inexperienced bureaucratic corps, and a structurally unstable financial system combined to produce outcomes that were far inferior to the more stable outcomes that had prevailed before 1875 under an automatic mechanism, and that could very well have been reestablished with the consummation of a multilateral solution to the silver problem. The folly of the unilateral solution to Britain's India problem, aside from the tumultuous monetary and financial outcomes, was especially evident in a trail of laws and policies that emerged in piecemeal and experimental fashion. They were a testament to a plan that was uncertain, unsystematic, and reactive. At best, the unilateral solution plodded along, leaving a trail of monetary and financial fallout (Keynes [1913] 1971, pp. 30–34). Indeed, the great financial power that was embraced by British perceptions as a viable solution to the silver problem ended up being largely illusory. But it was the only option Britain had, since its intransigence against monetary cooperation left it victimized by a vicious cycle of unilateralism.

Coping with Complexity: US Power and the War in Vietnam

The Vietnam War appears to feature classic characteristics of complexity, the foremost being an outcome that seems to violate intuition and prior expectations (Jervis 1997, p. 7). This is manifest in the perplexing question that has haunted US supremacy analysis since the end of the war (Komer 1986, p. 9): How could the United States have failed so miserably in dealing with insurgency in South Vietnam, given its preponderant military advantage and its success in all the major battles? Much of the explanation lies in the poor adaptation of the United States to the complex effects that unfolded in the course of the war. In explaining the failure in Vietnam, Robert McNamara's own postmortem account suggests that it was due to the inability of the United States to manage an "extraordinarily complex range of political and military issues" (1995, p. 323). This view is supported by General Maxwell Taylor, who blamed the US failure in Vietnam on the fact that US leaders were "particularly ignorant of the complex relationships" within and across Vietnamese society and politics (quoted in Komer 1986, p. 35). Ultimately, the victimization of the United States by complexity emanated from its preponderant military and economic power, a preponderance that made it less than perspicacious in conducting a well-adapted and effective war effort. Indeed, its preponderant power proved to be a curse in fighting the war.

Early on in the war, the US power curse in the context of complexity was starkly manifest in initiating military responses to Hanoi's support of Communist insurgency in South Vietnam. Ultimately, the problem of complexity engulfed President Lyndon Johnson, who ended up making the classic error of dealing with a variety of opposing goals through the use of only one instrument at a time.[54] In responding to attacks on US and South Vietnamese installations in early 1965, Johnson was faced with two fundamental sets of goals, each demanding a different response. There were four objectives that encouraged a large-scale assault on North Vietnam and its operations in the South: send a strong message to the Soviet Union, China, and North Vietnam to stay away (certainly the United States did not want the war to escalate the way Korea did and risk either Chinese or Soviet involvement); send a signal to Communist insurgents in Laos, Cambodia, and Malaysia about US resolve; embolden the government of South Vietnam through US support; and placate the American Right. On the other hand, a far more modest retaliation to the attacks attended better to four other goals: allay fears among the American Left; avoid alienating US allies, such as those among the North Atlantic Treaty Organization (NATO) and other nations that took a strong position against a large-scale war in Asia that might drag them in; give the South Vietnamese government an incentive to fight for itself; and preserve the domestic political support for Johnson to continue his Great Society program. The path chosen was the latter, more modest retaliation, but Johnson mistakenly believed that the response would attend to the first four goals as well, because the administration believed the power of the United States would effectively make North Vietnam perceive any military retaliation to be a highly menacing action (hence producing fears of the possibility of a large-scale assault).[55] In this mind-set it would be perceptions of the potential degree of escalation that would create the deterrent, rather than the actual initial military response. So, in Johnson's mind, all of the goals could be achieved merely by initiating a limited and gradual response (which began as a tit-for-tat strategy) that was backed up by the potential for limitless escalation.[56] Johnson's Rolling Thunder bombing strategy banked precisely on the effectiveness of a potentially escalated response in deterring the insurgency and North Vietnamese support of the Vietcong (Pape 1990, pp. 114–115; Komer 1986, p. 15; *Pentagon Papers* 1971–1972, vol. 3, pp. 312–340; Simons 1971, pp. 157–160).[57]

At the most direct level, rather than deterring insurgents and their supporters, the strategy of limited and gradual response emboldened them, as they had challenged the might of the imperialist forces and evoked only limited retaliation (*Pentagon Papers* 1971–1972, vol. 4, pp. 117, 128, 168).[58] But various other problems developed with this strategy, many unforeseen or discounted by the administration. The deterrent value of the limited-response gambit initiated by Johnson in hopes of stemming insurgency at an early stage lost much of its bite due to a number of factors. In playing such a game, there must be absolute clarity about the meaning of specific actions and an acknowledgment of where this game may lead—the "shadow of the future" (Axelrod 1984). The shadow of unlimited US escalation potential was not as salient nor frightening for insurgent fighters in Asia (who were not Cold Warriors and had little familiarity with the deterrence game) as it was for the Cold War adversaries of the United States. Furthermore, such measured-response strategies work well in conventional scenarios where enemy command and control functions derive from centralized sources, communication among adversaries is clear, and aggressive actions are clearly perceived. Such was hardly the case in Vietnam, as insurgency was being driven by many influences, both internal (among the insurgent factions) and external (China, the Soviet Union, and North Vietnam).[59] Moreover, Rolling Thunder was conducted very poorly with respect to generating a deterrent effect: it created little urgency to capitulate (*Pentagon Papers* 1971–1972, vol. 4, p. 113). The graduation was so limited that it was hardly perceptible.[60] It was carried out in a very disjointed manner with various pauses and irregular attacks.[61] But even in trying to generate a "shadow of the future" effect through retaliatory strikes, it missed key opportunities to respond strongly to provocative enemy assaults (Sharp 1978, pp. 85–86; Clodfelter 1989, pp. 63–65). But above and beyond that, operations were not accompanied by sufficient communication that made the nature of the game more clear to the Vietcong and North Vietnam.[62] Finally, targeting was far from effective in a military sense: it was often symbolic and of limited effectiveness in debilitating the enemy's war efforts.

Robert Pape (1990, p. 124) observes that signals of conventional escalation on the part of Johnson's Rolling Thunder strategy (from minor military installations up to bigger targets) worked poorly in Vietnam because of the limited size and importance of the industrial sector in North Vietnam (comprising 12 percent of gross national product in 1965). Furthermore, China and the Soviet Union were filling the shortfall of products with their own manufactures. In this respect, Pape notes that North Vietnam was "immune to conventional coercion." A number of important US decisionmakers, including McNamara, in fact voiced pessimism about the ability of US bombings to deter North Vietnam (*Pentagon Papers* 1971–1972, vol. 4, p. 116–118; Simons 1971, p. 146; Clodfelter 1989, p. 54).

It is clear in documents from military elites that in their opinion the war failed because targeting strategies were not left to the military. Very little bombing went on above the Twentieth Parallel early on, sanctuaries were not targeted, and principal targets in the South (all of which could have crippled the enemy) were left unscathed (Sharp 1978, p. 85). The *Pentagon Papers* (1971–1972, vols. 3–4) are a repository for military memos and reports lamenting the gross misuse of US military power in this regard. Many military postmortems on Vietnam issue a similar lament: that an immediate aggressive campaign run strictly by military elites would have ended the war in relatively quick fashion.[63]

Johnson purposely remained vague or silent about US strategy because he was aware of the conflicting goals with which he was faced, and hence remained noncommittal to avoid alienating groups who were fighting over US strategy: he wanted to keep China and the Soviet Union out of the conflict, in addition to not alarming the American public. But without such messages clarifying the intent to escalate and respond strongly to major incursions, this initial restraint worked against the United States through various feedback loops. First of all, as we would expect, Johnson's limited response worked against his goals: the Soviet Union and China adopted a more militant posture (with the Soviets moving further away from a preference for negotiated settlement), Hanoi became less fearful of supporting the Vietcong, insurgents in South Vietnam were emboldened, insurgency flared up in other Asian nations, some South Vietnamese leaders remained uncertain about US commitments, and the American Right stirred up political problems at home (*Pentagon Papers* 1971–1972, vol. 3, pp. 312–340; Clodfelter 1989, p. 60; Simons 1971, pp. 149, 196–197).

For Johnson, such vagueness was a response to the failure to take into account the need for simultaneous actions in order to address multiple, conflicting goals. Compounding his own disposition toward single formulas, the advice he was given often lacked a sense of coping with complexity, as many recommendations were oriented around simple plans. The problem with complex situations is that manifold effects may end up making the costs much larger than they seem in a world where all remains equal, which in a complex system is never the case. It is clear, however, that greater attention to the complementary use of action and rhetoric could have yielded superior results in achieving Johnson's goals, even if not all of them (Clodfelter 1989, pp. 61–64). Unfortunately, Johnson made similar mistakes in conducting the land war, which was subject to periodic phase-ins without sufficient rhetorical complements to raise their deterrent power (Clodfelter 1989, p. 71).

But above and beyond the obvious drawbacks to the strategy of limited and gradual response, other feedback loops created manifold effects that made the situation worse for the United States. It might have been better to take a position among these two sets of goals with action and rhetoric that were clearly in line with one set, and give up on the other, rather than trying to achieve all of the goals by walking a tightrope with rhetorical vagueness. The vagueness stirred up alarming perceptions on all sides: those who wanted large-scale military intervention and a strong US commitment feared limited US support for South Vietnam, and those who wanted limited US involvement feared the possibility of escalation. Uncertainty worked against the United States across all of its goals.[64]

As insurgency and North Vietnamese support increased in early 1965 (February through April), the United States stepped up its military response commensurately (staying within its strategy of limited and gradual response). This is the period when the United States more vociferously made a commitment both in rhetoric and in military action to fight Communist insurgency in South Vietnam. But in this respect, Johnson became an unintended and unforeseen prisoner to his own quest for flexibility, and in the end such a quest through a measured-response strategy had the opposite effect: boxing him into a rigid position. In essence, staying loyal to a strategy that was graduated in theory but flexible in reality essentially took control of the military engagement away from the United States and gave it to the Vietcong and North Vietnam, as US strategy became a predictable function of the strategy of insurgency (Sorley 1999, p. 4). The enemy found that it could influence US military responses by regulating the intensity of their campaign upward or downward with appropriate military actions and diplomatic gestures (Clodfelter 1989, p. 53; *Pentagon Papers* 1971–1972, vol. 3, p. 340). Also, the graduated and predictable targeting strategy and the escalation (moving from minor targets to more important military targets as insurgency and North Vietnamese support continued) gave the enemy immeasurable relief, because such a strategy allowed them to adapt militarily so as to limit their vulnerability.[65]

Such an escalation of the war, of course, also had predictable negative effects with respect to the second set of goals, as the American Left and US allies criticized the administration, fearing a large-scale war in Asia. Moreover, instability in the South Vietnamese government and the increased military commitment by the United States slowed South Vietnam's own indigenous capabilities of sustaining a war against insurgents, which called for substantial reforms domestically and an animated military effort (Macdonald 1992; Simons 1971, p. 159).[66] In the case of South Vietnam, the political instability experienced by the government (both before and during the war) emerged as one of the greatest obstacles to the United States in achieving its goals in Southeast Asia. US support for both junta governments and corrupt civilian governments weakened the war effort through manifold feedback loops (Pape 1990, p. 127; Simons 1971, p. 162).

The American Left was less supportive of joint efforts with such governments, thus cutting into US domestic soft power in support of the war; such governments fueled the insurgent cause for political reforms, thus strengthening the position of the Vietcong among the South Vietnamese people and hence diminishing US and South Vietnamese soft power among the Vietnamese people; and finally, junta governments sent a signal to insurgents that the machinery of the state could indeed be captured through violence. In this respect the United States would have been better served by adopting a more integrated and multitiered approach to the insurgency, one that combined efforts to fight insurgents with efforts to promote a stable and popular civilian government. Again, the complexity of the problem required complex solutions, which were not forthcoming (Komer 1986, pp. 12–13; Simons 1971, p. 162).

Moreover, the expected gains in terms of the first four goals that escalation was supposed to deliver were somewhat abated by problems of path-dependence. Those goals would have been more effectively achieved if larger-scale military responses had been delivered at the beginning. By sequencing, the United States lost many of the benefits of invoking a more aggressive response.[67] Once the limited-response strategy was invoked, it placed perceptions and relations within the theater of conflict and competition onto a different path. Perceptions of US restraint emboldened both the Vietcong and Hanoi, thus making them less deterred by later escalation. Since the intentions to respond to insurgency in kind were made unclear by vagueness about US strategy, it was difficult for Communist forces to distinguish among differing responses by the United States. The insurgent forces and their Northern supporters only saw a trail of military actions that did little to undermine their strength. Hence, contrary to the hopes and expectations of the Johnson administration, the great hard power of the United States was effectively diminished as a deterrent threat.[68] Johnson's escalation in his bombing strategy failed to undermine insurgent resolve, even at its peak in 1968 (Pape 1990, p. 112). Johnson and his top advisers also failed to appreciate several prevailing traits that made the North and the insurgents ever more committed to staying the course. They underestimated the power of Vietnamese nationalism and the desire to live in a unified nation, even if that goal cost numerous war causalities (Lind 1999).

But beyond the direct effects on Vietnamese insurgency, the greater theater of the Cold War was not impacted to the same degree that early escalation would have delivered, and this fed back onto the conflict in Vietnam. The Soviet Union and China, themselves, were emboldened by limited response, seeing their greatest fear—an all-engulfing Asian conflagration—diminished by US restraint. The more militant posture taken by these two great Communist powers gave Hanoi greater license and courage to step up its support of Southern insurgents. Even worse for the United States, it removed the Soviets from a path of diplomacy that might have delivered the optimal long-run solution to a peaceful resolution of the Vietnam problem. The Soviet Union had been pushing for a resuscitation of the Geneva Conference on Indochina, placing itself at the forefront through its own chairmanship of the conference. As US limited response progressed, the Soviet Union stepped back from such a role, as it was less fearful of a conflagration that would force it into war. Now, with China continuing to be recalcitrant about cooperating with the United States on Indochina and a newly hawkish Soviet Union, the dream of a stable negotiated settlement of Indochinese affairs (which absolutely required the support of Hanoi and the Soviets) withered with the emboldened Communist coalition.[69] In this respect the United States, through its own hard power, compromised the greater influence that its soft power (diplomacy) might have delivered by interfering with the most stable long-term solution with respect to US interests in the region.[70]

The United States was banking on Communist nations and insurgents cowering at the threat of military conflict with a superpower. But US hard power did not translate into enhanced influence. On the contrary, it diminished US influence by eliminating the support of powerful Communist nations (the Soviets had great influence over Hanoi and could have convinced it to negotiate as well) for a negotiated solution to the Vietnam problem (Simons 1971, pp. 153–154). Sequencing the military response may have also been worse for the US administration in terms of domestic politics. After an initial series of limited military engagements, escalation may have seemed all the more alarming to the American Left because psychological baselines were accommodated to a low level. It may have been a better strategy to start at a higher level and remain consistent, than to start modestly and escalate gradually.

The early war effort clearly demonstrated other important weakening effects that created a legacy that limited the capacity of the United States to realize its military potential in Vietnam. And these were, again, generated by a power curse process. The excessive hard power of the United States got in the way of a negotiated settlement early on as Johnson's combination of an early, limited response with a staunch refusal to negotiate a settlement diminished the incentives for Hanoi and Southern insurgents to negotiate. The response strategy gave insurgents control of the war, so they felt less urgency to negotiate at first. But as US response escalated along with pleas for negotiation, the appearance of US strategy suggested more weakness than strength (i.e., the military response was failing, so the United States was perceived as hoping for diplomacy to deliver), thus emboldening the insurgency and North Vietnamese support all the more. In this case, the hard and soft power of the United States were poorly coordinated (Simons 1971, p. 196). Furthermore, the early military targeting was oriented around conventional war operations: direct attack and bombings of military installations (Sorley 1999, pp. 4–9). And of course this derived from the United States being militarily muscle-bound because of its reliance on large conventional forces. The common perception was that the United States was much too powerful to have to worry about guerrilla wars, which it had never fought, nor needed to fight. Since the United States started and stayed with a targeting and operations strategy oriented around conventional war, it encouraged the insurgency to concentrate its campaign on guerrilla operations, something the US forces were least qualified and prepared to confront (Komer 1986, pp. 2, 16; Pape 1990, p. 127). Moreover, the targeting followed standard operating procedures in concentrating on enemy transportation and communication, which further drove the Vietcong to embrace guerrilla war as the means of conventional operations were taken from them (*Pentagon Papers* 1971–1972, vol. 4, p. 170). In this case, natural adaptation to the US campaign represented feedback processes that weakened the US military from an operations standpoint (Pape 1990, p. 115; Simons 1971, p. 186).

But moreover, and consistent with the literature on asymmetrical warfare, the perceptions of the relative strength of US forces introduced feedback processes into the US military and the insurgents themselves in the form of moral hazard and x-inefficiencies. In an asymmetrical war fought on the terrain of the weaker nation, it is common for the conflicting sides to face differing incentives regarding the outcomes and conduct of the war. Powerful nations are not fighting for vital interests, which creates moral hazard in planning the war, and x-inefficiencies in the field of operations—in other words, a relative lack of urgency limits the application of human capital on the part of military leaders and field operatives. Conversely, their counterparts among the insurgents or military of the weaker nations, facing greater vital interests in the outcomes and conduct of the war, are more x-efficient in fighting because their land is violated and occupied, and a smaller force encourages military planning to be at its best and most aggressive

(Mack 1975; Boserup and Mack 1975; Barnett 2003; Arreguin-Toft 2005; Ewans 2005). Such was the case in Vietnam, as the war devolved into a war of attrition between a weary titan that was applying its military force in a limited and suboptimal manner (concentrating more on conventional operations and strategies against infiltration) and a far more animated and flexible insurgency.[71]

Intelligence and military documents from the period attest to a general concern among the US administration and military elites that the United States would have to adapt to a guerrilla war, yet military strategy continued to rely on conventional operations for a large part of the conflict. But even when Creighton Abrams replaced William Westmoreland and embraced a "smaller war" strategy in military operations, a long trail of frustration had already worked in favor of North Vietnamese and Vietcong resolve, and against US and South Vietnamese resolve (among both the military and the general populations). In this respect, even with these superior tactics embraced by Abrams, the US military effort was the victim of adverse path-dependence (*Pentagon Papers* 1971–1972, vol. 4, pp. 108–112, 298–300, 396–400; Sorely 1999, pp. 17–30; Arreguin-Toft 2005, p. 166; Komer 1986, pp. 2, 5). Paranoia about infiltration of forces from North Vietnam to the South held up operations that would confront socially integrated insurgent operations and terrorism. It is interesting how poorly that US military strategy adapted to the course of the war, as guerrilla operations dwarfed conventional North Vietnamese operations (Vietcong insurgents outnumbered North Vietnamese troops five to one, and 96 percent of battles were fought at a very small scale). Once more we witness the power curse afflicting US operations through a muscle-bound effect (Pape 1990, p. 127; Simons 1971, p. 192). Komer (1986, pp. 48–51) reinforces the power curse aspect of this muscle-bound effect in noting that technology dictated US strategy. The emphasis on "big-war" weapons in US military research and development led US leaders to neglect the needs of "little-war" operations that prevailed in Vietnam.[72]

The deterioration of US soft power was among the most significant weakening effects of the US power curse in Vietnam. The United States compromised its soft power in various areas that fed back negatively onto its war effort. The deterioration of soft power manifested itself in three main arenas: within US politics itself, within the theater of war, and within the international community. In all three cases, the United States fell victim to power illusion: its preponderant military superiority in the face of a problem perceived to be small at first (rebellious activity at a local level) led it to discount the importance of soft power in dealing with the insurgency in the long run. In this respect, the United States manifested the classic problem of linear thinking with respect to Vietnam, and this linear thinking was encouraged by power illusion. Vietnam showed what might at first glance suggest extremely small differences from Korea: a more animated insurgency, a less stable and less popular government, and the advent of the information age, which brought the war graphically into American living rooms.[73] Great power advantages obfuscated the larger impact (nonlinearities) that these small difference might have. But this larger impact would neutralize the effectiveness of US hard power, and thus require greater soft power in all three areas to compensate for such weakening effects. Hard-power illusion essentially made US decisionmakers less perspicacious in applying models of complex decisionmaking, given their hard military superiority in the face of what were considered limited threats. Soft power impacted on the war effort in a variety of complex ways, many of which consequently were difficult to ascertain and address by decisionmakers.

Certainly, many strategists made recommendations that embraced this complexity, but often they came to differing conclusions. One way to filter out unsuccessful strategies would have been trial and error, but this too was limited by US power illusion: great powers don't have to be flexible about war strategies against inferior opponents. Again, consistent with complexity, even as these problems made more of an impression as the war effort continued to flounder, corrections became all the harder because of path-dependence. Failure to take these factors into account made the problems far more difficult to deal with than they would have been at the beginning, and perhaps even impossible to solve once a certain inflection point in the loss of soft power was reached: the point of no return for both Americans and Vietnamese in opposing US involvement and the South Vietnamese government. So once more we witness the manifestation of nonlinearities: problems did not evolve incrementally but in large, step-level processes.

With respect to the decimation of soft power in the theater of US politics, in all fairness to US strategists, the United States had never been severely hamstrung by adverse public opinion in a war. So it was not surprising that the role of domestic support was underappreciated before escalation began.[74] In this sense the United States was vulnerable to complexity effects as a result of overlearning from history (Jervis 1976). The Vietnam campaign proceeded as if it were not a scenario very different from those in the past. If anything, it was less menacing in light of the preponderance of US hard power. Hence, past experiences could be drawn on to guide strategies. But, as noted, in complex systems, even small changes can sometimes lead to large differences in outcomes (Jervis 1997, p. 17). In this scenario, differences in the Vietnam experience did make soft power more fragile, but rigid models of military and political strategies failed to compensate.[75] In the long run it proved to be the domestic antiwar sentiment (i.e., the deterioration of domestic soft power) that would deal a severe blow to the ability of the United States to conduct a successful campaign.

Over the course of the war, the growth of the antiwar movement in the United States represented perhaps the most important obstacle to sustaining the war with the full application of US military potential (Komer 1986, p. 54; *Pentagon Papers* 1971–1972, vol. 4, p. 126). And in this respect, it was the deterioration of such soft domestic power that produced one of the principal weakening effects for the United States in conducting the war.[76] The literature on asymmetrical war demonstrates how the antiwar movement was to a large extent a function of the power curse. The literature posits domestic political backlashes in the dominant nation as a major factor in explaining why very large powers can lose wars against much smaller states. Perceptions of relative power primacy condition the public to expect a short military campaign, or at worst a longer campaign with few causalities. As such wars devolve into longer campaigns of attrition, the public becomes all the more animated against the campaigns. The political machinery in the nation follows suit as legislatures are also frustrated by relative failure in the face of asymmetrical power levels. Both the public and the political machinery of the state become less x-efficient and become more x-inefficient, and consequently develop into a drag on the state in perpetrating its war efforts. The impact of this process is all the more pervasive in democracies (Mack 1975; Boserup and Mack 1975; Barnett 2003; Arreguin-Toft 2005; Ewans 2005).

Over the course of the war, the influence of American public opinion constrained military strategy, thus limiting the effectiveness of the US military campaign. From an operational standpoint, military campaigns cannot be effectively carried out when hostage to domestic political constraints (Sharp 1978, pp. 267–269).[77] US leaders were less than sufficiently effective in consulting and communicating with the American public and Congress about the strategies and course of the war. In drawing lessons from the war as to why the United States failed, both Robert McNamara (1995, p. 323) and Henry Kissinger (2003, pp. 558, 561) were adamant about the fact that the war created a backlash and schism that robbed US leaders of the kind of domestic political environment necessary to conduct a war effectively.[78] As they averred, the true power of the United States was in the "unity of the people," and this was sadly absent. In the case of Vietnam, American public perceptions were all the more animated and contaminated by the administration's continued rhetoric about seeking a negotiated solution, while continuing to escalate the war (Pape 1990, p. 105; Simons 1971, p. 185).[79] But the complex interactions between the conduct of the war and American public opinion conspired all the more to weaken the US war effort. In controlling the course of US military strategy, especially early on in the war when American public opinion was catalyzed, the insurgents effectively controlled that opinion. The insurgents could manipulate public opinion by carefully crafting the size, nature, and timing of their strikes. This gave them significant influence over a major weapon in the war. But even more significant as a feedback loop than the one created by controlling US domestic soft power was the deterioration of this soft power, which emboldened the Vietcong and North Vietnam to sustain hostilities in expectation that public opinion would force the United States to either pull out or sue for peace under more advantageous conditions (*Pentagon Papers* 1971–1972, vol. 4, p. 170; Gardner 2002; Simons 1971, p. 194). Several years into the war, it became apparent that the only way to root out insurgents, and thereby win the war, was to undertake an "antisocial" war: a war against civilians. And in the face of this realization, many Americans undermined the war effort all the more by proposing that such a war should not be waged, and hence the war should not be won under such conditions (Arreguin-Toft 2005, p. 168).

In terms of the role of soft power within the theater of Vietnam, the United States was also very much victimized. And as with the lack of soft power in US domestic politics, this is somewhat understandable. Along with the fact that the United States had never been involved in an unpopular war, it also had never fought a war where soft power in the actual military theater was fragile. Unlike European nations, the United States did not have to fight insurgents in decolonizing regions.[80] In the major wars of the twentieth century, popular support for the United States was ensured, as it was the liberator in the occupied territories it fought in. As with US domestic support, Vietnam was a different game. Both the consequences of the power curse and a failure to assess the role of indirect effects of political failure introduced important weakening effects on the war effort, specifically in the context of the theater of conflict. Even before the United States intervened militarily, it might have heeded its own warnings (issued to the French when the latter occupied Vietnam as a colonial power) to try to reduce a rising revolutionary fervor among the Vietnamese people by promoting a stable and popular governing regime. This would have meant allying with the South Vietnamese government in fighting a political war against poverty and political injustices, which would have required vigorous programs in land reform, redistribution, rural development, resettlement, and general political reform. But ironically, much like France, the United States did not fight such a war, which enhanced the appeal of Communist insurgency in the South. While numerous experts in Asian affairs warned of such an oversight, once again the great power of the United States made it somewhat blind to such indirect consequences, as the relative power balance sheet showed a superior, conventional military force against scattered insurgents. But the complex ramifications of fighting such an enemy in such an environment as Vietnam caused the United States to greatly underestimate the military potential of such a threat. In this respect, moral hazard emanating from superior, relative military resources made the United States less perspicacious in exploring the complex implications of domestic political instability in the South. Again, like France, the United States continued to side with political regimes that increasingly estranged the Vietnamese people, thus sowing the seeds of revolution all the more in the South, and making insurgent movements all the greater (Komer 1986, pp. 4–6).

Specifically within the theater of war, the United States found various adverse feedback mechanisms emanating from its deteriorating soft power among the Vietnamese people. In carrying out a successful counterinsurgency campaign, the United States needed the allegiance of the South Vietnamese people, which required effective political, economic, and social programs (the famous pacification strategy). Such a campaign was crucial to undermining support for the insurgents, as the Vietcong relied heavily on rural youth and villages for combatants and supplies. It was not until 1967 that strategies linked to pacification became a major issue for US war planners, but by then all such efforts had failed miserably, especially those by the South Vietnamese government itself (another path-dependent outcome that cut adversely against new US initiatives to gain local support for the war). Effective pacification strategies relied on significant reforms, indigenous operatives, and management, and required a local focus with close ties to rural villages and police functions administered in the form of local constabularies. The pacification functions by the South Vietnamese government violated such requirements across the board: they fell short on reforms and were administered through nonlocal and larger-scale military operations. Indeed, the Vietcong often proved to be better at pacifying local populations, because they more successfully addressed local grievances through the provision of public goods (e.g., fighting corruption), land redistribution, and economic engagement (*Pentagon Papers* 1971–1972, vol. 3, pp. 515–623, 698–704). While Richard Hunt (1995) and Lewis Sorley (1999) underscore the impact of the actual pacification efforts undertaken within the South, especially after General Abrams appointed William Colby as director of pacification efforts in Vietnam, the evidence they marshal does not dislodge the preponderance of evidence suggesting that such efforts were too little, too late. While the US military embraced pacification to a greater extent under Abrams, the South Vietnamese government never fully matched this concern, either with policies or resources. And success in pacification required more political than military engagement.

The United States continued to concentrate on military strategies at the expense of such programs, to the detriment of its war effort. In this respect, observes Robert Komer (1986, p. 41–42), the great mistake of the United States in managing the war was to excessively Americanize and militarize the conflict, when both indigenous and nonmilitary (civil) solutions carried the key to uprooting the insurgency. In this regard, the power illusion's interaction with complexity problems manifested itself once more. Superior military power limited US perspicacity in deriving lessons from both the French experience in Vietnam and the British experience in Malaya. Both experiences underscored the importance of integrating military and civil solutions in the face of insurgency (Komer 1986, pp. 44–45; Nagl 2002). Britain clearly demonstrated superior soft power compared to the United States in its greater talents for assessing local cultures and winning over local allies.[81]

The fight to root Vietcong insurgents out of villages was undertaken in a more conventional manner rather than one that was sensitive to the local needs and practices dictated by pacification criteria. Search and destroy operations, indiscriminate bombing, the use of defoliants, and crop destruction tactics applied to local theaters were disastrous for support at the local level, as such "occupation" tactics made US soldiers appear as thugs rather than liberators. This gave the Vietcong, who were far better at courting and controlling local villagers (through carrots), extensive ammunition to engender locals with their causes against US imperialism and the South Vietnamese regime.[82] But even when using sticks, the Vietcong were difficult to uproot without successful pacification programs in place. This led to extensive feedback effects that made the South Vietnamese less animated (x-inefficient) in their support of the US cause. To a large extent, the loss of the military war in Vietnam was intimately connected to the loss of the political war in Vietnam. As long as the South Vietnamese government continued with practices that had generated the insurgency in the first place (dictatorship, nepotism, corruption, elitism), even with the aid of the foremost superpower of the period it would prove impossible to uproot revolutionary activities in the country (*Pentagon Papers* 1971–1972, vol. 3, pp. 706–718; *Pentagon Papers* 1971–1972, vol. 4, pp. 374–400; Komer 1986, p. 1, 11–15, 23–30, 47–48, 111; Hilsman 1967, pp. 578–579).

Having been colonized by the French, it was easy for insurgents to play the imperialist card against the United States. Given the legacy of imperialism, a better strategy for the United States would have been to simultaneously fight both a military and a social war (the latter for the hearts and support of South Vietnamese villagers). It was in such a scenario that a revised Vietnamization strategy could have paid more dividends for US soft power, as indigenous Vietnamese operatives were more valuable as village liaisons for the Americans than as frontline troops. In this respect, the Vietnamization strategy of the United States paid scant attention to the value of soft power in winning the war. Again, this recalls the literature on complexity in vindicating multiple and complementary solutions to problems with extensive feedback loops (Jervis 1997, p. 221).

At the international level, the dearth in soft power also compromised the ability of the United States to achieve its goals in Southeast Asia (McNamara 1995, p. 323). Even in the experiences in Cuba and Korea, which were not accurately evaluated as models for Vietnam, international support was important. Certainly, soft power was instrumental in US successes there: legitimacy obtained through the Organization of American States, the United Nations, and principal allies for confronting a Communist threat garnered support internationally and domestically.[83] But in the case of Vietnam, for most of the war the United States never seriously embraced a multilateral solution to end hostilities, evident both in its lack of consultation with and support from allies as well as in its aloofness from other nations and international organizations. This alienated sources of diplomatic and military strength that could have helped conduct a more effective military campaign or facilitated a more effective negotiated settlement to the war.

First, with respect to the goal of encouraging China and the Soviet Union to pressure Hanoi to the bargaining table (an important condition for pushing a stable negotiated settlement with Hanoi, given Hanoi's resolve to stay the war), the ongoing course of hostilities through much of the war, as noted, had the counterproductive effect of alienating the two great powers all the more, thus driving them further from a role of brokering or encouraging a stable peace (*Pentagon Papers* 1971–1972, vol. 4, p. 107).

As the war unfolded it was also clear that the United States was not very successful in unilaterally bringing Hanoi to the bargaining table, whether using extensive force or olive branches. It is instructive that the Paris peace talks concluded favorably later in the war when Nixon skillfully dealt with China and the Soviet Union (through rapprochement) in ways that pressured and isolated Hanoi, and thus likely encouraged North Vietnam all the more to conclude a negotiated settlement. Earlier successes in achieving such Soviet and Chinese compliance might have been perpetrated with the help of engaged allies or third-party nations (Thies 1980, pp. 143–160, 189; Kissinger 2003, pp. 238, 240, 288, 295, 398, 431–432; *Pentagon Papers* 1971–1972, vol. 4, p. 353; Gardner 2002).

Furthermore, with respect to deterring Hanoi from supporting the Vietcong and compelling it to the bargaining table, the ongoing bombing made the North Vietnamese more patriotic and pro-war, thus reducing internal compulsion to negotiate (Thies 1980, p. 174; *Pentagon Papers* 1971–1972, vol. 4, p. 352–353). These effects demonstrate the nonlinear properties of outcomes in complex systems (Jervis 1997). While early military responses may have scored some points in inducing a negotiated settlement, it appears that such military actions created more vituperation than diplomatic leanings. Thus the enemy reaction showed an inflection point that threw their perceptions onto another path (a more militant one at that), rather than a linear progression toward a breakdown in their resolve and a need to sue for a negotiated settlement. Furthermore, US coercion set up a chain of events in the relations among Communist regimes that placed the United States in a position that was more vulnerable to North Vietnamese hostilities. The war enhanced fledgling ties between the Kremlin and Hanoi, which served several negative feedback functions against the United States. With the Soviets competing for Hanoi's favor, Hanoi found itself having greater freedom from Chinese political hegemony, which often served to restrain Hanoi from adventurism. This gave Hanoi greater freedom to act against US aggression, and the Soviet ties allowed Hanoi to maximize its aid from both superpowers, which were now competing for Hanoi's favor. This dual supportership emboldened the insurgents and North Vietnam to stay the course (Kissinger 2003, p. 238; *Pentagon Papers* 1971–1972, vol. 4, pp. 118–119).

U Thant and the United Nations had continually sent prompts to the United States to desist in its aggression so as to create a better environment for a negotiated settlement, thus demonstrating an acknowledgment of the deleterious consequences of the US strategy for a stable negotiated peace. But by the time that US power illusion was somewhat diminished by failure in the war effort, the inflection point toward vituperation was past and Hanoi and the Communist superpowers were less compelled by olive branches (*Pentagon Papers* 1971–1972, vol. 4, p. 136) Moreover, in pursuing a unilateralist course in planning and conducting the war, and in this respect disregarding the wishes of its NATO allies (which did not share the same fears of a Communist South Vietnam), the United States placed itself in a difficult position. With the United States lacking a NATO blessing, and even significant military support from nations such as South Korea, Australia, and Great Britain, the Chinese and the Soviets were all the more emboldened early on in taking a recalcitrant course in supporting revolution in the South (and concomitantly withdrawing from diplomatic solutions). Finally, lack of international support for the United States made the Vietcong and North Vietnam ever more militant in their expectations that an isolated United States would either buckle or sue for peace under conditions that were more advantageous for the insurgents. Also, this lack of allied support fed back in compounding the US antiwar movement, as well as in making international condemnation of the war all the stronger, both of which cut into US soft power (*Pentagon Papers* 1971–1972, vol. 4, p. 170).

All of this in turn emboldened the insurgents even more as alliance patterns shifted in their direction: they had the support of two great nations, while the United States was alone and hamstrung domestically (*Pentagon Papers* 1971–1972, vol. 4, p. 156; Simons 1971, p. 155). In this respect, losing NATO eliminated a plethora of soft-power (diplomatic) options that could have helped in securing a desirable solution in the South: through linkage to various issues in Europe and Asia, NATO and the United States could have courted the Soviets and Chinese in a number of diplomatic trades in order to secure their support in Vietnam (Simons 1971, p. 157). In essence, a multilateral effort would have invested a number of nations in the process of concluding the war. The unilateral posture that the United States adopted for much of the war robbed it of those opportunities.

In the end, the great giant was slain by a cadre of revolutionaries and their North Vietnamese allies. The way the United States conducted the war was driven by perceptions of preponderant asymmetries in power. But these perceptions proved to be illusory. They were all the more detrimental when they dictated a strategy that was poorly adapted to the complexity of conducting a war against insurgents.

Notes

1. The fact that Athens produced more silver than any other Aegean state made it naturally endowed to import goods without a concomitant rise in agricultural production (French 1964, p. 78; McGregor 1987, p. 50).

2. The issuing and standardization of coins to fit trading-partner practices greatly enhanced the prospects for Athenian trade under Solon (French 1964, p. 24).

3. The military campaigns gave Spartan and Athenian generals extensive experience in leading large-scale assaults, lessons that would be used frequently throughout the fifth century B.C.E. This gave Athenians confidence that, indeed, a large military force could be well managed in controlling an empire.

4. This also explains relative complacency on the part of Delian League members early on, as Athenian imperialism was less severe relative to Persian imperialism. That would change quickly with the expansion of the empire (McGregor 1987, pp. 13, 90).

5. In this respect, while the fifth century B.C.E. saw Athens victimized by the power curse, there was a distinct variation in the fundamental processes relating to the power curse, especially in the context of soft and hard power. And it is this variation in the relevant variables that somewhat abates problems of limited variation in the dependent variable across this case, and therefore renders greater inferential strength to the findings of the Athens case study (see the section on methodology in Chapter 5).

6. Jack Snyder (1991) identifies a historical tendency for imperial policies of self-destructive overexpansion to be fueled by domestic groups that have a vested interested in such expansion.

7. Scholars debate the precise level of Delian tribute. Estimates tend to gravitate toward an average total yearly take of 450 to 500 talents. One talent was roughly the cost of building a battleship. It is estimated that the Parthenon, Athens's

most expensive single public building, cost 400 talents to construct. This tribute indeed represented considerable money for what really was a small city-state with an urban population of about 16,000 people. The level of collected tribute varied, but was considerable; for example, in 431 B.C.E., it equaled the total revenue generated by domestic taxes. Military contributions have been less definitively estimated, but they too were certainly considerable, especially in times of war. Indeed, the Delian League brought great wealth and resources to Athens (Romilly 1963, pp. 74–76; Wilcoxon 1979, p. 176).

8. Imperial funding helped Athens maintain what became, at the height of the empire, history's first welfare state: large-scale financial transfers to citizens for various activities and services to the state (Wilcoxon 1979, p. 173). The easy money of empire allowed the state to conduct large transfers and maintain employment without resorting to the painful option of large tax burdens on Athenian citizens. The state, unsurprisingly, became the largest employer in Athens. Interestingly, Athenian citizens who earned money as jurors liked the fact that the expansion of empire would bring more court cases to Athens, and hence more opportunities to sit for trials. Moreover, it is no coincidence that the great public expenditures on the grandeur (the Acropolis) and defense (extensive fortifications) of Athens came at the height of the empire. Easy money fueled the Athenian appetite for imposing infrastructure and conspicuous consumption (French 1964, pp. 94–96, 148–153).

9. Interestingly, this migration promoted a weakening effect, as the people who might have stayed home to expand and diversify the economy of Athens went abroad. Above and beyond the siphoning effect, colonists produced agricultural goods that were exported back to Greece, thus further pressuring Athenian agriculture through competition (French 1964, pp. 49, 99).

10. Interestingly, economic historians find little evidence of an improvement in the living standard of Athenians during the height of the empire (480–430 B.C.E.). It is apparent that the wealth of imperial Athens went toward further expansion, protecting its empire, and large-scale infrastructural projects at home (French 1964, p. 159).

11. The Peloponnesian War was fought between Sparta and Athens, along with their respective allies. It comprised a series of military campaigns, with intermittent truces, from 431 to 404 B.C.E. The Spartan coalition would ultimately prevail. Arguments that this expansion could have persisted without becoming overexpansion (i.e., debilitating) had the Peloponnesian War never broke out fail to consider several points. First, the war was a direct outcome of this imperial process. Even earlier hostilities between Sparta and Athens in the 450s and 440s (often called the first Peloponnesian War) were fueled in large part by Athenian adventurism and expansion of footholds in the Aegean. Hence the system seemed bound to generate its own shocks, because growing spheres of influence in regions where several great powers exist inevitably collide if at least one of the powers is expansionist. Second, logistics cut against the possibility of a great empire being maintained by a relatively small city-state like Athens. Indeed, Persia, which was infinitely larger and better-endowed than Athens, could not maintain as great an empire as the Athenians aspired to. Interestingly, and ironically, this was a lesson Athens failed to learn (Souza 2002, pp. 13–14).

12. This is not to say that Athenian leaders expressed this political dependence on empire as supporting all imperial ventures. Indeed, in Thucydides' famous *History* (1985), particularly in chronicled discussions of imperialism in the Ecclesia, we

see quite a bit of disagreement among leading citizens of Athens. The issue became more controversial as the century progressed, especially during the Peloponnesian War (Romilly 1963, pp. 59–63; Souza 2002, p. 91). But leaders did feel compelled to maintain sufficient wealth to placate the urban masses and influential political groups, and this required vigorous support of imperial affairs. Moreover, Thucydides points out a bias in favor of aggressive action when Athenians were faced with debates over risky expansionist policies in the Ecclesia, noting that a lack of support for imperialism and military action tended to be equated with a lack of patriotism; hence critics of aggressive policies would be more circumspect in their objections. This bias was most glaringly evident during the debate in 415 B.C.E. over whether Athens should undertake the Sicilian expedition (Thucydides 1985, VI:24).

13. On Athenian tyranny, see especially Thucydides 1985 (I:3, 16, 58, 75–76, 99, 122, 124; II:63; III:37, 70; IV:60; V:18, 47, 92, 99; VI:47; VII:66), Forde 2000 (p. 166), Romilly 1963 (pp. 86–94), D. Kagan 2003 (p. 19), and Garst 1989.

14. The Athenians themselves were portrayed in Thucydides' *History* (1985) as acknowledging the pursuit of such a repressive strategy and the risks that it entailed, with perhaps the most vivid portrayals coming in the Mytilenian speech (III: 9–15), the speech of Pericles (II:63), the speech of Cleon (III:37), and the Melian dialogue (V:84–116). But the *History* is nonetheless permeated with references to Athenian tyranny and the hatred it generated among Athenian allies and subjects (see citations in endnote 13 above). See also Romilly 1963 (pp. 86–87) and Forde 2000 (p. 58).

15. Athenian tyranny had to be perceived as extensive indeed if allies were to break the sacrosanct pledges (consecrated in religious bonds) of alliance among Greek peoples, because Greeks were extremely moral in their relations with other Greeks. Violating such promises was perceived as carrying significant religious consequences. One especially debilitating consequence of this imperialistic style was that it discouraged neutral states from considering joining Athens's Delian League, thus forcing Athens to coerce membership among a number of these states. The effects of this repulsion were most devastating during the Peloponnesian War, the outcome of which was determined by alliance patterns (D. Kagan 2003, p. 19).

16. In modern history, cases of overstretch appear to invariably lead to dissolution of empires or spheres of influence. The cases vary in the speed and magnitude of the shocks, but the weakening effects of overstretch are felt unequally and sporadically rather than continuously (Snyder 1991).

17. Cleon, who had succeeded Pericles as Athens's leader, was especially severe in dealing with such problems during the first decade of the war (McGregor 1987, pp. 139, 151).

18. In this respect, Alcibiades manifested a common myth of empire: the idea of cumulative gains and losses. Alcibiades convinced the Athenians that failure to join the Sicilian campaign, after being called upon by allies (Egesta) to help them fend off military action by the Sicilians, could result in a domino effect of allies leaving in droves, which could in turn threaten the empire. In keeping with Snyder's analysis of the myths of empire (1991), convincing the Athenian people of such a belief was instrumental in gaining the political support required to sustain such policies of overexpansion (Wilcoxon 1979, p. 176).

19. Associations with the Spartans, especially for coastal Greek states, were far less ominous, because Sparta was less harshly imperialistic compared with Athens. It was much more a regional presence, having no need for great commercial

networks, and remained fairly contained, surviving on agriculture and inland trade. It had little need for a large network of allies it could squeeze for tribute. Furthermore, besides the effects of sending Spartan spies into Delian states to foment rebellion against Athens, alliance with Sparta became increasingly desirable as it fought the war under the self-affirmed title of "liberator of Hellas." For lesser powers, these factors made Sparta a better bet as a leader (Romilly 1963, p. 36; Thucydides 1985, IV:81–85, 105, V:9; Souza 2002, p. 85; McGregor 1987, p. 134).

20. On British primacy, see especially Lindert 1969 and Kindleberger 1984.

21. This is consistent with Joseph Nye's treatment (2002, 2004b) of hard power as the ability to impose direct physical control over resources.

22. The counterfactual is based on the actions that other governments took in major financial centers. While these measures differed across nations, they were still more closely related to each other than to the prevailing style of financial oversight in Britain. There was a distinct gap between British practices and those in other leading nations.

23. This episode is a distinct manifestation of a change in the relevant variables comprising the power curse within the case of Britain itself: as the power of the bank became greater, the British state became a greater victim of financial moral hazard.

24. Indeed, both parliament and the treasury had much less involvement in financial matters than did their counterparts outside Britain. The treasury shied away from matters of private and central banking, concentrating on its fiscal mandate. Aside from the aftermath of the few major financial crises experienced in Britain in the nineteenth century and colonial financial problems, parliament generally tended to be less involved (relative to other matters) in questions of banking and finance (Ziegler 1988, p. 249).

25. Early industrialization generated other interesting moral hazard effects. Much has been made in economic historiography of Britain's decline in industrial competitiveness across the late nineteenth century. One important factor accounting for this decline was Britain's reticence to adopt newer, leading industries. Early industrialization generated less incentive to shift to these industries, which in Britain would have meant dismantling existing industries that were still somewhat profitable and whose physical plants were already built and paid for. Conversely, late developers had greater incentives for and fewer obstacles to adopting newer industries, since they were starting from scratch. On this tendency in leading economic powers, see especially Gilpin 1996.

26. No central bank was more "private" in terms of its charter and relation to government than the Bank of England. It was run by directors taken from private banking who supervised as agents of the shareholders, who were all private citizens and private companies (US Senate 1910, p. 8).

27. John Maynard Keynes ([1913] 1971, p. 13), in one of his first major works, underscored how the relative weakness of the rates of foreign central banks led them to develop more extensive tools of influencing credit conditions than were practiced by the Bank of England.

28. Open-market operations entailed the buying and selling of government securities to influence financial conditions in private markets.

29. The US financial system also featured competitive note issue during the nineteenth century, which accounted for a significant amount of its own financial instability. The Bank of France had a monopoly on note issue, while the Reichsbank had a near monopoly (US Senate 1910, p. 209).

30. Gold devices were instruments through which central banks changed the buying and selling price of gold in order to influence gold flows and effectively manage their reserves.

31. It was regarding its role as lender that the Bank of England faced most of its criticism from the financial community at the time. Walter Bagehot's complaints ([1873] 1921) were representative of a common theme in the financial press of the late nineteenth century.

32. One prominent British banker testified that a prevalent idea among his colleagues was for joint-stock banks to amass a secondary gold reserve to buttress the one already held by the Bank of England. Such ideas manifested the apprehension generated by the bank's frugality in holding reserves (US Senate 1910, p. 58).

33. Differing performances across central banks serve as a testament to the impact of the power curse, and demonstrate significant variation in the relevant variables comprising its manifestations in the context of financial moral hazard (thus raising the inferential value of the British case). Because they were relatively weaker financial institutions compared to the Bank of England, other central banks were far less victimized by complacency. They proved far more enlightened and perspicacious in all aspects of central banking.

34. See especially the testimonies of Georges (US Senate 1910, pp. 196, 201, 225, 374).

35. As I have noted elsewhere (Gallarotti 1995a, 2005), relative stability in British finance, especially in the late nineteenth century, was more a function of the prevailing conditions in the British economy and in the global political economy. There were few significant exogenous political and economic disturbances that seriously tested the strength of the Bank of England. The smaller disturbances that did occur were well within the capacity of the bank to correct. In actuality, the financial stability of the nineteenth century prevailed despite British central banking rather than as a direct result of it.

36. The case of the Bank of France will be briefly discussed in Chapter 5 as a vehicle for assessing variation in the principal variables comprising the financial power curse and thus for confronting problems of selecting on the dependent variable (King, Keohane, and Verba 1994, pp. 129–149).

37. On the factors contributing toward this stability, see especially Gallarotti 1995a and Gallarotti 2005.

38. The designations of multilateralism as a soft-power solution and unilateralism as a harder-power solution fit squarely into the most common descriptions of soft power, especially Nye's conceptualization (2002) when applied to US foreign policy.

39. This is the classic manifestation of what economists call "network externalities" or "synergistic effects." For example, as a product begins to win out over others, people are more inclined to adopt it because of compatibility incentives. In terms of money, being on the same standard meant better access to financial markets and fewer transaction costs in commerce.

40. Interestingly, some of Keynes's earliest work—notably *Indian Currency and Finance* ([1913] 1971)—addressed the silver problem in India.

41. The three commissions have become known as the Gold and Silver Commission (Great Britain 1888), the Herschell Committee (Great Britain 1893), and the Fowler Committee (Great Britain 1899).

42. A report by the Herschell Committee (Great Britain 1893, pp. 39–40) provides a detailed and cogent analysis of the problem regarding trade with silver-standard nations.

43. The monetary commissions presented evidence that trade flows did not respond in perfect step with changes in the exchange rates, but a look at the pattern of British trade over the last quarter of the nineteenth century did show sluggish performance in a variety of major product groups traded with silver-standard nations (see Saul 1960, pp. 19, 33, 53, 88, 111, 191, 199, 202, 215). The commissions all explicitly affirmed that indeed trade was most probably affected in some way. Their main objective was to dispel the gravest fears of the consequences for British trade (Great Britain 1888, 1893, 1899). But even here there is the problem of the counterfactual. We do not know what British trade performance would have been without the depreciation of silver. We do know, however, that Britain's relative industrial decline occurred in the period when its own trade performance was spotty.

44. Interestingly, discussion of potential effects on Britain's domestic currency situation were largely absent in the reports, even though such effects proved potentially dangerous. Solving the silver problem would have maintained much of the demand for silver (for monetary use), thus diminishing the competition for gold, which the British system relied on exclusively. Certainly, given the thin film of gold at the Bank of England, the British system in some ways was more fragile in a world where other nations were making greater use of gold. In this respect, the power curse manifested itself in the form of moral hazard in another context. The significant power of London to attract gold made British decisionmakers less vigilant in addressing problems that might arise from increased international competition for gold.

45. As with noncolonial trade, the various monetary commissions pointed out that Indian trade did not end up showing the tumultuous adverse secular effects prognosticated by the most vigorous naysayers. It did, however, show adverse effects in periods of especially large depreciation of the rupee in the mid-1880s and mid-1890s. Furthermore, as with noncolonial trade, we should consider the counterfactual. We do not know what Indian trade patterns would have been with a stable rupee. It is possible that new industries might have obtained a greater foothold in Britain as a result of more lucrative trading possibilities in India. This edge might have allowed Britain to keep up with other European nations in new industrial technologies and hence stave off elements of its relative industrial decline. Moreover, the fact that secular trade patterns with India did not deteriorate significantly only came to light years after having lived with prescient fears. And we do see evidence of a strong export performance on the part of India from 1880 to 1900 (De Cecco 1974, p. 70). In the final analysis, the three monetary commissions surely presented enough evidence that the fears were large enough to have rendered the British government culpably deficient as a result of not taking sufficient action in rectifying the silver problem (Great Britain 1888, 1893, 1899).

46. The Gold and Silver Commission (Great Britain 1888, p. 199) underscored how maniacally resistant Britain was to any changes in its monetary practices, thinking that even small changes might have great consequences. The famous financial pundit of the times, Walter Bagehot, summarized the general feeling about avoiding change in a system that had "been so successful" (quoted in Bagchi 1989, p. 69).

47. An apt analogy to this power curse process relates to getting nicked to death. Great power can make an actor insensitive to many small wounds, especially if they occur gradually over time. Each wound registers little alarm, yet together they may eventually prove fatal. It remained easy for Britain to tolerate the depreciation of silver through the 1870s and 1880s because each incremental devaluation

of silver did not yield a large blow to the British economic machine. Yet in the end, the depreciation took its toll on British economic interests, especially with respect to its destabilizing consequences for India's economy.

48. Keynes ([1913] 1971, pp. 41–42) suggested a system that relied primarily on nonmetallic financial assets (two-thirds) rather than gold (one-third) to serve as a reserve currency, precisely because India would have so much trouble maintaining sufficient stocks of gold for bank reserves.

49. The Indian government of course enjoyed direct responsibility for the management of Indian monetary and financial policy, but there was much indirect influence over such policy from the British government. Hence I will speak of "government" and "financial officials" as comprising elements of both.

50. Marcello De Cecco's analysis (1974, p. 67) supports this view.

51. The banks faced limits on long-term lending, could only deal with restricted securities, and could not engage in international business or have foreign branches. The banks also had few regional branches and no presence in smaller towns (Roy 2000, p. 203).

52. Keynes ([1913] 1971, pp. 143–163) provides a penetrating and detailed analysis of the state of the Indian financial market in the late nineteenth and early twentieth centuries. The picture painted suggests that it would be an understatement to say that such a system would be almost impossible to effectively rationalize and effectively regulate. Indeed it was impossible, as the actual historical track record demonstrated. It was reflective of the poor integration and poor coordination in Indian finance that the various president banks often quoted different discount rates in the same country (p. 140).

53. In fact, the need to maintain the value of the rupee with tight credit conditions often superseded the need to relieve financial pressures at harvest time.

54. Robert Jervis (1997, p. 221) notes that in complex systems, manifold effects can neutralize single actions; hence, successful strategies for coping with complex relationships require doing several things simultaneously to make up for counteractive feedback processes. This is especially true when trying to achieve several contradictory goals. This is familiar to economists who argue that the number of policy objectives has to be matched by an equal number of policy tools.

55. Robert Komer (1986, p. 15) underscores how dominant the "rational process model" was for US strategists: the idea that no rational enemy would continue a war in which the United States was committed. Both Komer and Stanley Hoffman (1968) cite this "arrogance" of the United States—its power illusion—as a major factor that plagued its policies and distorted perceptions throughout the war.

56. Military documents of the period showed a tendency to underscore the effectiveness of America's "superior military force" to bring about US goals in Southeast Asia. Johnson and many of his close advisers were just as victimized by this hubris as were the majority of the military elite. These groups never believed that the United States could ever lose the war (*Pentagon Papers* 1971–1972, vol. 4, p. 300).

57. Military strategists of the early 1960s were compelled by a belief in the efficacy of coercion. After all, it had won the day in Cuba and was believed to hold the key to a quick victory over insurgents in Vietnam if vigorously employed. In this sense, they were victims of hard-power illusion (Simons 1971, p. 148).

58. Admiral Grant Sharp, the commander of Rolling Thunder, lamented that the strategy of limited and gradual response sent a clear and unfortunate message

to the enemy: "we were lacking the will to fight" (1978, p. 80). In a memo to Johnson, Central Intelligence Agency director John McCone warned the president that such a strategy sent a signal of American fear (Clodfelter 1989, pp. 66–67).

59. Even within the North Vietnamese high command, there was hardly a unified military view prevailing (Thies 1980, p. 182).

60. Indeed, even Admiral Sharp lamented that in the crucial period of mid-1965, Rolling Thunder was expanded "with the rapidity of a tortoise" (1978, p. 85).

61. At a general level of military operations, Lewis Sorley (1999) underscores just how poorly the Vietnam War was conducted with respect to a coordinated effort on the part of the US armed forces. He notes that "nobody" was ever in command (p. 32). This is an especially disastrous outcome in the face of complexity, which creates problems requiring the utmost coordination among actors.

62. Fearing that ultimatums would provoke adverse reactions among Communist nations, the US administration purposely delinked bombings with compliance by North Vietnam and the Vietcong. Moreover, the administration never made clear to North Vietnam the potential consequences of its support for the Vietcong, nor did it create urgency by invoking a timetable for compliance (Simons 1971, pp. 196–197).

63. See, for example, *Pentagon Papers* 1971–1972 (vol. 4, p. 128) and Sharp 1978 (p. 268).

64. Contributing to the uncertainty were statements by various important players in the administration that made the United States appear conflicted about its plan for Vietnam. This also emboldened the insurgents, who viewed this disagreement among US leaders as conveying a sense of confusion and bewilderment (Simons 1971).

65. In a sense, Johnson doomed himself to this escalation trap when his initial limited-response strategy sent signals of weakness to elements of the insurgency, whose resulting escalation thus ensured later escalation by the United States (Clodfelter 1989, p. 52). Robert Pape (1990, p. 128) underscores the logistical advantages that the insurgents reaped from this control, in being able to better manage resources and optimize the impact of their strikes.

66. Douglas Macdonald (1992) and Hilton Root (2008) refer to this as a "commitment trap" and an "alliance curse" respectively: greater commitment on the part of a patron generates moral hazard effects on the part of the client. In Vietnam this manifested itself in the South Vietnamese government becoming more complacent about undertaking the sacrifices necessary to undermine insurgency in the South. Interestingly, as later de-escalation in the land campaign sent signals of decreasing commitment, the South Vietnamese government responded with more substantial land reforms. But this ended up being too little, too late. Lewis Sorley (1999, p. 5) cites a debilitating moral hazard effect on the South Vietnamese military that resulted from Westmoreland's reluctance to integrate it more effectively into the early war effort.

67. Path-dependence manifests properties of nonlinearities and hence is a common characteristic of complex systems (Jervis 1997, pp. 17–27).

68. In this respect, the United States learned poorly from the lessons of the victories of the Vietminh over the French in the 1940s and 1950s.

69. The adverse feedback in this respect was all the more pernicious for the United States. Menacing Hanoi precisely at a time when it was developing closer ties with the Soviets enhanced Soviet support in Vietnam, but this greater Soviet support generated positive feedback in bringing China into the circle of Communist

revolution, as China feared Soviet competition for the allegiance of Hanoi. On the complications generated by the looming presence and actions of the Soviets and Chinese, see especially Christensen 2005.

70. Early on, both Hanoi and the Soviets were primed for a negotiated solution, as the Soviets feared the consequences of escalation and Hanoi was beginning to industrialize and had meager funds to conduct a war (Simons 1971, p. 147).

71. It is interesting that later in the war (1972), the insurgents and North Vietnam fell into the same power trap as had the United States, as great successes in guerrilla operations and ongoing Vietnamization of the war emboldened them to undertake larger-scale military ventures that were, as one might expect, dealt with easily by US air strikes (Pape 1990; Simons 1971).

72. John Nagl (2002, p. 49) notes that the strategic myopia of the United States was built upon the legacy of a military culture that embraced big-war tactics throughout the nineteenth and twentieth centuries. The legacy was so strong that the military learned few lessons from its own experiences with guerrilla wars.

73. In this case, complexity theory suggests that even scenarios that appear very similar should not produce precisely similar lessons, because of the possibilities for small differences to generate largely different outcomes (Jervis 1997). The United States was most guilty of this shortcoming in the lessons it drew from Korea and in not realizing just how unique the Vietnam experience was (Kissinger 2003, p. 557; Clodfelter 1989, p. 39).

74. Certainly public opinion flared up during the Civil War and Spanish American War, but such public engagement was not as pervasive and compelling as the popular uprising during the Vietnam War.

75. In addition to the seemingly small change in which information technologies had brought the horrors of war into the public consciousness more graphically, Americans had never fought in a broadly unpopular war. Both these changes interacted in a way that compounded problems in dealing with the war.

76. Komer (1986, pp. 85–88) observes that the administration became especially vulnerable to public opinion because the management of the war was so decentralized across the US governing bureaucracy. Such lack of unified management robbed the administration of a countervailing political force to fend off public opinion.

77. Two compelling manifestations of this became visible in the management of troop levels throughout the war. Both Johnson and Nixon remained reluctant to mobilize reserves in fear of riling the American public, but all major military contingency plans relied on such mobilization. Moreover, the fact that the strategy of increasing troop levels after escalation had achieved limited success made both presidents less hopeful that further increases would be worth the political backlash (Sorley 1999, pp. 2–4).

78. A less emphasized feedback loop relating to public opinion appears to be the adverse manner in which shifts in public opinion hurt US diplomatic efforts. Kissinger (2003, p. 559) notes that, as with military strategy, diplomacy also became hostage to public opinion, and this undermined the ability of the United States to sustain an effective bargaining position.

79. In this respect, it may have been possible to enhance public support for the war if Johnson had sincerely pursued a negotiation option consistently. Such a scenario might have been more plausible if a larger military response from the United States had come at the very start of the campaign to drive the Soviets and North

Vietnam to the bargaining table. The Joint Chiefs of Staff were in fact behind such a response early in the war as a means of deterring further hostilities and opening other avenues for resolution. But such a strategy was not pursued, and further escalation after a limited response did little to enhance willingness to negotiate and drew further ire from the American public (Komer 1986, pp. 13–14).

80. While the US military did have some experience in fighting insurgents in the Philippines and Cuba in previous military campaigns, the lessons were all too distant and far less salient given the size of operations in Vietnam.

81. An especially insightful comparison of the disjuncture between British strategy in Malaya and US strategy in Vietnam is marshaled in Nagl 2002.

82. This outcome cut strongly against Westmoreland's strategy of attrition, which sought to eliminate more insurgents than could fill their ranks (Sorley 1999, p. 2).

83. In both cases, the United States also benefited from hard-power support: troops in Korea, and persuading African nations to deny landing rights to Soviet planes during the Cuban missile crisis.

CHAPTER 4
The Bush Doctrine and Power Illusion

WHILE GEORGE W. BUSH campaigned on promises of a "humble foreign policy," events that would confront the fledgling president called off all bets. After September 11, 2001, the United States embarked on a new course in global affairs, one that painstakingly and autonomously sought to blaze a crusading trail that would leave those who menaced Americans charred in its path. According to Bush, the new threats to the American people ("radicalism and technology") created conditions that altered US foreign priorities (White House 2002a, p. 3). This in turn called for new solutions. While grand diplomacy and alliances were the appropriate strategies for confronting security threats in the old world of international politics, the new world of terrorism and weapons of mass destruction vitiated the effectiveness of these cumbersome and slow strategies. The new threats called for anticipation, speed, and resolve, none of which accorded with the lethargic processes of international organization or alliance commitments in the face of threats. The strategy must be to "destroy threats before they reach [American] shores," and this would necessitate that Americans "not hesitate to act alone, if necessary, to exercise [their] right of self defense" (White House 2002a, p. 6). Moreover, as Bush proclaimed in the National Security Strategy of 2002 and reiterated in the preface to the National Strategy to Combat Weapons of Mass Destruction: "The only path to peace and security is the path of action" (White House 2002a, p. 6; White House 2002b, p. 1). Indeed the premise of security policy under Bush was that "America is at war," so it was a "wartime national strategy" (White House 2006, p. i). In war, the United States could not afford to be passive. The policy mandated an unapologetic imposition of US will and hence it was strongly grounded in an orientation of assertive nationalism. This strategy was dubbed the Bush Doctrine. The doctrine designated vigorous use of US strength and unilateralism as the foundations upon which to construct a more effective style of US foreign policy.[1]

Deriving from what was termed "roll-back theory" in the 1950s, this updated neoconservative version (first manifest under Ronald Reagan) of roll-back theory strongly embraced the same fears against overly passive foreign policy in the face of ever-growing menaces (akin to the critique of containment in the 1950s).[2] This neoconservative view of US foreign relations designated force, coercion, and assertive unilateralism as crucial means of effectively confronting the pervasive evil forces that threatened US interests. In this respect, the doctrine was fundamentally grounded in a hard-power orientation.

The strategies dictated by the Bush Doctrine strongly exuded elements of the power curse, as it was the primacy of the United States that was touted as firmly buttressing the "action" that these strategies entailed. In Bush's own words from the National Security Strategy: "Today, the United States enjoys a position of unparalleled military strength and great economic and political influence." This "strength" and "influence" should dictate the configuration of US global security strategies. Indeed, Bush proclaimed that "the great strength of this nation must be used to promote a balance of power that favors freedom" (White House 2002a, pp. iv, 1). Tony Smith (2007) has concisely identified the neoconservative world view that comprised the premises driving the Bush Doctrine: the United States must remain dominant across global issues and versus all competitors, must adopt an active foreign policy stance to thwart its enemies, and must foster its image across the globe (what Smith calls "liberal imperialism"). This brash and aggressive orientation in foreign affairs, as would be expected, drew differing responses from the public and intellectuals alike: critics condemned it as arrogant, parochial, and chauvinistic, while supporters hailed it as redeeming.[3]

The implications for US foreign policy have been compelling. Rather than strengthening the United States in the face of these new and old threats, Bush's foreign policy has in many ways weakened the nation.[4] In short, the greater influence deriving from US material power, which was supposed to deliver the United States from the immanent dangers facing it, was illusory. Bush's foreign policy proved self-defeating in promoting the administration's major goals: abating terrorism, promoting democracy abroad, and reducing the threat of WMD. The policies of strength followed by the Bush administration delivered only weakness instead. Like the other nations in the cases presented in Chapter 3, the United States under Bush was victimized by the power curse and power illusion. But under the Bush Doctrine, susceptibility to the power curse and power illusion was all the greater. The fundamental premises of the neoconservatives compounded

US victimization (Smith 2007).[5] Fred Kaplan captures the nature of this victimization well in noting that "Bush and his top advisors began their administration believing that America was so peerlessly strong that it could impose its will unilaterally" (2008, p. 183). The hypnotic allure of US primacy as a strategic springboard produced a rather myopic and limited foreign policy based on force and coercion. But in being so myopic and limited, it fell into the duel trap of neglecting alternative means of policy that could enhance national influence (soft power) and of becoming desensitized to the debilitating effects of force and coercion.

Indeed, after eight years of the United States flexing its muscles from a position of perceived primacy, the state of world affairs at the end of Bush's tenure appeared worse with respect to US interests then it had before Bush took office. Politics in Latin America moved to the left and anti-US sentiment arose concomitantly. All of the posturing and coercion by the United States hardly dented the development of WMD in North Korea, India, Pakistan, and Iran. The Doha Round failed. Peace in the Middle East was as elusive as ever. Political instability and poverty both increased in Africa. US-Russian relations were at a post–Cold War nadir. The new economic titans of Asia—China and Japan—were ever more recalcitrant and independent-minded. Democratic statebuilding in Iraq, Afghanistan, and the Balkans was precariously held together through military occupation. The price of oil for most of Bush's second term was higher than ever, resulting in a choke-hold on the US and global economies. And finally, polls showed that the United States and the Bush administration were held in very low esteem by the international community. The state of world affairs was a compelling reflection of the decline of US influence during the Bush presidency, its hard power notwithstanding.[6]

The analysis in this chapter attempts to trace the power curse as manifested under the Bush Doctrine with respect to its four elements (complexity, moral hazard, vicious cycle of unilateralism, and overstretch), and the power illusion to which that curse led. Compared to Chapter 3, where a different element of the power curse was scrutinized in each case study, here all four elements are scrutinized in the case of US foreign policy under the George W. Bush administration. Such a congruence across cases will hopefully enhance the inferential value of this historical analysis. Furthermore, the Bush case is especially salient for several other reasons. First, it is a case of general global primacy. Hence it allows us to scrutinize the consequences of a more pervasive global influence. Second, it is a recent event, which allows us to inspect the consequences of the power curse and power illusion in the most current historical context. Moreover, as with the cases presented in Chapters 3, it features an aspect of primacy and therefore fulfills the requirements for a most-likely crucial case. Finally, and most important, the case of US foreign policy under Bush appears to be an especially crucial historical laboratory for assessing the manifestations of the power curse and power illusion. The Bush Doctrine was oriented around the neoconservative belief that US primacy in the world must dictate the course of US foreign policy: this primacy imparted special roles, responsibilities, and privileges to the United States. Hence, foreign policy itself was strongly grounded in perceptions of power. Moreover, since the doctrine embraced the use of hard power, it is an especially critical case for assessing how the power curse and power illusion manifest themselves within a hard-soft power context.

The Bush Doctrine in a Complex World

Arnold Wolfers (1981) made a perceptive distinction between direct goals (which he calls "possession goals") and milieu goals in foreign policy. The former represent outcomes that can be directly and immediately attained (such as forcing a trading partner to eliminate a tariff), while the latter represent attempts at influencing the greater international environment within which a nation-state functions (continuing the tariff example, the aggrieved nation would work to build an enhanced, global free-trade regime). Wolfers has sensitized his readers to the complex relationship between the two: sometimes they can reinforce each other, while at other times they may work at cross-purposes. In fact, it is possible for the attainment of direct goals to be self-defeating if they create an international environment that is antithetical to national interests. Unfortunately, the lessons of Wolfers were lost on the Bush administration, as the manner in which the United States tried to attain its goals—through aggressive unilateralism—created an environment that was hostile to US foreign interests. The interesting thing about this outcome is that the Bush administration had a very clear sense of both the direct and the milieu goals it sought, as articulated in the National Security Strategy (White House 2002a): enhance the safety of American citizens against terrorism, limit the proliferation of WMD, enhance the power of moderate Muslim regimes, promote democratic state-building and capitalism around the world, maintain strong bonds with allies, enhance respect for human rights and international law, and defuse regional and ethnic conflict. Unfortunately, the manner in which the United States chose to effect the direct goal of protecting Americans significantly undermined the foundations for the stated milieu goals, thus dealing a significant blow to US interests in the world at large.

In terms of the administration's three major goals—limit the spread of WMD, promote democracy, and combat terrorism—the direct solution to such problems in Iraq and Afghanistan served as perfect examples for counterproductive outcomes (because of negative feedback) in complex systems. There are striking parallels between the fight against terrorism under Bush and the fight against insurgency in Vietnam. In both cases, US tactics compromised the very soft power than might have undermined the ability of terrorists and insurgents to recruit new members. Furthermore, fighting the war against these menaces exclusively with hard power proved counterproductive due to the negative feedback generated by coercion.[7] Robust initiatives based on pacification strategies would have produced far better results against an enemy that was invulnerable to conventional military solutions. Even the military underscored the need for pacification strategies in Iraq ("US Military Index" 2008). Indeed, Iraq stands as a poignant testament to the complex dynamics that breed the power curse and power illusion.

In Iraq, the invasion and occupation proved counterproductive to the goal of combating terrorism. Like Vietnamization, the transfer of security functions to Iraqi forces proceeded slowly, hence keeping the United States in a despised position as an invading and occupational force. Aside from the resentment due to outright occupation, the United States generated resentment from all three major political groups in Iraq. For the Sunnis, de-Baathification made the United States an enemy; for the Shiites, US insistence against popular elections was reminiscent of political and religious oppression under Saddam Hussein; and for the Kurds, the United States failed to deliver on its promise of true political autonomy and power for the group (Allawi 2007, pp. 132–146). The problems facing the United States were compounded by indirect effects with respect to Israel. Preemptive operations by the United States emboldened Israel to also act preemptively itself against erstwhile threats. Both Shaikh Ahmad Yassin and Hamas leader Abdel Aziz al-Rantissi were assassinated in 2004, which in turn compounded the terrorist and Palestinian problems and set back Bush's "Road Map for Peace in the Middle East" (Gardner 2005, p. 149).

This general resentment generated by US hard-power strategies, which fueled terrorist sentiment in Iraq (as well as in other nations), was compounded by crucial decisions regarding the management of the transition to self-rule. Ali Allawi, former Iraqi minister of defense, stated that "the entire process of planning for a post-war Iraq was mired in ineptitude, poor organization and indifference" (2007, p. 83). Decisions to disband the Iraqi army and the policy of de-Baathification both put into motion a process that significantly fueled the causes of terrorism and insurgency. These decisions put hundreds of thousands of people out of work: 50,000 Baathist workers and 400,000 soldiers (Kaplan 2008, p. 151; Allawi 2007, pp. 150–160). The causes of terrorism and insurgency appeared especially appealing to Baathists and displaced soldiers, as they experienced both the anti-Western resentment and economic hardship that made them especially impressionable to the anti-US cause of militia groups (Allawi 2007, p. 177). Aside from fighting the perpetrators of the economic hardship, these new insurrectionist recruits found militia groups to be essential to their economic welfare. The militia groups became all the more important in Iraq given the refusal of US occupying forces to undertake police functions in the early months of the invasion. With no police, the Iraqi army disbanded; and with US soldiers not policing Iraqi streets, there developed an environment of lawlessness that made the situation in Iraq all the more menacing. Hence the militias fulfilled a fundamental role of protection for displaced Iraqi soldiers, bureaucrats, and their families.[8] The instability was compounded by the dismissal of thousands of experienced Baathist bureaucrats, who were replaced by inexperienced counterparts (Kaplan 2008, pp. 150–151; Allawi 2007, p. 161). In a lawless environment, the militias were able to obtain resources and weapons. They were also headed by ex-soldiers who knew the art of war well. Statebuilding to restore order was set back significantly through the dismissal of many competent public servants. And to compound matters, all the displaced and deprived parties were now targeting the United States as the principal villain.

One of the rationales for invading and occupying Iraq emanated from the conviction that the country was a breeding ground for terrorists. In actuality, Hussein himself was despised by the majority Shiite population due to his religious repression of the sect, and Hussein was a fierce enemy of terrorism (Halper and Clarke 2004, p. 212).[9] If anything, the replacement of Hussein by the US occupying force increased the threat of anti-Western terrorism in Iraq. Strictly with respect to suppressing terrorists, keeping Hussein in power would have better served the United States.

But de-Baathification and the disbanding of the Iraqi army led to feedback processes that also cut against the goals of democratizing Iraq in the Western style and limiting the proliferation of WMD. With respect to the first goal, the growing Iraqi dependence on militias for economic welfare and safety was a major roadblock along the path toward a stable coalition and a democratic government in Iraq. The proliferation of militias fueled rather than diminished sectarian divisions in the country. In effect, US strategies allowed a process of counterinsurgency versus a weak government to devolve into civil war (Allawi 2007, pp. 233–248). So now rather than just facing insurgents, US forces had to prepare themselves to fight larger and well-endowed military units. And in setting itself in opposition to armed indigenous groups, the United States effectively became an enemy to all.[10] As the strategy of de-Baathification set back the pace of state reconstruction, the Iraqi population came to equate US occupation with political and social chaos (Kaplan 2008, p. 185; Allawi 2007, p. 83). In this respect, as in Vietnam, the building of a stable government in the face of insurrectionist forces necessitated policies that were better sensitized to the need for effective pacification strategies based on political reform, institution building, and economic relief.[11] In both cases, an external presence intervened to promote political stability in the face of a vibrant insurgency and extremely difficult economic conditions for the population at large. But in terms of the indigenous political environment, Iraq appeared to be Vietnam on steroids. South Vietnam was not as seriously fractured politically from sectarian or ethnic divisions. Hussein overcame those divisions through brutal repression of the Shiites. The United States hoped that some coalition government could eliminate those divisions democratically, yet there was no historical precedent for such fractured societies being stabilized within a democratic environment (Walt 1999).

With respect to WMD, while the development of nuclear capacity may have been avoided in Iraq for the time being, the aggressive and preemptive solutions undertaken by the United States have made its cause all the more difficult with respect to Iran. The net effects of shutting down some nuclear research and development in Iraq may in the end generate more actual weapon systems in Iran and other Middle Eastern nations that consider such systems to be the only viable means of averting a US invasion. In this respect, the coercive strategy of eliminating WMD has in fact raised the deterrent value of such weapons for other nations, and hence has made development of such weapons all the more desirable (Johnson 2004, p. 285; Kegley and Raymond 2007, p. 102; Jervis 2003a; Gardner 2005, p. 12; "The Other Struggle" 2007, p. 16).[12]

Considering all three goals of the United States in Iraq (promote democracy, combat terrorism, limit WMD), the shadow of complexity has loomed large, generating negative feedback effects that actually cut against US interests and intentions. Instead of pursuing concurrent, complementary solutions to achieve these tightly coupled goals separately (Jervis 1997), the Bush administration attempted to achieve all three with a single strategy: a military invasion. The result was an outcome common to complex systems: actions targeted toward bringing about certain objectives actually made those objectives all the more difficult to realize.

But even beyond Iraq, the aggressive and imperialistic crusade of the United States to bring about these three goals has proved counterproductive in other ways. Indeed, Zbigniew Brzezinski (2007, p. 148) has identified the campaign, in its international reverberations, as a "geopolitical disaster" for the United States. The militaristic and coercive methods used to root out terrorists even outside the Middle East have further fueled the cause of anti-Western militancy and alienated the governments and societies of target nations. Both Robert Jervis (2005, p. 353) and Richard Betts

(2002, p. 19) aver that the use of US power in the war against terrorism has actually increased "American vulnerability."[13] Aside from creating new and greater enemies in the nations invaded, the web of fear and vituperation created by US coercion has spread to other countries (especially Muslim nations), undermining the global image of the United States and hence its influence at large. According to a Pew Research Center survey (2003), a majority of the population in seven out of eight Muslim nations saw the United States as a military threat. The survey also showed support for the United States shrinking significantly in such nations. But even more than creating hostile coalitions where fewer had existed before, negative feedback in the key area of terrorism has been even more devastating and self-defeating for the United States. Hostility breeds the rise of more martyrs among Muslim populations who are likely to perpetrate the very acts that unilateralism was supposed to eliminate (Brzezinski 2007, p. 149; Halper and Clarke 2004, pp. 313; Smith 2007, p. 198; Kaplan 2008, p. 184; Betts 2002, p. 26; Jervis 2005, p. 353; Calleo 2003, p. 14).[14] In this respect, excessive reliance on hard power to deal with terrorism has proved counterproductive.[15] Utilizing soft-power solutions would have proved far more effective (Nye 2003; Lennon 2003).

In terms of spreading democracy, the coercion and aggressive posturing employed by the United States in marshaling the liberal crusade for democracy have taken on an air of "imperialism" (Smith 2007). But rather than generating domestic political dynamics favorable to the spread of democracy, these methods have generated countervailing processes that cut against such an outcome. The crusade has often undermined the power of moderate Muslim regimes by fueling support for anti-Western hard-liners in politics. This has retarded possibilities for democratic statebuilding and capitalist transition within these nations. Indeed, in this respect, the US crusade to spread democracy has backfired also because it has equated indigenous democratic movements with US pressure. But even well before the invasion of Iraq, the hard line taken against these nations through menacing rhetoric and sanctions had polarized politics and skewed the balance of power toward conservative groups. So the United States may have eliminated or attempted to force out more autocratic regimes, but in doing so its coercive and interventionist actions have sown the seeds of discontent that may undermine more democratic regimes (Gardner 2005; Nye 2003). The height of this deleterious process was visible in Bush's rhetorical campaign against autocratic regimes; his use of pejorative terms such as "Axis of Evil," "rogue states," and "outposts of tyranny" alienated general populations not only in target nations, but also in other autocratic nations that had experienced erstwhile problems with the United States. The pejorative rhetoric set into motion political shock waves that set back reformist politics in many of these states (Kaplan 2008, p. 62). The anti-US sentiment generated by this confrontational style fueled nationalism in the target states, and consequently undermined indigenous liberal transformation processes as the populations and regimes became less amenable to reform (Gardner 2005, pp. 164–165; Halper and Clarke 2004, p. 262).[16] Furthermore, the poorly tailored imposition of a US vision of democracy—without sufficient sensitivity to the particular sociopolitical conditions in the target nations—has delegitimized not only US-style democracy but also democratic transition in general.[17] Tragically, the United States has squandered significant opportunities to promote democracy and capitalism in these nations, as fairly recent surveys show that resounding majorities of many populations (even in autocratic Muslim nations) support the idea of Western-style democracy and capitalism (e.g., Indonesia, 64 percent; Jordan, 63 percent; Lebanon, 75 percent) (Inglehart and Norris 2003; Pew Research Center 2003). Hence it would appear that doing nothing at all would have been superior with respect to US interests than trying to coercively impose Western-style governments in these nations. Smith states that in promoting democracy through imperial aggression, the "liberal internationalism [of the United States] has seriously damaged its own cause" (2007, p. 235).

In terms of WMD, the effect seen in Iran has also been seen elsewhere. North Korea has certainly vindicated the idea that the US policy of coercion in dealing with weapons of mass destruction raises the utility of such weapon systems as deterrents, but in this case it is clear that they also hold utility as bargaining chips (Jervis 2003a; Gardner 2005, p. 12).[18] As the six-nation talks over North Korea's WMD program faltered in September 2003, its chief envoy announced that his nation intended to formally declare that it had, and would test, atomic weapons, as well as an improved missile delivery systems. But he added that such weapon programs would be stopped if Washington agreed to an ironclad nonaggression pact with North Korea. Shortly after that declaration, North Korea's parliament, even if largely symbolic politically, expressed support for Kim Jong Il's policy of maintaining a "nuclear deterrent force" to counter a hostile United States. While Bush perfunctorily pushed diplomacy through the six-party talks, he gave little leeway to negotiators, as he was opposed to negotiating with militant autocrats like Kim Jong Il.[19] Bush saw the deal as "blackmail" (Kaplan 2008, p. 68). All the while, Bush never relinquished a coercive posture in dealing with North Korea. In fact, he reinforced this orientation, and undermined the more positive diplomatic relations built with North Korea under the Bill Clinton administration, by ordering the Joint Chiefs of Staff to prepare military operations against potential North Korean targets, some of which were suspected weapon centers (Operation Plan 5030). When Bush's plan was leaked to the press, North Korea pushed ever harder to develop

WMD in hopes of building a viable deterrent against military strikes (Kaplan 2008, p. 68).[20] But Bush's posture had other feedback consequences that made the quest to limit North Korean WMD all the more difficult. In pushing the hard line versus Kim Jong Il, Bush undermined diplomatic efforts by South Korea's Kim Dae Jung to bridge testy issues (including WMD) between the two Koreas. Lack of US support undermined Kim's political initiative for a new South Korea and eventually led to his electoral loss to new leader Roh Moo Hyun. This hurt the US cause significantly because Roh harbored strong anti-US sentiments and proved more difficult to influence. A key to US hopes of limiting WMD in North Korea has been to foster better relations on the peninsula and thus reduce the tensions that contributed to Kim Jong Il's need for deterrence capabilities. But with a less amenable leader in South Korea, such designs have been dealt a serious blow. In 2007, Kim Jong Il appeared to accept a number of US terms to curtail his nuclear energy program under international surveillance, but the agreements have been ambiguous and his compliance has been problematic. Further, Kim has nonetheless been able to refine enough weapons-grade plutonium to build several nuclear devices. In the end, Bush's militant crusade to deliver the United States from terrorism and WMD made these threats even greater because of the negative feedback generated by his confrontational strategy (Gardner 2005, p. 154; Kaplan 2008, pp. 68–76).

In many cases, these three principal goals of the Bush Doctrine have often come into conflict. Certainly, democratic institutions in various nations have in fact enhanced the cause of terrorism: Hamas in Palestine, Hezbollah in Lebanon, and the various militant elements represented in Iraqi politics (Kaplan 2008, p. 175). But complex relationships and conflicting objectives often necessitate numerous, simultaneous solutions (Jervis 1997). The United States has failed to do this many times. Certainly in Iraq, a strategy geared toward winning a war compromised all three major goals of the Bush Doctrine. In the case of Hezbollah, its attacks on Israel from southern Lebanon in July 2006 suggest that choosing to root out terrorists in favor of invigorating democracy in the Middle East proved counterproductive in both respects. Israel responded to Hezbollah's attacks with retaliatory strikes against Lebanon. The United States in fact missed a crucial opportunity to bring about some cooperation among Muslim states in brokering a peace settlement on Palestine, as such states were unified in condemning the acts of Hezbollah. But the United States sat back and allowed Israel to root out as many insurgents as it could in southern Lebanon. As the Israeli offensive persisted, former critics of Hezbollah now turned against Israel and the United States. The Israeli aggression destabilized an already shaky government under Fouad Siniora that was struggling to promote democratic reform, as the Lebanese now felt more vulnerable to external aggression. While the United States issued limited economic aid to bolster the

Siniora government after the raids, Syria and Iran poured in over $1 billion of aid, much of which was distributed through Hezbollah. In the successive elections, Hezbollah gained significantly more seats in parliament, thus increasing its political influence. With the windfall relief and greater political influence, Hezbollah was able to better entrench itself and better supply its militias with weapons and resources. In this case, US hopes of sacrificing some democratic reform for rooting out terrorism in fact generated the worst possible outcomes in respect to both (Kaplan 2008, pp. 168–174).

One of the most devastating weakening effects of the Bush Doctrine was in undermining the domestic soft power that buttressed foreign policy. Coercive solutions, especially as manifest in preventive war, generate elements that undermine the solutions themselves. First, such solutions must often be sustained to succeed, as the kinds of things that are being sought require ongoing security functions (rooting out terrorists, disarming WMD, and transforming political regimes). Preventive war must be repeated if it fails to deter. Hence this requires exceptional support from Congress and the American public. This domestic soft power that is crucial to propagating such solutions is often fragile, even if the public is convinced that the national interest is at stake.[21] But such solutions, especially preventive war, are by nature ill-equipped to deliver assurances of success. Rationales for preventive war are based on speculation regarding the future (what is supposed to happen) and limited information about the past (since little has already happened, there is less of an informational base on which to predicate war). In conjunction with the natural fragility of domestic support for coercive foreign policy in democracies, the limited evidence for its rationales is an ongoing obstacle to public and congressional support and undermines the very soft power required to sustain such policies (Jervis 2003b, 2005). But the weakening effects do not end here, as domestic political shocks from the policies, and possible backlashes if the policies ultimately fail, create a debilitating shadow of the future (syndrome effects). And indeed, developments in public opinion and in congressional politics under Bush revealed a growing backlash against his policies. Bush's approval ratings deteriorated concomitantly with congressional confrontation (Halper and Clarke 2004, pp. 221, 237–240). The adverse manifestations of asymmetrical war processes (frustration over military campaigns that were expected to be "cakewalks") were heightened all the more by broad perceptions of deception. The rationales used to invade Iraq were never corroborated, and the prognostications for the course and expense of the war diverged greatly from reality (Halper and Clarke 2004, pp. 215–221; Piven 2004).[22]

Just as the Vietnam syndrome hamstrung the United States in conducting its regional geostrategies during the Cold War, a similar Iraq syndrome has already hamstrung the United States in effecting its three major goals in the future, and has acted as a debilitating factor by hamstringing US foreign policy in general (Piven 2004). The hamstring effect has been exacerbated all the more by a propensity to overlearn from history: in this case, the United States would be more restrained than it should otherwise be in pursuing its goals in the world polity because of perceptions that the Iraq case will be repeated in other scenarios (Jervis 1976). Indeed, the United States has had to backtrack from its confrontational position against Iran and North Korea; it has been far more restrained in its relations with Pakistan and the Palestinians in promoting democratic reform and political stability; it has retreated to a softer approach in dealing with Russia (outside the Georgia incident); it has been much less antagonistic in the face of the transition of Latin American politics to the left; and it has relented in its pressure on China with respect to liberalization and human rights. Clearly, the depreciation of political capital in the wake of the Iraq failure has enervated foreign policy (Kaplan 2008). This is all the more troubling considering that the military itself feels ill-prepared to take on a significant campaign elsewhere in the world, even with full domestic support ("US Military Index" 2008).

Geostrategically, the shadow of complexity has revealed numerous menacing outcomes for the United States as well. In the Middle East, the complex dynamics generated by Bush's foreign policy gave birth to America's worst nightmare: political-strategic solidarity among Muslim nations. The lack of such solidarity over the years has been crucial to US interests in protecting Israel and influencing the price of oil. Certainly, the confrontational posture toward Iran and Syria over WMD has forged bonds among those nations as partners in the cause against US coercion. Even more frightening is a potential alliance between Iran and Iraq forged in Shia religious solidarity and anti-Western sentiment. While Saddam Hussein was demonized by the United States, he had in fact served important functions in promoting US interests in the Middle East. His militarism against other Muslim nations (Kuwait, Iran) had maintained a schism in the Middle East that blocked the formation of any grand alliance against the West or Israel. His secularism promoted a political balance in the Middle East that prevented a religious solidarity that might also menace Israel and the United States. Removing Hussein loosened Shiite religious fervor, which could eventually produce the same outcome as in Iran in the 1970s once the United States and its allies have unlatched the political shackles presently placed on restoring self-rule in Iraq. Ironically, the war for Iraqi freedom may produce the outcome that the Gulf War was fought to prevent: an alliance between two of the largest oil producers in the world. An Iraq-Iran alliance forged in Shiite politics would be even more troubling than an Iraq-Kuwait alliance, because of the greater strength of Iran. Hence, Hussein's removal seems to verify the famous American cliché "be careful what you wish for" (Brzezinski 2007, p. 148).

More generally, the invasion of a Muslim nation without the support of the international community poisoned relations with all Muslim nations (as aggrieved populations placed pressure on the ruling regimes to withhold support, as is evident in the Pew survey previously), which has dealt a serious blow to US interests in the Middle East as well as in the world at large. One glaring manifestation of this was the difficulty in obtaining permission from even erstwhile supporters (Saudi Arabia, Turkey) to set up bases from which to conduct the invasion of Iraq. Similarly, Egypt and Pakistan, two large recipients of US aid, proved quite aloof in the face of US requests. This cold posture has continued to turn negotiations sour on a variety of issues, from oil pricing to terrorism. Moreover, in light of the feedback mechanisms that have cut against US objectives in the Middle East, it is clear that the Bush Doctrine, rather than advancing the "Middle East Project" (liberal transformation), placed significant roadblocks in its path (Smith 2007, p. 208).

In Asia, of course, the menacing posture toward North Korea undid much of the progress for better relations on the peninsula, which has been a mainstay for stability in the region. North Korea has retrenched in a way that has gone against US goals in Asia: integrate Communist nations into the global economy and maintain a wedge in potential Communist alliances. China, which has shared some of North Korea's vituperation against US confrontationalism, may have been driven to better relations with North Korea more than it otherwise would have. Certainly the fear of Taiwan, coupled with US aggressive unilateralism, has placed China in a more defensive position. One manifestation of this enhanced feeling of vulnerability has been a campaign on the part of China to build security agreements and regimes across the globe: from the Middle East to the South China Sea. And although Bush's hard line may have generated more cooperation from Russia and China in some areas, potential backlashes could create a ripple effect that poses a major problem for the principal allies of the United States in Asia, as they must carry a large part of the burden of strained relations in the region. US-Chinese relations represent an especially promising vehicle to stabilize relations in Asia, as China shares a number of goals with the United States on trade and North Korea. China, like the United States, seeks a politically stable Asian theater so economic relations can flourish. Both nations also wish to limit the proliferation of WMD in the region. Finally, both would welcome some liberal reform among the autocratic governments of Asia. But the neoconservative bent toward confronting rather than working with autocratic states has limited the possibilities for forging agreements on the greater geopolitical fate of Asia. Once more, the

Bush Doctrine and hard-power solutions only made things worse, and have made the case that more soft-power solutions through the venues of diplomatic rapprochement are needed (Gardner 2005, pp. 155–156; Shambaugh 2004).

In US-Russian relations, what started as a positive alliance in the aftermath of 9/11 has deteriorated significantly. After a warm start with a conciliatory phone call from Vladimir Putin in 2001, the Bush administration and Putin left office amid talk by some experts about a renewal of the Cold War, or at least the beginnings of a Cold Peace. In this respect, Bush's quest for liberal transformation in Eastern Europe and the fight against terrorism there have been dealt a blow. Once again, balancing US-Russian relations with these broader goals required multiple and diverse solutions. Bush's myopic response with his unilateral-confrontational style generated feedback that soured the relationship. Bush's proposed missile defense shield to protect against Iranian attacks generated suspicion and a new fear on the part of Russia. Ironically, the fallout with both Russia and Iran over the missile shield might drive them even closer together, as both continue rapprochement based on oil, nuclear technology, and weapon sales (Gardner 2005, p. 140).[23] As the United States aggressively pushed to expand NATO and support of independence movements in Eastern Europe (mainly in Kosovo), Russia became excessively isolated in orchestrating its foreign relations in Europe. Moreover, US criticism of Russian reversion to autocracy alienated Russia all the more. The backlash manifested itself adversely for US interests, with Putin suspending an arms control treaty and issuing menacing language (comparing the United States to the Third Reich) and even more menacing threats: targeting missiles at US allies (Gardner 2005, p. 130). Putin and Bush left office with a mutual gesture of extending olive branches, with bilateral talks over multilateralizing the missile shield so Russia could oversee and manage it as well, but the US-Russian rivalry has once more flared up over the question of Georgia. In this respect, nonlinearities in the form of path-dependence have worked against US efforts at rapprochement (just as earlier strategies of confrontation placed relations on a less amicable path), and hence a negotiated solution to the problems facing the two superpowers has become all the more difficult (especially since the Georgia incident).

Dealing with Pakistan will perhaps be the greatest challenge for the United States. The complexity effect is especially visible there, where the US quest to reduce the threat of terrorism and WMD has instead exacerbated these problems. A war against their ethnic Pushtun kin in Afghanistan and support for an unpopular Pervez Musharraf turned the general population against the United States, thus fueling support for anti-US activity. This in turn fueled the position of radical elements in politics, which manifested itself in part in the assassination of Benazir Bhutto. The path blazed by Bush has left the United States poorly equipped to deal with Pakistan. But in terms of the intersection of the three major goals of US policy under Bush, Pakistan represents the "perfect storm": it has fully operational WMD, it has an extremely large Muslim population pervaded by a plethora of extremist elements, and it has become extremely unstable since the assassination of Bhutto. Given the deteriorating image of the United States among Muslims, it has limited its leverage in reducing the threats from terrorist cells and WMD in Pakistan ("The World's Most Dangerous Place" 2008, p. 7; Halper and Clarke 2004, p. 210; Kaplan 2008, p. 167).

Ultimately, the anti-US sentiment generated by the Bush Doctrine has given birth to a "counter-Americanism" that carries manifold adverse consequences for the United States and Americans within the global arena. Stephen Halper and Jonathan Clarke lament that, indeed, these consequences are pervasive in a complex global system: they are "diplomatic, commercial, educational, cultural, touristic" (2004, p. 237). Nations will be less receptive to US overtures, which will serve to deprive the United States and Americans of resources, experiences, and agreements that would enrich them. Examples include the European Union's opposition to US-produced genetically modified food, and Brazil's decision to discontinue the use of Microsoft Windows in government offices. In essence, the counter-American posture abroad represents an extensive deterioration of US influence in the world: a devastating weakening effect when considering the global scale of US activities (Halper and Clarke 2004).

In sum, the United States has fared poorly in dealing with the complexity of the power curse generated under Bush. Indeed, the greater influence that his doctrine was supposed to deliver has been largely illusory. The challenge in dealing with such complexity is extensive even for the most enlightened of administrations, yet even here it is not unreasonable to have hoped for a better result.

Moral Hazard

Moral hazard, a principal component of the power curse, derives from the adverse behavioral consequences of strength. In the case of the United States, great military primacy has led to an overreliance on the efficacy of coercion in bringing about desired goals in the international arena, at the neglect and deterioration of other power resources and important means of statecraft. In effect, the Bush Doctrine made the United States musclebound. More generally, the fundamental tenet of the Bush Doctrine—that the United States still enjoys primacy in a plethora of international issue areas—led the administration to believe that it was fairly invulnerable, and hence a classic effect of moral hazard arose: the tendency to neglect development of the flexible array of tools needed to effectively conduct foreign relations. This perception of invulnerability led to actions that in effect made the United States even more vulnerable. Many of the adverse consequences of this muscle-bound effect created by moral hazard manifested themselves as a deterioration of US soft power. And in undermining such important power elements, these consequences carried significant weakening effects with respect to US influence. A trail of these weakening effects can be seen across the major goals of the Bush administration. As with complexity, the consequences of moral hazard proved antithetical and often counterproductive to the Bush administration's cherished goals of eliminating terrorism, promoting political transformation among nations, and limiting weapons of mass destruction.

With respect to terrorism, primacy in hard power led the Bush administration to attack the problem using conventional weapons, which, as already noted, has generated a more hazardous position for the United States in a world fraught with potential terrorists. Richard Betts avers that "American global primacy is one of the causes [of the terrorist] war" (2002, p. 20). Interestingly, even before the invasions and military occupations that followed 9/11, perceptions of invulnerability led the United States to undervalue the threat of terrorism even after several Al-Qaida attacks and Osama bin Laden's declaration of a holy war in his *fatwa* of February 1988. In this case, moral hazard had manifestations both for hard and soft solutions to terrorism.[24] But after 9/11 the Bush Doctrine introduced different kinds of moral hazards into the fold: invasion, military occupation, political intervention, and coercion. These had manifold consequences for compounding the threat of terrorism. In essence, the reaction to terrorism produced reckless policies in the form of solutions that proved overmilitarized, excessively coercive, imperialistic, authoritarian, and diplomatically injudicious (Betts 2002, pp. 20–22). Directly, this hard assault actually created more targets for terrorist insurgents in occupied nations, in the persons of the occupying forces and complementary-service personnel. Indirectly, it made Americans abroad and their allies greater targets of terrorism, as the greater incidence of terrorism since 9/11 attests (Piven 2004, p. 6). Moreover, as in Vietnam, military primacy and reliance on conventional military operations to thwart terrorism actually increasingly channeled global and local insurgencies against the United States into terrorist initiatives, something that even the US military itself admits to be especially difficult to deal with ("US Military Index" 2008).

As Richard Betts (2002) and Steven Lambakis, James Kiras, and Kristen Kolet (2002) observe, terrorism has a multitude of tactical advantages that render it a more elusive target of conventional coercive and military strategies.[25] In this respect, terrorism represents an asymmetric threat that occupies what Betts refers to as the "soft belly of American primacy." Terrorism is rooted in civil society. Uprooting such a well-integrated and concealed phenomenon is challenging at the least. Furthermore, globalization has provided terrorists with a plethora of opportunities to organize, strike, and disappear. Even in the case of state-sponsored terrorism or terrorist-friendly political environments, the networks and operational logistics of the initiatives have always proved to be well concealed within the civil societies of the host nations, as the many failed attempts to uproot terrorists from such environments have consistently demonstrated (e.g., Pakistan, Lebanon, Syria, Egypt, Saudi Arabia).[26] This battlefield hardly lends itself to the weapons that have delivered military primacy to the United States and in fact places greater currency on soft-power solutions (Thomas 2008; Halper and Clarke 2004; Lennon 2003). Furthermore, terrorists enjoy the tactical advantage of being the insurgent force in an asymmetrical war. This lowers the requirements for success (in that they win simply by not losing—i.e., maintaining some capacity to inflict harm) vis-à-vis state actors, who only succeed by completely rooting out terrorism.[27] But a further advantage of inferiority in an asymmetric war is that the difficulty of winning a quick and decisive victory frustrates the domestic societies of the stronger parties, thus inhibiting the ability of the latter to effectively marshal a vigorous and sustained military effort.[28] Furthermore, terrorists have the tactical advantage of attack: they can strike with surprise and make extraordinarily large impacts with limited means (e.g., consider the small number of men who hijacked the airplanes on 9/11, or the small number of envelopes used to deliver anthrax). Finally, terrorists enjoy a targeting advantage. They are difficult targets because of their elusiveness and limited exposure, but their targets are infinite and cannot be fully protected: power plants, bridges, airports, stadiums, waterways, skyscrapers, and people (Betts 2002; Thomas 2008). Indeed, Charles Kegley and Gregory Raymond have reminded us that America's "preponderant power is not reducing global terrorism" (2007, p. 69).

In this sense, terrorism requires a different cure: soft power is the key to addressing the weaknesses of America's soft underbelly (Kegley and Raymond 2007, p. 69). But it is precisely this more effective solution that has been compromised by the moral hazard of hard-power solutions. From a military standpoint, the moral hazard emanating from conventional primacy has caused military operations to undermine the most effective means of promoting "sustainable security" (Thomas 2008; Halper and Clarke 2004, p. 281). Fighting terrorism through coercion and conventional military strategies (large-scale interdiction, troop deployment, occupation, threats) has come at the expense of more progressive tactics. Moreover, such approaches at best have fared poorly and at worst have proved counterproductive.[29] Jim Thomas (2008) and Rob de Wijk (2003) demonstrate that the tactical systems required to confront terrorist threats are founded on prevention, indirect methods, disaggregation, and limited-scale engagement. Prevention requires civilian and military personnel working in potential trouble spots with domestic institutions and personnel to set up infrastructures for deterring or anticipating threats that might migrate internationally. This strategy highlights the benefits of indigenous constabularies that would interdict terrorist threats at the grassroots. Indirect methods would work through nonconventional military channels and through the development of domestic security functions in allied and partner nations. These methods would feature pacification-type strategies that encourage better governance and the socioeconomic development of indigenous civil societies. Disaggregation would stress the need to frame security strategies based on local and regional conditions. Limited engagement would stress the use of small numbers of military and civilian personnel in developing indigenous security capabilities. The main functions of these personnel would be oriented around training, advising, intelligence gathering, and paramilitary and covert operations. Such a sustainable security initiative would rely extensively on soft power in terms of implementation and success ("US Military Index" 2008; Thomas 2008; Lambakis, Kiras, and Kolet 2002).[30]

Soft initiatives would rely fundamentally on the access of US military, diplomatic, and civilian personnel to potential troubled spots, as the joint-security operations would require extensive cooperation between the United States and foreign political entities (Newhouse 2003; Jervis 2005; de Wijk 2003). Local and national receptivity to such cooperation with the United States would determine the success of these joint operations.[31] But moreover, this bilateralism needs to be complemented and integrated into a multilateral security network.[32] This would rely on international regimes and international organizations to broker and participate in the security initiatives carved out by the United States and selected nations. This multilateralism would also be predicated on the receptivity of participating nations to US overtures for sustainable security. Bush's policies dealt a strong blow to this receptivity at both levels (Gardner 2005, p. 80). In this respect, the Bush solution to terrorism proved a double-edged sword in undermining sustainable security. First, it proved counterproductive by generating even greater security threats through enhanced terrorism. But it also undercut the soft power necessary for launching and maintaining such an initiative, both in the United States and abroad: allies and partner nations proved to be a coalition of the unwilling, indigenous populations were repulsed by Americans and their initiatives for local security, and the US Congress and

American public showed bipartisan condemnation rather than bipartisan support for foreign policy (Jervis 2005; Kaplan 2008; Johnson 2004, 2006; Allawi 2007).

Above and beyond the link between soft power and military strategy, the moral hazard effect of the Bush Doctrine in neglecting the soft-power consequences of hard-power strategies compromised US security at an even more fundamental level (Halper and Clarke 2004, pp. 280–281). Enhancing this soft power would have rendered many of the sustainable security initiatives less necessary, because such soft power could have effectively addressed many of the root causes of terrorism. But this would have required a multifaceted diplomatic campaign that aimed for regional political and economic stabilization, based on a willingness to work with governments rather than beyond or above them (Fukuyama 2006, p. 185). The United States should have worked in a multilateral context, both within and outside the Middle East, to bring about a resolution to the Palestine problem. This would have required a normalization of relations with nations that Bush targeted as rogue states. Relations between India and Pakistan, as well as relations between North and South Korea, should have been approached in a similar way. The United States should have guaranteed the civil liberties of all who were being held under suspicion of terrorism, both within the United States and at foreign bases. It also should have improved relations with the other major regional power brokers whose domains contained most of the asymmetric threats to the United States: China, Russia, Pakistan, and Saudi Arabia. These domains also featured many of the autocratic regimes that were holding back liberal democratic transitions, regimes that themselves proved to be breeding grounds for terrorism. Finally, the United States should have more vigorously provided the economic public goods to deliver many parts of the world from deprivation. All such soft-power initiatives would have addressed the problems of asymmetric threats at the grassroots. Ultimately, the grassroots approach relies on x-efficiencies in civil society (i.e., the United States having allies in foreign populations). The Bush Doctrine, unfortunately, generated primarily x-inefficiencies (Gardner 2005, p. 3; Halper and Clarke 2004, pp. 279–282).

A soft war would be an entirely different kind of war in that it would hope to "win the hearts and minds" of populations in potentially dangerous regions (Lennon 2003). Interestingly, it has been the more radical elements, against which the United States has been fighting a hard war, that have done a better job in conducting such a war. Throughout the Middle East and the Muslim world at large (especially Afghanistan and Pakistan), radical Islamic groups since the 1990s have been actively engaged in providing public goods to populations that are deprived or experiencing turmoil.

Often these groups have been far better than the domestic governments in these states at providing general relief and social activities (welfare, education, healthcare, food aid). The generosity on the part of Hamas, Hezbollah, and Al-Qaida has become legend among Muslim populations in a number of countries. It is little wonder that recruitment into the ranks of extremist organizations has been vigorous, and has shown no signs of declining (de Wijk 2003, p. 20).

Like terrorism, weapons of mass destruction, as asymmetric threats, enjoy a plethora of tactical advantages against conventional US security strategies. The geographic size and global presence of the United States creates a fairly indefensible network of targets. The freedom of American society and the level of globalization create manifold opportunities to obtain materials to build WMD, develop them through small numbers of perpetrators, hide them effectively, and deliver them with alarming speed and consequences (Lambakis, Kiras, and Kolet 2002; Ellis 2004). All of this is especially true of chemical and biological weapons. As we have seen in the past (with anthrax and the use of such weapons in the Iran-Iraq War), only very small levels of input are required to produce devastating consequences, making the problem extremely difficult to root out of global civil society.[33] Given the indefensibility of potential targets (especially agriculture and water systems) and the ease with which perpetrators can inflict damage, the United States is alarmingly vulnerable to such attacks.[34] But even nuclear weapons, given technological advances, have evolved to a point where state sponsorship is no long necessary to build and use them. Indeed, an especially vigorous market in missile and nuclear technology has been visible since the end of the Cold War, with the United States being a major player as well. Moreover, much takes place in the black market, where monitoring of these devastating weapons is almost nonexistent.

As with terrorism, sustainable security against WMD requires a soft-power solution (Newhouse 2003). Regional security communities in which the United States has a strongly integrated role would need to be constructed. Again, as with terrorism, strategies of prevention, indirect methods, disaggregation, and limited-scale engagement would be required for sustainability. And these communities would need to be implemented in ways that are fundamentally similar to those used in the war against terrorism. This, again, would rely on foreign receptivity to US involvement in national and local security initiatives, as well as receptivity among allied and partner nations in building multilateral initiatives to support plans for sustainable security. And again, as with terrorism, the Bush Doctrine, in undermining this receptivity among host and potential partner nations, also undermined sustainable security possibilities against WMD (Gardner 2005, p. 160). As with terrorism, reliance on big-war strategies has generated moral hazard in developing the more viable strategies enumerated above (Thomas 2008; Lambakis, Kiras, and Kolet 2002). Big-war mania under the Bush regime crowded out the more finely tailored operations required to confront such asymmetric threats. The problem of WMD, as an asymmetric phenomenon, is manifest at the undercurrents of world politics (terrorist activities, concealed activities in so-called rogue states); hence effective penetration is the very lynchpin determining the success of counter-WMD operations (Jervis 2005; Newhouse 2003).

And again, as with terrorism, above and beyond the link between soft power and military strategy, the moral hazard effect of the Bush Doctrine in neglecting the soft-power consequences of hard-power strategies has compromised US security at the grassroots level as well. Enhancing this soft power would render many of the sustainable security initiatives unnecessary. The strategies for confronting terrorism through the multifaceted diplomatic campaigns enumerated above, in a quest for geostrategic pacification outcomes (i.e., regional, political, and economic stabilization), would also work well for WMD, given the asymmetric qualities they share with terrorism. Effective preventive strategies against asymmetric threats, as noted, require strong x-efficiencies to root out the threats, which means having foreign populations favorably disposed to US interests. Only soft power can effectively deliver such x-efficiencies (Halper and Clarke 2004, p. 281).

Eliminating security threats, political instability, and economic deprivation are three essential objectives for reducing the incentives to rely on WMD. These objectives can only be delivered through multilateral venues. Such venues have shown far more success in delivering such outcomes than did Bush's hard campaign. The Nuclear Non-Proliferation Treaty, Biological Weapons Convention, Chemical Weapons Convention, Comprehensive Nuclear Test Ban Treaty, and the Nunn-Lugar Cooperative Threat Program (Commonwealth of Independent States) have produced numerous positive accomplishments. Enhancing these initiatives and adding more of an economic-relief dimension to them would hold far more promise than did Bush's unilateral crusade (Heisbourg 2004, p. 17; Guoliang 2004, pp. 79–83).

As with terrorism and WMD, the Bush Doctrine's hard-power approach also proved counterproductive to the goal of promoting democracy. In fact, there have been a number of empirical studies on the effectiveness of using force to promote liberal democratic regime change. The results across these studies strongly suggest that force consistently fails miserably in bringing about regime change (Kegley and Raymond 2007, pp. 117–119). Overly militarized and overly coercive strategies for promoting regime transformation have in fact set back prospects for such outcomes.

Indeed, the heavy-handed approach, which has generated perceptions of victimization by "liberal imperialism," has discredited much of the ideological appeal and undermined the power of political forces attempting to consummate the change within the regimes themselves (Smith 2007, p. 235). This has effectively undercut the soft power necessary for such a political transformation (Lennon and Eiss 2004). Hence, by relying on these methods for promoting change, the United States has failed to embrace the more viable means of effecting sustainable change, and in this sense hard power has again victimized the United States through moral hazard in neglecting viable strategies for political transformation.

Sustainable political change has to be indigenous, as history has shown that stable and lasting regimes cannot simply be imposed onto nations without sensitivity to prior political culture and prevailing socioeconomic conditions. Sustainable change is founded on general ideological receptivity for regime change and a vigorous domestic initiative on the part of political leaders.[35] Both create the requisite soft-power foundations for new regimes to flourish (Lennon and Eiss 2004). As with terrorism and weapons of mass destruction, US goals for true regime change in the long run are better effected through strategies of positive engagement. This would mean regime enhancement through diplomacy, cooperation, economic partnerships, and disaggregated political engagement (local, regional, national). In effect, these would essentially be strategies of "political pacification" that would both promote and reduce the burden of political and economic transformation (Ansari 2004, p. 280).

Moreover, the United States should be more interested in state success than democracy. Failing states and failed states are the most likely breeding grounds for terrorism and tyranny (Kegley and Raymond 2007, p. 59). And it is far easier to strengthen states than to rebuild them after they have failed or collapsed. In this respect, the major goals of US foreign policy are best served if the focus of US soft power is on helping forge legitimate domestic institutions that deliver political goods rather than on regime orientation specifically (Fukuyama 2006, p. 185). In fragile states, it is not imposition of a regime that delivers a stable democracy, but rather it is political stability. This kind of stability can only be delivered multilaterally, as unilateral attempts can never generate the legitimacy needed to build stable institutions. Hence the foundations of soft-power initiatives are forged through political cooperation. But this cooperation must be pervasive, which is something the Bush Doctrine did not permit. Cooperation must include all relevant parties irrespective of regime types and diplomatic legacies. In this respect, it would also require engagement with erstwhile enemies of the United States. Hence rapprochement has remained one of the most important but elusive requirements. The moral hazard generated by the Bush Doctrine unraveled a significant diplomatic fabric that might have enhanced such rapprochement, and thus consequently set back the cause of statebuilding and state rescue (Rotberg 2003; von Hippel 2003).

The belief in the idea of "incorrigible rogue regimes" (that regimes are void of the indigenous progressive ideas and forces needed to support liberal transitions, and therefore such transitions must be imposed) is not only misleading but also dangerous. It has in fact encouraged just the kind of imperialistic assaults that have set back the liberal democratic cause across many such perceived regimes. Globalization and economic progress have been instrumental in stoking these indigenous progressive forces in all political systems. All such perceived regimes have a sizable number in their populations who embrace liberal political and economic ideas, and many of them are extremely influential political actors (Inglehart and Norris 2003; Pew Research Center 2003). Iran, for example, has headed this list of purported incorrigible rogue regimes for some time, and has therefore remained a principal concern for those who have been pessimistic about the possibilities for indigenous reform. But Iran, in fact, has demonstrated a strong veneration for republicanism for over a century. Starting with the constitutional revolution of 1906, desire for liberal political institutions has remained strong in Iran. Ali Ansari (2004) avers that, in fact, the past century in Iranian political history reveals a vigorous process of "organic democratization." Iranian politics, according to Ansari, has always reflected a dynamic and pluralistic nature. Even the crucial political events that ended up producing more autocratic regimes (under the Shah and Khomeini) began as democratic upheavals. The constitutional spirit of 1906 has never died and has in fact been compounded by the present-day forces that are continually modernizing Iranian society.

The economic need to deliver desirable outcomes (especially employment opportunities to the growing mass of educated young) in a globalized world has forced all modern regimes to make accommodations to political freedom and the market. Moreover, even the most autocratic regimes in the modern era have relied on a capitalist proletariat and bourgeoisie as important pillars of political support (Ansari 2004). In this respect, powerful indigenous forces for change are always fighting against the development of a political gap (Huntington 1971). And these conditions are also prevalent in other such regimes that have been branded as politically arrested. Saudi Arabia, Syria, Jordan, Libya, and Lebanon have been continuing to feel the pinch of a modern and materially grounded society facing economic difficulties in a globalized world. This has led to economic, political, and educational reforms in all these nations. Hence the underpinnings of organic democratization have apparently manifested themselves across the "rogue" world (Alterman 2004).

Even in what might be the most repressive regime among the purported rogues, North Korea, progressive forces are promoting a "quiet revolution" in government and society at large, claims Sergei Lankov (2007). While Lankov's claim would generally appear to be exaggerated, certainly a number of factors are emerging in North Korea that might constitute agents of change. The Kim Jong Il regime has continued to face great internal pressure from these progressive forces and has found it increasingly difficult to repress a greater transformation emerging in North Korea. Irrespective of massive attempts to keep people and information under control, there is far greater freedom in North Korea today than has been the case in preceding decades. A number of access points along borders with China and South Korea and greater elusiveness made possible by a globalized environment have allowed private markets to emerge, people to migrate out, and information to flow freely in. The levers of control have also been compromised by a debilitating corruption that has continued to delegitimate the regime among the greater population. Lankov, in fact, sees striking similarities between present-day North Korea and the Eastern-bloc nations shortly before the fall of the Berlin Wall. While most would see the potential for political change in present-day North Korea as limited, the indigenous forces that can marshal a transformation there are nonetheless manifesting themselves.

Indeed, the Bush Doctrine's reliance on hard power generated a type of moral hazard that rendered the United States muscle-bound in its foreign policy. The use of coercion and force both undermined the most important power resources (soft power) for achieving its most vital and treasured foreign policy goals through counterproductive effects and fundamental neglect. At a more basic level the Bush Doctrine undermined the credibility and legitimacy that was necessary for building multilateral networks in pursuit of those goals. This was compounded by the discarding of such networks in favor of independent action. Hence the Bush Doctrine limited flexibility in accessing the power resources necessary to marshal effective US foreign policy. Zbigniew Brzezinski (2007, p. 147) is representative of a large cross-section of scholars who lament the power curse caused by this muscle-bound state and inveighs for a new and more flexible policy orientation that is founded on a softer core. Indeed, only through such change does the United States have a "second chance" to reclaim its international influence.

Overstretch

As Paul Kennedy (1987, pp. 357–360) chronicles, the United States in the post–World War II era was a prime candidate for overstretch. It had emerged from the war with unquestioned primacy. In fact, all other competitors were in ruins from having been theaters of war. The US economy was intact and boosted by war-capacity production. US expansion was predicated on the dual opportunities of benefiting from this economic primacy, and also of building an international political milieu that accorded with US interests. Hence, beside the liberal economic policies that gave US products and businesses access to the international arena, geostrategic considerations emanating from a mandate to promote democracy demanded an international political and military presence. Building a new postwar international order promoted a new global presence. That presence mirrored a series of mutual dependencies. The growth of the US economy became dependent on this greater political-military presence in the world. And the greater presence was financed by the growing economy (Gilpin 1975). Mission creep was a natural outcome of the new internationalist orientation of the United States, as a growing stake in the system became naturally self-expanding in terms of maintaining the global political-economic milieu. Fueled by the Cold War, domino theory, and a growing international economy, the inclination toward further expansion and mission creep grew all the more.

The global presence of the United States is in fact larger today relative to the late 1940s. Most of the engagements forged in the ashes of World War II are still active today. US alliance commitments have neither diminished nor declined in number. These security functions have been increased all the more by a greater role in regional peacekeeping and an expansion in alliance membership. Hence the United States maintains greater global security functions then ever before. The US economy has become ever more integrated into the global economy, thus increasing the international presence of US business and banking. American society has followed suit as the main vehicle for globalization. Therefore, as the United States faces its greatest level of internationalization in the postwar era, it also faces a natural tendency toward overstretch (Kennedy 1987). But three interacting developments under Bush raised the ante and predisposed the United States all the more to a tendency of overstretch. First, the post–Cold War primacy of the United States placed it in a position similar to that of the late 1940s. Second, the Bush Doctrine was inspired and in fact mandated by this primacy to encourage the United States to play a greater role in the international arena in order to promote its vital interests. Finally, the new problems of nuclear proliferation and weapons of mass destruction were cast by the Bush administration as so menacing and pervasive that security could only come through extensive foreign engagement (Smith 2007).

The course of US unilateralism and vigorous engagement under Bush increased the tendency for mission creep, thus self-feeding the growth of US foreign presence (Johnson 2004, 2006; Gardner 2005; Jervis 2003a).

This presented a variety of burdens for the United States that served to weaken it. As the United States took on a bigger and more aggressive unilateral presence in the world as a global policeman, the costs of carrying on its international operations grew proportionally. So the maintenance costs of involvement in foreign affairs naturally grew along with the size of the stake in the system. Iraq and Afghanistan provide a lucid microcosm of the self-aggrandizing nature of a growing international presence. Military operations there have begotten further military operations to reinforce the gains and military positions carved out in the theaters of war (logistics and support, more bases, expanded regional operations, etc.). Furthermore, military operations in both countries have generated a need for complementary and ancillary functions and services, which have in turn expanded the foreign policy mandate and responsibilities. Private companies servicing military operations (Halliburton, DynCorp) and companies contracted to provide postwar reconstruction services (Bechtel, Perini) have considerably expanded the US presence in these countries. In turn, this presence has generated further needs from both civil society and the state. Dozens of companies, employing over 20,000 personnel, have been contracted to guarantee security functions in order to protect ongoing projects and services. But as the United States expanded its presence under Bush, and did so unilaterally, so many more manifold needs for complementary and ancillary functions arose, and all of these ultimately required a growing public mandate by the US government (Johnson 2004; Piven 2004, pp. 15–17).

But above and beyond Iraq and Afghanistan, Bush's three major objectives effectively bound the United States to a global commitment in furthering these goals, thus enhancing the self-feeding nature of the commitment itself. This emanated from the cumulative effects that Bush identified in the promulgation of these three major goals of US foreign policy. Because the goals were envisioned by the Bush administration as subject to cumulative gains and losses (domino effects), the United States had to commit to exploiting all opportunities to protect or promote these goals, and this required extensive global engagement.[36] Hence the United States had to commit to stabilizing many fledgling democracies, especially in Muslim regions (like Kosovo and Iraq), in order to promote momentum for democracy in the Middle East by showing that democracy can indeed succeed in all political environments.[37] Similarly, the quest against terrorism and weapons of mass destruction generated the same demands for an extensive global commitment on the part of the United States to engage in every major opportunity with respect to abating such dangers. Missing one important opportunity could reverberate globally in ways that undid the fabric of success that the United States was constructing. Moreover, the three goals of the Bush Doctrine were just one part of US "mono-containment" or "mega-containment" strategy under Bush. The strategy exhibited other grand goals: contain the influence of Russia in Europe and Asia, contain the economic and military rise of China, protect Taiwan and Japan, contain the activities of rogue nations, contain the rise of Communism in Latin America, protect Israel, keep Europe from achieving a unified foreign policy, pressure China and Japan economically, contain European economic independence, and contain the spread of dangers from the third world such as disease and drug trafficking (Gardner 2005, pp. 25, 127). But even the great material wealth and power of the United States have appeared humble in the face of such a burden. Indeed, Chalmers Johnson (2004, 2006) has averred that the "ruinous" burden of this global presence could very well destabilize the democratic foundations of US government.

The resulting self-feeding growth in US military presence has shown up starkly in a global geostrategic context. Hal Gardner (2005, p. 127) has referred to it as a "third wave" of US overseas imperialism. Johnson (2004, 2006) has labeled it an "empire." Indeed, aside from traditional overseas operations, the United States has expanded militarily into other regions in which it has had little historical experience: Eastern Europe, the Caucasus, Central Asia, North Africa and the Horn, the Far East, and the Persian Gulf. The United States has been actively engaged in opening new bases in these regions as well as in attempting to renegotiate or reobtain base privileges that have lapsed (Vietnam, Philippines, Japan). Much of the downsizing seen in both Europe and the Middle East in specific nations (Germany, Great Britain, and Saudi Arabia) actually represents more of a regional shift in forces (to Italy, Qatar, Bahrain, the United Arab Emirates, and Oman). A great deal of this expansion has been a manifestation of the tactical needs of the Bush Doctrine: "to defend rimlands, shatterbelts and chokepoints by developing rapid reaction and expeditionary forces that are ready to move as fast as possible versus a 'virtual' enemy" (Gardner 2005, p. 129). Such a global military capability is of course extremely taxing on a nation's resources. To compound the burden, the United States has continued its traditional Cold War strategic role of allocating large numbers of troops for deterrence and reassurance. The resulting military presence has been indeed gargantuan, with over 700 military bases in over 130 nations employing approximately 2.5 million people. This is complemented by a military force of approximately 1.5 million, with another 1.5 million in reserve (Johnson 2006; US Department of Defense 2007).

Just the burdens of the Iraq and Afghanistan wars themselves stretched the United States very thin both militarily and diplomatically, thus imposing significant weakening effects. These burdens have severely weakened the military capacity of the United States, both to effectively continue engagement in present campaigns and to respond to new threats around the world (Jervis 2005, p. 354). In one of the most comprehensive military surveys of the past fifty years, respondents emphasized the significant weakening effects of the Bush campaigns ("US Military Index" 2008).[38] They overwhelmingly (60 percent) declared the US military to be weaker relative to its capabilities five years earlier (25 percent believed the military to be stronger). Of the 60 percent who identified a weaker military, 20 percent cited the Iraq and Afghanistan campaigns as the main reason. When respondents were asked to judge the present health of individual branches of the US military (1 = not concerned, 10 = very concerned) and their readiness to respond to a crisis immediately (1 = not ready, 10 = fully ready), the average rankings for present health were Air Force 5.7, Army 7.9, Marine Corps 7.0, and Navy 5.9, and the average rankings for readiness were Air Force 6.6, Army 4.7, Marine Corps 5.7, and Navy 6.8. In responding to the statement "The demands of the war in Iraq have broken the U.S. military," 41 percent either strongly or somewhat agreed. In responding to the statement "The demands of the war in Iraq have stretched the U.S. military dangerously thin," 88 percent of respondents either strongly or somewhat agreed. In identifying the country that had gained the greatest strategic advantage from the Iraq War, more respondents cited Iran and China than the United States. When respondents were asked about the readiness of the US military to fight a war in various regions (1 = not prepared, 10 = fully prepared), the average rankings were as follows: Taiwan Straits 4.9, North Korea 4.7, Iran 4.5, Syria 5.1. In responding to a question about how reasonable it was, given the present campaigns in Iraq and Afghanistan, to expect the United States to wage a war elsewhere in the world, 80 percent considered that expectation to be either very or somewhat unreasonable. In identifying specific initiatives that should be undertaken to improve the fight against terrorism, a majority of respondents cited increased diplomatic functions, more special-operations forces, and better intelligence. Clearly, according to this extensive polling, the military itself has underscored the weakening effects of the Bush campaigns and has voiced serious concern about its subsequent abilities to confront new challenges and engage new enemies (Gardner 2005, p. 23). Jim Thomas observes that "more than six years on from the 9/11 attacks, America's position in the world and the course that lies ahead are uncertain. The high costs of current wars in terms of blood and treasure contribute to a growing sense of strategic exhaustion. Given its global goals, responsibilities, and values, America's current course is unlikely to be one that can be sustained for the long term—politically (both domestically and internationally), economically, or militarily" (2008, p. 3).

Moreover, a growing military force and a pronounced military presence in the world make it increasingly difficult to control national security. Stories of the Iran-Contra affair attest to the warning of political theorists: a growing military bureaucracy is increasingly difficult to manage (Halperin 1974; Yarmolinsky and Foster 1983). The foreboding possibilities emanating from this tendency are that mistakes in the field may compromise the position and interests of the United States in sensitive areas. Hence, military occupation, such as in Iraq, is always a potential powder keg for US foreign policy, as accidents (which raise the ire of indigenous populations against the United States) can completely unravel the greater and dearly sought goal of political transformation.

The imposing international role of the United States under Bush also generated diplomatic overstretch that cut adversely against US foreign interests. The growth in attention on Iraq in many ways debilitated the capacity of the United States to manage other important foreign relations and attend to crucial issues in other parts of the world. In 2007, for example, the president, secretary of state, and secretary of defense all canceled important diplomatic missions to Asia, Africa, and Latin America because developments in Iraq had trumped those missions. The consequences of this "Iraq tax" have continued to manifest themselves throughout the diplomatic landscape. Terrorism has been allowed to flourish in many other places, especially places where governments are either sympathetic to or incapable of limiting it (Lebanon, Syria, Pakistan, Indonesia). The political environment in Lebanon has deteriorated, with Hezbollah rising in political influence and popularity. Hamas has become an increasingly influential player in Palestine. North Korea has muscled its way to developing significant amounts of weapons-grade plutonium. Leftist regimes have proliferated in Latin America, all touting at least some anti-US platform. In Africa, poverty and infectious diseases, as well as political instability, have increased, all of which carry significantly adverse consequences for the United States. And in Eastern Europe, democratic reform seems to be moving in reverse (Kaplan 2008, pp. 186–187). In this respect, such adverse outcomes are consistent with a historical trend cited by Stephen Walt (1999): limited diplomatic resources across an excessively large international agenda have resulted in a debilitated capacity over a broad range of important issues and regions.

Furthermore, since a large hegemonic presence in the world necessitates multi-tasking, there is a tendency for some initiatives to unravel others (Walt 1999). This tendency rises as overstretch causes nations to take on more commitments then they can coordinate effectively, as indeed happened in the United States under Bush. In pursuing direct goals with a heavy hand, Bush undermined the broader foundations (the milieu) within which

US interests play out, thus making the pursuit of those direct goals all the more difficult to sustain. The quest to protect Israel has had adverse consequences in terms of terrorism, WMD, and liberal transition; the need to contain Russia has weakened its commitment to fight for US interests inside and outside Europe; the quest to keep Europe divided on foreign policy has made NATO and European nations less cooperative in helping the United States realize its three major goals; and more generally, confrontations over terrorism and WMD have undermined the quest for democratic transition, and vice versa.

Under the Bush Doctrine, the mandated global presence generated overstretch and mission creep through another sort of dependence, one that resides in the dynamics of US politics. The requirements of the doctrine had to some extent become domestically self-reinforcing and self-expansive. After having staked his political fate and legacy on the doctrine after 9/11, Bush could not extricate himself from this position. Retracting US commitments and engagements around the globe would have been an admission that the doctrine was in fact either mistaken or a failure. Hence, even a failing international presence, as has been the case in a number of situations, had staying power (i.e., rational failure). But failure did not lead to retraction; rather it encouraged even greater US engagement so as to preserve the possibilities for success, or at the least not create an impression of failure. Even in the face of extreme pressure from the public and Congress to scale down military operations in Iraq and Afghanistan, the administration resolved to stay the course. The legacy has clearly made an impact on future administrations, as no mainstream candidate for the post-Bush presidency advocated a cut-and-run strategy. This is a manifestation of the undesirability of admitting that seven years of war and thousands of deaths have been borne in vain.

The most glaring consequence of overstretch has been the enormous burden it has imposed on the US national economy and domestic society. As Johnson blandly states, "military domination of the world is an expensive business" (2004, p. 306). The arguments on this point are fairly straightforward and have been a mainstay of the critique against Bush's foreign policy.[39] But the problem grew significantly more onerous in the face of the administration's fiscal policy: conterminous tax cuts in the face of expensive domestic and security initiatives that put the United States on a trajectory toward a $2 trillion deficit. The policy was eerily reminiscent of events under the Reagan administration, whose combination of tax cuts and profligate funding of domestic and security programs coincided with the highest real interest rates in US history; its domestic and international economic shock waves left an indelible impression on the US economy in the 1980s. Recently, while interest rates have remained low and the price tag on the Iraq campaign benefited from the relative brevity of the war, a continuation of this policy mix looms forebodingly, especially in the face of the government's financial bailouts in 2008 and 2009 (which carry a price tag of several trillion dollars). Given the financial meltdown, the accompanying recession, and the fragility of the stock market, the US economy remains highly vulnerable. Essentially, the strength of the United States derives from its economy, and hence any policies that imperil this foundation of US power threaten to significantly weaken the nation (Stiglitz and Bilmes 2008, p. 125).

The real and hidden economic costs of the Iraq and Afghanistan wars have represented significant weakening factors, suggesting that US economic resources have been significantly overstretched. And in this case overstretch and mission creep have been tightly interconnected. As has always been the case, the United States has faced mission creep in spending large sums rebuilding nations decimated in its military campaigns. Both wars have led to expensive occupations. In fact, a lion's share of the costs of the wars have emanated from US reconstruction mission creep. By early 2008, the joint campaign in Iraq and Afghanistan, at an accumulated cost surpassing half a trillion dollars (by official government estimates), had become the second most expensive US military campaign in real dollars, surpassing all campaigns but World War II. And while World War II was five times greater in real (2007) dollars, at $5 trillion, that war employed over 16 million troops.[40] Moreover, in terms of real cost per soldier, the Iraq and Afghanistan wars have far surpassed all wars, at $400,000 per troop, with World War II costing $100,000 per troop (Stiglitz and Bilmes 2008, pp. 5–6). As the occupations and stabilization missions with both Iraq and Afghanistan progress, the mission creep will manifest itself all the more in terms of expenditures. Both campaigns are headed toward longer-term economic and security missions that will generate ever larger bills, as has historically been the case with such US military campaigns. Already the campaigns have caused the Pentagon to pursue a variety of new access and basing arrangements throughout the Middle East and Central Asia (Jervis 2003a).

Most of the expenditures on Iraq and Afghanistan have come through emergency supplemental spending bills, which are designated outside of the annual budgetary process. These have been financed through government borrowing, which essentially places the burden on future generations to pay.[41] With the yearly federal deficit hovering between $150 and $500 billion over the period 2003–2008, the direct costs placed on the future populace, who have already been burdened by the government's financial bailout, are significant. Adding to this already extreme US indebtedness is a current account deficit that has hovered at about half a trillion dollars in recent years. Joseph Stiglitz and Linda Bilmes (2008, p. 54) estimate that interest on the war debt will be about $1 trillion in 2017. This not only carries great financial burdens, but may carry significant potential for macroeconomic instability (with its consequences for interest rates and growth). And given the still dominant role of the United States in dictating terms in the international economy, US macroeconomic developments may generate international outcomes (recession, weak dollar) that feed back adversely on US economic performance. But the burden is also compounding other domestic fiscal problems. The viability of future social security outlays has become questionable, given a shrinking pool of funds. Moreover, large military budgets have squeezed numerous programs that provide health, social, and educational services to Americans, which are far less visible than simple, nominal war expenditures, but they are nonetheless large and debilitating for the US economy.

In fact, the hidden costs of the Iraq and Afghanistan wars dwarf the overt costs if we take into account their impact on the lives of American citizens. In this respect, two types of hidden costs appear compelling: the deprivation costs due to direct budgetary outlays, and the opportunity costs of supplementary allocations. Deprivation costs represent the adverse impact on American lives due to the budgetary impact of the wars. In this respect, there will be more limited social and health spending, which in turn will impact negatively on the health and human capital of Americans (Johnson 2004, p. 285). But the costs of the wars must also consider the opportunity costs of the supplementary expenditures. These costs would represent the social impact that the same expenditures might have had on American citizens if the money were spent on domestic programs—what Stiglitz and Bilmes (2008) refer to as "switching costs." It is fairly certain that in terms of benefiting Americans materially, domestic investment (jobs, better healthcare, greater education) would have been much more productive. This productivity would have manifold effects in raising the standard of living in the United States. While it would be impossible to quantify both sets of hidden costs, it appears compelling that both are in fact significant additions to the costs of the wars. Hence if one defines national strength in terms of a broad conceptualization of public well-being—protection from economic deprivation, ensured healthcare, investment in human capital—then the direct and indirect costs of the Iraq and Afghanistan campaigns have had a significant weakening effect on the United States. Stiglitz and Bilmes (2008, p. 31) estimate that the hidden and nonhidden costs of the campaigns might very well end up costing $3 trillion, and that even this might be a conservative estimate.[42] In this sense, the war effort may generate far more casualties in the United States—from economic deprivation and opportunities forgone—than it ever will on fields of battle (Stiglitz and Bilmes 2008).[43]

Some estimates on the human costs of the US war effort are revealing in terms of both switching and deprivation costs. Just in healthcare alone, switching costs appear to be relatively significant. In early 2008 there were approximately 45 million Americans without health insurance. Excessively conservative estimates would place the costs of insuring those Americans through a standard private health maintenance organization at approximately $225 billion for one year.[44] Let us further assume that, because of the lack of healthcare for that year, one-half of one percent of those people would either die or develop medical conditions that lead to premature death. This would mean that 1 out of 200 of these uninsured Americans would be affected, which would seem to be a fairly conservative estimate considering the incidence of terminal and serious diseases even among individuals who obtain regular medical attention.[45] Using this figure, we would estimate the death toll in United States from the Iraq War, simply in terms of medical-insurance switching costs, to be 225,000 for one year. This is infinitely greater than the 4,000 official war deaths amassed by the spring of 2008.[46] Even if these estimates have been exaggerated by a factor of ten, which would be pathologically conservative, the numbers still suggest that many more Americans would have died in terms of switching costs (22,500). But these are just the most conservative estimates in terms of switching costs with respect to medical-insurance opportunities forgone. Money forgone just from the emergency outlays alone could go to a variety of health and human services, economic assistance, transfers, and a plethora of other social investment that would ultimately save lives through one relief mechanism or another. There is no way of even attempting suggestive estimates of such human costs, but it is prudent to believe that a considerable number of lives could be saved with an investment of half a trillion dollars in American society. Furthermore, the significant deprivation costs—the funds channeled from social investment into the military budget—would have to be factored into the equation.[47]

Additionally, economic costs have not been counterbalanced by wartime macroeconomic growth or greater power over the oil market. Neither the Gulf War nor the recent Iraq War produced wartime booms, because regular budgetary military expenditures did not increase significantly as a result of the campaigns. Gulf War expenses were paid largely by the Saudis and other nations, while the current campaign has been largely funded by supplemental spending. In this respect, these wars broke the iron law of wartime booms: both led, in the short run, to declining economic indices. William Nordhaus (2002, p. 32) points out that a modest increase in budgetary defense spending meant that compensatory expansionary stimulus was not provided by public sector spending; hence the dominant factor in driving short-run economic consequences were psychological, and these psychological factors produced bearish economic behavior. With respect to the Iraq War, Stiglitz and Bilmes (2008) factor in the macroeconomic opportunity costs of the war, as they argue that economic growth would have been greater in the absence of war. But even with respect to compensatory outcomes in other economic areas, the principal venue of oil has proved disappointing. The United States has not used its military domination of Iraq in any way that would influence the price of oil to the benefit of American consumers. It refrained from orchestrating the management of oil in Iraq in ways that would confront or even threaten the Organization of Petroleum-Exporting Countries (OPEC). If anything, jitters about instability in the region due to the US occupation and confrontational posture toward Iran contributed to buoying oil prices to record levels.[48]

In examining how overstretch was promoted under the Bush Doctrine, it is instructive to look at the ways the administration was able to garner domestic support, which historically has always proved to be important political currency for the survival of expansionist policies (Snyder 1991). It was not difficult to bring big business on board, since a significant number of US corporations benefited from the military operations, from defense industries to service industries contracted to provide logistical support in occupied areas. But big business was never a hurdle for a big-party Republican like Bush. The ongoing allegiance of the Republican rank and file in Congress was a manifestation of this political synergy. American society at large and liberal elites were harder to convince, but Bush's public relations campaign was vigorous and ultimately effective to a large extent. For elites, important bureaucrats, and politicians, the administration built extensive networks across think tanks and policy institutes that were managed by powerful sponsors. Dissemination of pro–Bush Doctrine material was perpetrated through a variety of effective venues, from direct outreach to conferences. For the greater conservative public, the administration forged connections to conservative news and radio talk shows, as well as within editorial circles in charge of large newspapers and magazines. Furthermore, the administration developed strong associations with various conservative groups, the most important being the Evangelical Christian community (Piven 2004, p. 27; Halper and Clarke 2004, pp. 182–200). The campaign proved instrumental in swaying mind-sets among the targeted groups (Halper and Clarke 2004, p. 183).

But perhaps Bush's greatest public relations success was in framing the need for such policies in ways that persuaded the general public, both liberals and conservatives. In this case, two factors conjoined to propagate a compelling vision. The first was the use of fear emanating from 9/11 (Piven 2004, p. 9). Halper and Clarke (2004, p. 203) cite the use of 9/11 fear as instrumental in creating a "synthetic neurosis" within American society that predisposed it to adopt a mind-set consistent with Bush's objectives.

The synthetic neurosis proved instrumental in helping Bush frame the issues of WMD, terrorism, and democratic statebuilding as essential to the security of the United States. But moreover, the neurosis made American society more amenable to the message that rationalized the fundamental expansionist policies of the Bush Doctrine: that such menaces were in fact subject to cumulative gains and losses.[49] This was the rationale created to justify an extensive global presence to confront the menacing forces that pervaded the international system.[50] An image of interconnections and dominos undergirded this rationale.[51] Terrorism was linked to global networks that were well concealed within global civil society. The menace was all the greater when supported by states, so invasions of those states (like Iraq and Afghanistan) were supposed to deter other states from supporting terrorists lest they too be targeted. Furthermore, breaking any one link in the chain was supposed to reverberate globally to weaken the entire chain. And hence the dominos would fall and make Americans safer. So too with WMD, the dominos supposedly lined up. Standing up to rogue nations that sought to wield WMD would have similar compellence and deterrence effects on other nations.[52] Since both terrorists and WMD programs could be so well concealed and so pervasive, the United States had to be prepared to monitor and intervene almost anywhere in the world. And this is where the third goal, democratic statebuilding, became instrumental and added to the cumulative framework. Regime types were pitched as important factors of influence. Democracies were portrayed as less likely to sponsor terrorists or confront superpowers with WMD. But the creation of democracies was also subject to a cumulative dynamic. The growth of liberal political regimes in heretofore autocratic political bastions such as Afghanistan and Iraq would compel reformist groups in other nations to promote their own political transitions. Furthermore, this dynamic would benefit the United States by promoting cumulative gains through bandwagoning. New democracies as well as other nations that supported the US cause would forge a greater coalition of strength.[53] Conversely, failure in promoting any one of these doctrinal goals in just a single place would have a cumulative destabilizing effect, encouraging the dominos to fall against the interests of the United States. Allowing one state to sponsor terrorists would embolden other states, as would failure to confront a nation about possession of WMD. Similarly, failure to promote democracy in one state would reverberate through the political systems of other nondemocratic states, thus turning the domestic tide against reform.[54]

Despite the Bush administration's efforts to sell the war on terrorism and the rest of the doctrine early on, public support declined precipitously across Bush's second term (Jervis 2005). North Korea stands as a glaring microcosm of the Bush administration's ever-weakening ability to generate the domestic backing needed to sustain its foreign policy. Kim Jong Il's recalcitrant stand against US coercion reflected numerous sources of confidence about declining public support for Bush. Foremost, any US strike against North Korea would risk retaliation by North Korea against the South Korean capital, as Seoul sits extremely close to the border between the two Koreas and is in dangerous range of military assaults from the North. In recognizing that the United States would not risk another Korean war, especially with its resources stretched to the maximum, Kim was emboldened in terms of both his political resilience and his pursuit of weapons of mass destruction. US threats marshaled on hard power had become far less credible in this environment of overstretch and dwindling domestic support from the American public (Kaplan 2008, p. 65).

In sum, a greater international presence for the United States was stoked by perceptions of US global primacy under the Bush Doctrine. Expansion was an enticing goal for a nation perceived to have the capabilities to unilaterally transform many aspects of world politics. But in the end, such preponderant influence was only illusory. And in trying to fulfill such a mission, the United States compromised much of its strength.

The Vicious Cycle of US Unilateralism

It is interesting that Bush hailed the invigorating benefits of multilateralism in the 2002 National Security Strategy: "We are also guided by the conviction that no nation can build a safer, better world alone. Alliances and multilateral institutions can multiply the strength of freedom-loving nations" (White House 2002a, p. v). Irrespective of this rhetoric, it was a disposition toward unilateralism that emanated from the Bush Doctrine—a clear manifestation of the power curse. Premised on the neoconservative belief that the United States enjoyed primacy in the global power structure, the doctrine embraced independent action as the optimal means of securing US interests abroad. In this vision, the entangling and restraining chains of multilateral commitments could only weaken the ability of the United States to protect its vital interests in the world (Smith 2007). In short, it was a clear rejection of the venues of soft power (power through cooperation) and a commitment to the instruments of hard power. Bush himself blazed a unilateralist trail both before and after 9/11, and even independently of national security issues. The trail was extensive: a recalcitrant posture toward the United Nations; withdrawal from the International Criminal Court; rejection of a UN ban on germ warfare as well as a UN resolution designed to protect children against slavery and forced labor; refusal to sign the Kyoto Protocol; continued waffling on Law of the Sea negotiations; withdrawal from the Anti-Ballistic Missile Treaty and pursuit of a missile defense shield in the face of worldwide opposition; reluctance to sign the Biological Weapons Convention; reluctance to participate in a grand UN initiative designed to address racism in the member nations; remaining a lethargic observer with respect to the Land Mines and Comprehensive Test Ban Treaties; and attempting to weaken UN resolutions designed to limit illegal trafficking in small arms. This abdication from cooperation far from vindicated neoconservative expectations.[55] The rejection of important soft venues for pursuing its global objectives in fact weakened the United States. Moreover, the quest for independence led the United States into a vicious cycle of unilateralism that clearly revealed the insufficiency of its unilateral hard power to guard its interests in global issues. In fact, this unilateral hard power proved far inferior to multilateral venues as a lever to obtain its most cherished goals. The influence perceived as deriving from this hard power was an illusion, vindicating those who maintained that the United States, notwithstanding its primacy, was not in fact strong enough to "go it alone" (Nye 2002, p. 158).

The aloof posture of the United States compromised its global power position. Disregard for its allies, especially the UN Security Council and NATO in dealing with Iraq, sent shock waves through those constellations of relations, damaged the credibility of both organizations as important power brokers, and compromised the standing of the United States in both bodies (Gardner 2005, p. 129).[56] This rift is not as inconsequential as some, like Robert Kagan (2003), believe, because the United States has historically used both bodies as important venues to pursue its global interests, especially when it has sought multilateral legitimacy as a seal of approval and direct support for its actions (Jervis 2005, p. 354).[57] The United States has been critically dependent on both for its principal international goals: postwar stabilization in Iraq (with the Security Council now being invited to play a greater role), peace in the Middle East, combating terrorism and WMD, peacekeeping, and statebuilding in Eastern Europe. Without the backing of such bodies, the United States has been rendered less able to attain its international goals and has been left with fewer cards to play when protecting its interests. As a result, the United States has been confronted by a vicious cycle: as unilateralism has alienated allies and supporters, unilateralism has become even more necessary because of a diminished recourse to multilateral forums (Smith 2007, p. 198).

NATO support has been especially crucial, and given US unilateralism, it has been especially fragile as well. The United States has always been assisted by its allies in carrying out its most important international objectives. But it chose a different path after 9/11 with respect to NATO. While the United States was pursuing its own conceptions of retaliation and already planning for war with Iraq, NATO was left on the margins of both efforts. Bush focused on Britain as a key coalition ally, but continued to alienate his NATO allies by pursuing wars and occupations without substantive consultation and accountability. As the disdain for US unilateralism grew, it became more difficult for NATO allies to muster either the popular support or the elite disposition to help the United States when the latter found itself targeted as an imperialistic occupier. In this case, NATO's reluctance to provide enough muscle to both lighten the burden for the United States and legitimate the occupations left the United States in a vicious state of isolation in attending to its goals in Iraq and Afghanistan (Kaplan 2008, pp. 179–183).

NATO has been intimately involved in the three major goals of the United States concerning terrorism, WMD, and democracy. But above and beyond those goals, a supportive and vibrant NATO is essential to US interests throughout the world (Smith 2007, p. 198). NATO is the principal instrument through which the United States is presently brokering and securing it geopolitical interests in Europe. Furthermore, NATO's support is a boon to US goals in every principal global region. It continues to be the peacekeeper in Kosovo, but has also allocated a large number of troops in Afghanistan and has been instrumental in training Iraqi security forces. It has even been engaged in Africa by providing airlifts for African peacekeepers. The United States seeks to expand this peacekeeping role for NATO in order to obtain both logistical help and legitimacy for its own foreign ventures. It has pushed NATO to develop a vigorous program against cyber-terrorism and undertake a greater role in long-term civil reconstruction and peacekeeping operations in Iraq and Afghanistan. Furthermore, the United States has pushed for European support in its coercion of Iran and North Korea. But the alienation resulting from US impunity has scarred the alliance, with NATO recoiling at the very times the United States has needed it most.

At the NATO summit in Bucharest in April 2008, European leaders contemplated a change in the alliance toward a more limited focus in operations. The resulting rift between the United States and the European Union mirrors a splintering of the US-NATO alliance in recent years.[58] There has already emerged in the alliance a two-tiered system in terms of which nations supply frontline troops versus those that undertake less hazardous duties. Furthermore, the operations in Afghanistan are hardly well coordinated, but verge on a free-for-all. Moreover, the politics of NATO are absolutely crucial to US interests in Europe. The question of expansion is intimately intertwined with US-Russian relations, and hence is of immense importance to the United States. The Bucharest summit demonstrated the importance of NATO when the allies voted to endorse Bush's plan for a missile defense shield in Poland and the Czech Republic, agreed to send more French troops to Afghanistan, but nixed Bush's objective of expanding the alliance by not announcing a plan to include the Ukraine and Georgia.[59] Clearly the alliance still holds crucial leverage over important US geostrategic interests in Europe. And with associate status for Russia in the new cooperative council, NATO provides the principal multilateral forum for cooperation on European security matters with Russia. This is significant for the United States because it provides a rare multilateral reinforcement venue for addressing issues between the two great powers. Being marginalized in the alliance removes the United States from an important position of influence in the course of alliance politics, and hence diminishes its ability to orchestrate its most vital European relations. Indeed, its drift from grace in NATO has left the United States increasingly isolated in facing some of its biggest challenges (McKinnon 2008).

But even more than NATO, the United Nations as a whole and the UN Security Council in particular are absolutely essential forums for the United States, which has significantly disempowered itself by forsaking them. So while unilateralism may have given the United States more freedom to act with impunity in the short run, it has weakened the United States and in fact limited its wiggle room in the longer run. Indeed, the United States has squandered significant opportunities to pursue its interests through resort to meta-power in such well-respected multilateral venues, which could have been energized by greater US engagement. It somewhat defies reason that the United States would spend decades building these institutions in order to promote its direct and milieu goals and then abandon them when vital interests are at stake. In terms of the goals of combating terrorism and WMD, the institutional framework of the Security Council has provided a compelling problem-solving venue. The Council has passed sixteen major resolutions demanding Iraqi disarmament. Security Council Resolution 1368 contemplates a broad and effective mandate to hunt down terrorists throughout the world. More generally, the Council provides extensive latitude to its permanent members (the United States and allies) to manage security in the world at large.

With respect to nation building, decolonization has cast the United Nations in the leading role, something that the United States is finding difficult to compete with in reestablishing political order in Iraq (Heisbourg 2004, p. 11). While the use of meta-power through multilateral forums lacks the speed and directness of unilateral approaches, it may nonetheless prove a greater source of influence over the long run, as lasting solutions to international problems must be grounded in legitimate and influential structures of governance. The imposition of illegitimate or weaker structures will be ultimately self-defeating. The six-party talks on WMD in North

Korea are a case in point. The United States has been quite vocal in its disappointment with the historic progress of the talks. But the Security Council has not engaged the issue as resolutely. In this case, there are particularistic considerations that dissuade the permanent members of the Council from miring themselves in a contentious issue that might prove risky for their foreign affairs. In any event, bringing in regional powers, especially China, has made a significant difference in addressing the problem of WMD in North Korea with respect to US diplomatic goals.

In terms of global peacekeeping, the preemptive policy of the United States has threatened to unravel the legal fabric of the security regime contemplated under the UN Charter. The United States has relied heavily on this regime to promote its goal of limiting regional and ethnic conflict in the postwar period. While Article 51 of the Charter expressly affirms the right of unilateral militarism, it clearly precludes preemptive attacks, allowing military action only in self-defense. The United States has in fact made use of this clause in legitimating multilateral and unilateral responses to acts of aggression that go against its interests, from Korea to the Balkans and the Gulf (Wirtz and Russell 2003, p. 118). Setting precedents that undermine this clause can only increase military action in the world at large, as nations gain greater legitimacy for preemptive invasions. In fact, US impunity, in breaking with Security Council and NATO obligations in dealing with Iraq, unleashed a wave of responses on the part of other nations (a vigilante effect) that conflicted with US foreign goals (Guoliang 2004, p. 77). In the wake of Bush's 2002 national security statement, India, Russia, Iran, Israel, and Japan all issued statements proclaiming their right to perpetrate preemptive strikes for self-defense (Kegley and Raymond 2007, p. 102). Hence the US desire for a world of fewer regional and ethnic conflicts will become increasingly frustrated. Moreover, US preemption in this respect is inconsistent with the milieu goal of enhancing respect for human rights and international law. At a more general level, US policy appears to have been guilty of a "paradox of peace," in that it has sought to disseminate a commitment to peace through a preponderance of weapons and unilateral militarism (Yarmolinsky and Foster 1983).

By forsaking multilateral forums in a quest to protect its vital interests, the United States has missed some extraordinary opportunities to galvanize and shape these forums in ways that are consistent with those interests. The lesson learned by the Soviets in the early years of the United Nations was somehow lost on the Bush administration. The Soviets responded to disagreeable votes in the Security Council by simply walking out and boycotting proceedings. While this did not hurt them on procedural issues, it took a heavy toll on one important substantive issue: the Soviets boycotted Security Council deliberations on the Korean question because the Council had earlier voted to allow Nationalist China to keep its representative on the Council even after the Communist Revolution. Because the Soviets were not there to veto the resolution that called for a multilateral retaliation against the invasion of South Korea, this gave greater legitimacy to the US cause against North Korea. The lesson was clear: nations may gain independence by relinquishing multilateral obligations, but they also lose power over the proceedings in those organizations and hence sacrifice opportunities to shape the agenda. But such organizations can have considerable influence over the vital interests of those nations. In the worst-case scenario, absence may cause outcomes to become more hostile to the interests of the recalcitrant nations, which introduces perhaps the most pernicious consequence of the vicious cycle of unilateralism: continued politico-strategic aloofness may create more enemies than it eliminates if the abandoned organizations take a confrontational turn. And such contests produce a very uneven playing field, as organizations carry far more legitimacy for their causes, all other things being equal, compared to individual nation-states. At a minimum, if the organizations do not take a confrontational turn, they may produce additional roadblocks for a nation's foreign initiatives. In this case, the old axiom holds: "If you can't beat them, join them."

From a more general structural perspective, institutions that circumscribe and restrain sovereign actions in the international system tend to work in favor of the dominant nations. This has been fundamentally acknowledged across the political spectrum of international relations theory, from neomarxists to neoliberals (Krisch 2003; Cox 1980; Keohane 1984). But the benefits of this "institutionalization of hegemony" are all the greater due to the fact that the United States has been the most prolific international "legislator" of the postwar era. The possibilities for enjoying metapower in these institutions are all the greater because decisionmaking structures that have guided the institutions have been configured to a large extent by the United States itself (Krisch 2003). Hence the status quo fundamentally has rested on institutions built and supported by the United States. Compromising the effectiveness and even existence of these institutions will consequently undermine important traditional sources of US leverage in the international system. Moving outside these arrangements for slightly more flexibility in the short run carries the risk of weakening the United States across most issues in the long run. If we look at all of the arrangements that Bush forsook in his quest for more effective foreign policy, we see a trail of decimation in multilateral initiatives that have heretofore protected and promoted vital US interests: the Anti-Ballistic Missile Treaty (enhancing the power of US deterrence), the Kyoto Protocol (delivering market-based solutions to environmental problems), the International

Criminal Court (exporting US criminal law to the international system), the Law of the Sea (establishing definitive property rights on uses of the sea), the Biological Weapons Convention (limiting possibilities for devastating assaults on US soil), and the Convention on Small Arms (limiting the resources for asymmetric strikes against the United States and Americans abroad).

As the United States has alienated its allies within the context of existing arrangements, the latter have diverted to alternative arrangements that do not include the United States, and such arrangements may even turn out to generate competition for US interests themselves (Ikenberry 2001, p. 19). There were a number of such cases under the Bush presidency. US allies in Europe sought alternative and additional security arrangements outside NATO. European nations sought to forge their own rapid deployment force due to dissatisfaction with US willingness to compromise on the management of NATO's deployment. France reached out to Russia, North Korea, Iran, and Chechnya in search of new security arrangements. France and Germany reached out to China in order to consolidate arms dealings. Russia sought an alternative security arrangement with NATO outside the NATO-Russia Council. France, Britain, and Germany prompted Russia to form a multilateral security initiative to negotiate with Tehran over nuclear arms. Russia and China joined the Shanghai Cooperative Organization, alongside various Eurasian republics, to promote trade, limit drug trafficking, and fight terrorism. Russia sought to bring China and India into an arrangement that would fight pan-Islamic terrorism. Even Israel affronted US pride by joining India to form a security pact against terrorism (Malone 2003, p. 23; Gardner 2005, pp. 134–139). Above and beyond the competition over security arrangements involving the United States, these crosscutting commitments may create significant problems if non-US regimes require US allies to forsake their commitments to the United States. This is akin to the problem of crosscutting vassalages (vassals having more than one lord) during the Middle Ages, which made feudalism such an unstable political system.

If nations choose to maintain their present arrangements with the United States instead of seeking other venues, a corollary effect of alienation could manifest itself in another deleterious outcome: the US reputation for impunity within multilateral forums may generate a backlash that leads other nations to impose greater de facto (if not de jure) restraints against the United States in order to counterbalance the inclusion of what might be considered a maverick nation. In this respect, a history of restraint and cooperation under international agreements and legal instruments may paradoxically accord greater net benefits in terms of legitimacy and flexibility than a history of impunity (Krisch 2003, p. 64). Ongoing loyalty will place a nation in a better position to ask for exceptions to rules when they accord most with vital interests. A disloyal and recalcitrant nation will have compromised the political capital to ask for such favors. One stark example of this was manifest in the differential treatment by NATO allies in the Security Council with respect to the cases of Kosovo and Iraq. America's NATO allies were reluctant to give a Security Council mandate to justify US military action against Iraq even though Iraq was found to be in breach of Resolution 688 for over a decade. But the same nations allowed NATO air strikes against Kosovo without even requesting such a mandate. Legally, the basis for US action against Iraq differed little from that of Europe against Kosovo, but America's allies raised the institutional barriers in reaction to what was considered a trail of unilateralist impunity (Heisbourg 2004, p. 10). Another example has been the manner in which members of the International Criminal Court have been increasingly reluctant to grant the United States exceptions because of perceptions that the United States will never compromise on the statute (Krisch 2003, p. 64).

There is no question that strong alliance relations are key to US milieu goals of democratic statebuilding, combating terrorism and WMD, promoting economic liberalism, and forging regional and ethnic harmony. Ultimately, in both Europe and Asia, these goals can only be viably pursued within a multilateral framework. Hence the United States has to strengthen rather than weaken its colleagueship in regional alliances. Interestingly, greater and more crosscutting ties would be a boon to peace in the Middle East, a lesson that is obviously making an impression on the United States as it seeks a more multilateral solution to the Palestine question. The United States must act quickly and with resolution to consolidate its standing in regional alliances, as harbingers of potential disassociation have recently emerged. A Pew Research Center survey (2003) reported that a majority of Western European populations want more independence from the United States in diplomacy and security. In addition, US allies have for the first time refused to reelect the United States to the UN Human Rights Commission (Nye 2002, p. 156). The image of the United States within alliance networks deteriorated significantly with the overwhelming refusal of Bush's overtures, after September 2003, for help in rebuilding and stabilizing Iraq. More disconcerting for the United States, this refusal of support reflects not just disapproval, but also strategic burden avoidance. Staying out of such controversial undertakings not only saves resources for nations, but also reduces their security risks. Allowing the United States to supply the lion's share of occupation forces in Iraq and Afghanistan makes it the target of vituperation. This trend is visible in North Korea as well, where NATO allies can avoid risk by keeping WMD talks in a regional context rather than making them a prime focus of the Security Council (Heisbourg 2004, p. 11).

The unilateralism encouraged by Bush has served to weaken multilateral venues for addressing the most pressing problems facing the United States, and in doing so has introduced a vicious cycle that increasingly forces the United States to carry more of the burden without help from others (Guoliang 2004, p. 79). This has compounded the problem of overstretch and raised the costs of foreign policy all the more. A legacy of brash unilateralism has further enhanced the problem of overstretch, because it has given allies legitimate grounds for avoiding burden-sharing. While alienation and vituperation explain much of the reluctance to share the burden, NATO allies certainly have used US impunity in starting the campaigns without proper consent as justification for skirting logistical support. And even when the United States was able to procure partners in the Iraq campaign such as Britain, the difficulty of sustaining the campaign without communal contributions caused political backlashes that undermined the limited support the United States enjoyed (Halper and Clarke 2004, pp. 264–267). The 2003 Pew survey, in fact, reported that faith in the UN system was very low in the world at large. Such an absence of confidence can only mean more dependence on the United States to provide international public goods heretofore doled out by international organizations. Certainly this fear has been vindicated in the context of a variety of issues, as nations appear to be targeting the United States as the champion that will deliver them from their problems: Liberians and Palestinians have sought US intervention, Afghanistan wants more US aid, and Indonesia and the Philippines seek more US assistance in fighting terrorism. While such dependence may indeed increase the influence of the United States in these regions, perceptions of imperialism and other sources of negative feedback might also generate countervailing forces that could compromise US influence.

One of the principal adverse effects of the vicious cycle of unilateralism, as noted, is the fact that unilateral solutions are often far inferior to multilateral solutions in dealing with a nation's international problems. This has certainly been the case for the United States in pursuing its vital goals: combating terrorism and WMD, regional peacekeeping, environmental protection, democratic statebuilding, and promoting international law and human rights. US primacy has generated a tendency for unilateral solutions that are not only inferior but also counterproductive in attending to these goals. Indeed, as has been suggested in the context of moral hazard, softer-power solutions grounded in multilateralism present the most viable long-run opportunities for dealing effectively with many of these problems.

Developments in the Middle East and Asia represent a lucid microcosm of the intersection of the three main goals of the United States and the concomitant inferiority of unilateral solutions in attending to them. The unilateralist orientation in this case was heightened by Bush's neoconservative disdain for diplomacy with autocratic governments, especially those targeted within the "Axis of Evil" or fingered as sponsors of terrorism. But this disdain of working multilaterally with Iran and Syria has severely hamstrung the possibilities of substantive solutions to the Palestine problem. Both nations would have significant pull in negotiations with the most militant Palestinian factions, and hence peace agreements could very well be forged. These peace agreements would constitute a potential pillar from which the United States could achieve all of its goals in the Middle East: discouraging the need for WMD, abating terrorism, and promoting liberal political and economic reforms. Yet the United States not only shunned Iran and Syria, but also continued to coerce and isolate them. In this web of vituperation, greater confrontation made cooperation with these states ever more difficult, hence leaving the United States increasingly isolated as a champion of democracy and political stability in the region (Kaplan 2008, pp. 168–172).

Similarly, with respect to WMD and democracy in Asia, Bush chose to unilaterally confront Kim Jong Il in his disdain for diplomacy with North Korea and China. The China card has been especially important and fragile, as China is the most influential nation in Asia and any viable multilateral solution to the North Korea problem would have to feature China prominently.[60] Once more, the neoconservative disposition against working with autocratic states hampered the only viable long-term solution to WMD and liberal transformation in Asia. As Bush spurned such diplomacy, Kim Jong Il became ever more politically entrenched and all the more anxious to develop a deterrent against a US invasion. And given that the US neoconservative disposition hamstrung efforts to integrate China and North Korea effectively into a multilateral solution to the problem, the United States was increasingly forced to continue contemplating unilaterally coercive solutions, solutions that continued to prove counterproductive (Kaplan 2008, pp. 69–76).

With respect to peacekeeping and statebuilding, the superiority of UN and other multilateral solutions compared to unilateral initiatives such as those employed in Iraq and Afghanistan has been starkly demonstrated. Haiti and Kosovo provide interesting foils to Iraq and Afghanistan. The problems of unilateral engagement in the latter states have been duly chronicled in this chapter. But the results of collective engagement in the former territories attest to the utility of such strategies. In both Haiti and Kosovo, multilateral strategies promoted effective burden-sharing agreements that helped eliminate security threats and condition political forces to coalesce around expectations generated by the peacekeeping forces. Much of this derived from the greater legitimacy accorded to multilateral peacekeeping operations and solutions. But above and beyond the obvious advantages in terms of burden-sharing and legitimation, the multilateral solutions provided relatively low-cost exist strategies for the United States. Disengagement was enhanced by multilateral commitments for postconflict stabilization. Moreover, the United States never became a principal target for retaliation, given that it avoided an imperialistic presence. But more generally, statebuilding proceeded on perceptions of political stability in the emerging domestic regimes and institutions. Conversely, in Afghanistan and Iraq, the United States has found itself cursed with a lack of all three outcomes: little burden-sharing, even less legitimacy, and high-cost exit strategies (Malone 2003; Thakur 2003).

With respect to human rights and international law, the principal goals of the United States have been adversely affected not just by its preemptive security posture, but also by its reticence to support the International Criminal Court. US support for the Court would be a classic example of how moderation in attending to direct goals can create milieu effects that enhance those goals far more than would an audacious unilateral posture, and hence glaringly attests to the inferiority of unilateral solutions. Present US reticence to support the Court centers around the protection of US peacekeepers in international operations (to ensure their constitutional rights even when abroad). Fears center around erstwhile enemies of the United States using the Court as a legal platform from which to attack Americans. Such might be the case if initiatives arise that target the actions of US peacekeepers as crimes under the jurisdiction of the Court (e.g., an accidental firing on a civilian target that results in deaths). But such fears of a politicized court are unfounded. Since the Court is an ancillary mechanism to national courts in prosecuting international crimes, the United States would have first right to investigate and prosecute cases involving US peacekeepers. The argument that US peacekeepers should be completely unaccountable for their actions is indefensible. The only possible glitch in the first-right clause would be if a nation harboring a US peacekeeper refused to extradite, and chose to prosecute that suspect itself. Even here the likelihood is remote, as extradition is a diplomatic question and the United States has firm agreements on extradition with virtually all other nations. So while the downside of supporting the Court appears slim, the upside is substantial for US interests (and this upside represents opportunities lost if the Court is weakened by a lack of US support). First, the Court would allow the United States to step back from its role of world policeman and the negative image it has generated. Spreading the burden of prosecuting international criminals would help abate perceptions of US tyranny, which in turn would enhance the safety of Americans overseas and promote the desirability of US democracy and capitalism.[61] Second, prosecution of suspects would be enhanced, as erstwhile enemies of the United States would be more likely to extradite suspects to the Court than to the United States or any of its allies. Finally, the charter of the Court is heavily grounded in US law and constitutional rights. For all intents and purposes, it gives the appearance of having been written by US lawyers. Supporting the Court gives the United States the opportunity to export the US system of jurisprudence, concerning selected crimes, to the world at large. What better way to extend the protection of constitutional rights to Americans in the international system? Furthermore, by staying outside the jurisdiction of the Court, the United States also risks the consequences of leaving international criminal law in the hands of others; it might find itself powerless to prevent others nations from passing laws that conflict with US interests (Gallarotti and Preis 1999; Nolte 2003).

Multilateralism also appears superior to unilateralism in promoting environmentalism. The Kyoto Protocol shows similar opportunities lost with respect to US business and economic interests. As in the International Criminal Court, the United States used its participation in the Kyoto Protocol to shape it significantly to its own interests (staggered cuts, emissions trading). So a weakening of Kyoto due to US departure interrupted the exportation of US environmental policies to other countries, leaving the fate of multilateral environmental control in the hands of others—clearly an inferior position from which to prevent undesirable international policies. In short, departure enervated US international environmental influence. The argument that adhering to the emission limits of Kyoto would burden US businesses with extra costs and reduce economic growth fails to appreciate the opportunities that Kyoto carries for the United States. First, greater environmentalism would promote the US environmental industry, an industry in which the United States has both an absolute and a comparative advantage. Hence, what some industries burdened by environmental costs might lose in international sales will at least in part be recovered through increased sales in other industries. Moreover, since US firms are highly adaptable to changing environmental standards, because of stricter and frequent changes in domestic regulations, general limits may give US companies an international competitive advantage if they can adapt to the limits faster than other companies in other nations. It is therefore not certain that the US economy would suffer a net decrease in growth as a result of stricter emissions standards. On the contrary, a stricter environmental milieu may carry opportunities both for the macroeconomy and US business (Gallarotti, 1995b; Assunção 2003).

Above and beyond the comparative advantage in environmental technologies and production methods enjoyed by the United States, it is clear that the call for reductions in greenhouse-gas emissions has become politically compelling in all developed nations. The United States itself is faced with political pressure to enact these reductions even in the absence of a Kyoto treaty.[62] Interestingly, much of this pressure to consolidate some national initiative to curb greenhouse gases has come from US industry itself, which feared more draconian measures by a new administration and hence pushed to lock the nation into a system of more moderate cuts before future administrations could propose more drastic regimes. Bush, however, opted for a more decentralized system of cuts whereby nations would unilaterally select appropriate levels. In conjunction with its own unilateral cuts, the United States would prod other nations (first China and India, in this iteration) to follow suit and thus generate a sort of additive regime for promoting a solution to global warming. Such a regime would be far inferior to a multilateral regime; its decentralized character makes it inefficient and ineffective in dealing with the main problem of carbon emissions: the collective level of such emissions across nations. Appropriate collective levels can only be determined and managed within a multilateral regime, as iterated-additive diplomacy lacks the institutional capacity to set such levels. A multilateral regime provides the obvious advantages of an international market for emissions trading, opportunities for the United States to negotiate relief through quota realignments, and the domestic political capital needed for US politicians to sell painful cuts to their constituents. A decentralized regime such as that championed by Bush, based on unilateral and limited multilateral standards, would in fact introduce a type of moral hazard, locking nations into an essentially bounded free-for-all system whose existence would dampen initiatives for other international greenhouse-gas regimes (McKinnon and Power 2008; Assunção 2003).

In sum, the United States has been victimized by a vicious cycle of unilateralism under the Bush Doctrine. Indeed, by forsaking important venues and sources of international influence, the United States has found itself in the unenviable position of having to bear a greater unilateral burden in a period of already excessive international burdens. Although in the waning years of the Bush administration the United States became increasingly aware of the power curse inherent in this vicious cycle and sought repentance and greater multilateral support, it could not overcome its legacy of disdain for international law and organizations.

It is indicative of the victimization of the power curse and power illusion under the Bush Doctrine that even Stephen Brooks and William Wohlforth

(2008), in work that emphatically embraces the US influence generated by unrivaled global primacy, are highly critical of the doctrine with respect to its consequences for US power. Indeed, for them, the policies under Bush often took the route "least likely to persuade others"; they identify the "Bush administration's travails" as emanating from a foreign policy of overly coercive and unilateral activism (p. 214). Moreover, even their attempts to debunk conventional arguments that US influence was significantly hamstrung by oft-cited constraints (balancing, interdependence, reputation, legitimacy) are tempered by a concern for other factors that may indeed have constraining effects on US influence.[63] But it is precisely these constraints that the Bush Doctrine reinforced, thus compromising US influence in the world. Through Bush's unilateral coercive activism, these potential threats—overstretch, insurgency, terrorism, proliferation, ethnic conflict, environmental degradation—were compounded. Ironically, it was Bush's central foreign mandate to abate these threats. Interestingly, even such a vigorous vindication of US primacy as offered by Brooks and Wohlforth ends by prescribing a policy of activism "softer" than that chosen by Bush. The authors underscore the "benefits to the United States of legitimizing its hegemony, institutionalizing its preferred solutions to problems, and furthering the globalization of economic activity" (p. 216). Hence, even this fire-breathing vindication of American primacy underscores the importance of soft power.

Notes

1. The Bush Doctrine was spelled out in the National Security Strategy of 2002 and reinforced in the National Security Strategy of 2006 (White House 2002a, 2006). For insightful descriptions of the doctrine, see especially Smith 2007, Jervis 2003b, Jervis 2005, and Monten 2007.

2. On neoconservatism, see Kristol 1995.

3. For representative arguments defending the Bush Doctrine, see "Defending and Advancing Freedom" 2005, D. Kagan 2003, and Rice 2000. For diverse critical responses to the policy, see especially Kaplan 2008, Fukuyama 2006, Smith 2007, Nye 2002, Nye 2003, Jervis 2003b, Jervis 2005, Kegley and Raymond 2007, and Calleo 2003.

4. It is interesting that in a world structure where the United States is still unrivaled in terms of military and economic power, it has become increasingly common to see scholars talking about a new US decline; see Cox 2007 and citations to the literature therein. Stephen Brooks and William Wohlforth (2008) have issued a scathing critical response to this literature (see below).

5. Indeed, the very first sentence of the 2002 National Security Strategy reads: "The United States possesses unprecedented—and unequaled—strength and influence in the world" (White House 2002a, p. 1).

6. Stephen Walt (1999) commented on the adverse state of world affairs before Bush took office. Clearly, with respect to US interests, world affairs were worse

when he left office despite eight years of employing extensive hard resources to improve them.

7. In the 2002 National Security Strategy, Bush underscored the principal means of fighting terrorism as hard-power resources: "To defeat this threat we must make use of every tool in our arsenal—military power, better homeland defenses, law enforcement, intelligence, and vigorous efforts to cut off terrorist financing" (White House 2002a, p. iv).

8. We see path-dependence effects (i.e., nonlinearities) in the evolution of the militia problem. While police functions were strengthened with the development of new Iraqi armed units, the prior existence of militias made these militias difficult to uproot. Hence, the militia problem would have been better addressed preemptively, before they came into existence.

9. At best, Hussein's relations with terrorists were murky (Garner 2005, p. 12; Jervis 2003b, p. 371).

10. In an influential poll, 100 foreign policy experts gave the Iraq campaign a collective score of 2.9 out of 10 points ("Terrorism Index" 2007).

11. Military elites vociferously criticized military operations in Iraq. Much of the criticism centered around the incompatibility between the needs of effective counterinsurgency and the large-force and apolitical strategies employed in Iraq. As in Vietnam, a successful campaign that would deter terrorism and promote democracy required far more vigorous civil-military solutions (Kaplan 2008, pp. 49–50, 84, 162).

12. Robert Jervis (2003a, p. 86) argues that attempts to force disarmament would actually quicken proliferation. In fact, a survey by the Pew Research Center (2003) showed that, indeed, a great many people in Muslim nations fear a US invasion.

13. While only five Al-Qaida attacks were documented between 1993 and 9/11, seventeen more occurred over the next two years (Piven 2004, p. 6). In the 2007 "Terrorism Index" poll, 91 percent of respondents saw the world as a more dangerous place for the United States since the inception of its war on terror. Moreover, 84 percent believed that the United States was losing the war.

14. The statistics on suicide bombings bear this out. In 2007 there were 658 reported attacks worldwide, more than double the number in any other previous year. Of all such incidents from 1983–2008, 86 percent have occurred since 9/11 (Wright 2008).

15. Brent Scowcroft proved to be quite intuitive in his warnings that invading Iraq would actually increase the terrorist threat (Halper and Clarke 2004, p. 227).

16. In the 2007 "Terrorism Index" poll, only 3 percent of respondents believed that Iraq would become a beacon of democracy among autocratic states. Moreover, 35 percent of respondents believed that the war would actually discourage Arab autocrats from promoting liberal reforms.

17. Interestingly, it is clear in the Iraq and Afghanistan cases that the United States is more intent on building pluralistic political regimes (with competing political interests) than democratic regimes per se (i.e., popular determination of the political regime). Indeed, democracy may produce outcomes that cut against US interests if radical groups (e.g., Hamas, Hezbollah) win competitive elections. The difficulty here is that pluralistic systems work well where competition is channeled into political institutions. But in these fractured societies, in which political groups have competed through violence, pluralism is a recipe for civil war (Gardner 2005, pp. 164–165, 189).

18. François Heisbourg refers to this process as "precautionary proliferation" (2004, p. 16).

19. The six-party talks have proved valuable in addressing the Korea problem because of the involvement of China and because of the multilateral legitimacy they bring. It may in fact be the case that these talks carry greater potential than does the Security Council, which the United States has turned toward a more confrontational direction on issues of WMD.

20. Kim Jong Il became more sensitized to the utility of WMD against US threats by his growing perception that Iraq could have avoided invasion if it had in fact built a nuclear device (Gardner 2005, p. 153; Kaplan 2008, p. 74).

21. Jervis's argument (2005) that public support for the Bush Doctrine would ultimately erode proved prescient. Indeed, support showed a continual decline, as approval ratings of the president and foreign policy polls demonstrated.

22. A plethora of arguments have been made about the so-called true motivations of the war, from securing power over oil, to war as a vehicle to promote the Republican Right's domestic policy agenda. See Piven 2004 for a survey.

23. The missile shield has also reinforced an existing energy partnership between Russia and China, and brought the two great powers together into a strategic front against the United States, with Dmitry Medvedev and Hu Jintao issuing joint protests against the shield. Zbigniew Brzezinski (2007, pp. 168–171) is especially outspoken about the dangers that a Russo-Chinese strategic partnership carries for the United States.

24. Betts (2002, p. 22) notes that other events in the 1990s contributed to this false sense of security generated by primacy: winning the Gulf War easily, facing no casualties in Kosovo, and being able to disengage in Somalia so easily when military operations went awry.

25. Lambakis, Kiras, and Kolet (2002) underscore the general tactical advantages of "asymmetric" threats (i.e., threats that conventional weapons are poorly suited to defend against), with terrorist operations being a subset of asymmetric war.

26. Results of the 2007 "Terrorist Index" poll suggest that policy experts envision many nations as being possibilities for future Al-Qaida strongholds.

27. This recalls Henry Kissinger's famous statement about the war against insurgency in South Vietnam: that the insurgents win simply by surviving.

28. The frustration effect emanates from the fact that primacy raises domestic perceptions of quick and decisive victory, but as this outcome is frustrated and the costs of war continue to mount, societies can quickly turn against and hence hamstring the war effort. On the frustration effect and asymmetric warfare, see Mack 1975, Boserup and Mack 1975, Barnett 2003, Arreguin-Toft 2005, and Ewans 2005.

29. In addition to the extremely poor results from the use of direct force against terrorism, Martha Crenshaw (2003) notes that even coercive diplomacy has fared poorly in containing terrorism.

30. An extensive survey of military officers has revealed a belief that the US campaigns against Iraq and Afghanistan have not only debilitated the US military conventionally, but also served to undermine the development of more effective operations against terrorism ("US Military Index" 2008).

31. Stephen Halper and Jonathan Clarke (2004, p. 282) draw on the failure of Britain to contain insurgency in Palestine as a case reflecting the need for local cooperation as the fundamental means of combating terrorism.

32. Robert Jervis (2005) and John Newhouse (2003) underscore the difficulty of effective intelligence when acting unilaterally to solve the terrorism problem. It has become evident that the kind of information required to confront terrorism can never be delivered with the United States acting independently of target states. Reliable information can only be consistently generated from indigenous sources, hence the need for cooperation.

33. The 2007 "Terrorism Index" poll showed that policy experts envisioned numerous nations as possible sources of nuclear technology.

34. Response time to such attacks must be rapid in order to avoid extreme consequences, but many biological and chemical agents are not easily detectable (Lambakis, Kiras, and Kolet 2002, p. 32).

35. It is in this respect that analogies to the war-induced political transformation in Japan and Germany fail. The soft-power foundations for such change were far more abundant in those countries than in Iraq. In Germany the Nazi ideology was discredited, while in Japan the emperor supported reforms that already had a long historical legacy (from the Meji Restoration). Moreover, both societies were highly structured and not ethnically or religiously fractured, and the military occupation of each was brief. In Iraq, however, the occupation has lasted and Western ideas have become targets rather than models for reform. Moreover, sectarian and ethnic divisions make a stable pluralistic political system in Iraq tenuous at best (Rubin 2004).

36. The National Security Strategy of 2002 states: "To contend with uncertainty and to meet the many challenges we face, the United States will require bases and stations within and beyond Western Europe and Northeast Asia, as well as temporary access arrangements for the long distance deployment of US forces" (White House 2002a, p. 29).

37. Indeed, the United States has expanded its efforts to promote political stability in places like Kosovo, Iraq, and Pakistan in order to generate a signal to Middle Eastern nations that democracy can work in a Muslim culture.

38. *Foreign Policy* magazine and the Center for a New American Security surveyed more than 3,400 officers (both active and retired) at the highest levels of military command. See "US Military Index" 2008.

39. Joseph Nye (1990a, p. 157) underscores the increasing expenses of militarism as historically undermining US strength.

40. In 2002, economist William Nordhaus projected estimates of between $121 billion (for a short and favorable campaign) and $1.6 trillion (for a protracted and unfavorable campaign).

41. As of early 2008, the public debt of the United States stood at $9.3 trillion. Just the interest payments on this debt in 2007 amounted to $430 billion.

42. Even though Barack Obama has planned to scale down the occupational forces in Iraq, this decision has been conditional on some level of political stability in the country. Things could change rapidly in this respect. Furthermore, Obama increased the military presence in Afghanistan in 2009.

43. Joseph Stiglitz and Linda Bilmes (2008) also underscore hidden costs in terms of undercounting casualties (which are far greater than official casualties if nonwar injuries are counted), using cash as opposed to accrual accounting, and underestimating the human valuation of war losses (much higher in economic terms than compensation given to the war victims' families).

44. This estimate is based on an individual policy under a United Healthcare network plan in spring of 2008: $3,495 in premiums and a $1,500 deductible. The estimate is purposely inflated to make a point. The premium price assumes full

premiums for each individual, while in reality many of these Americans fall into families who can be entirely insured for a marginally smaller amount over the normal individual premium. Moreover, if this health coverage were being provided by the government, it would be far less expensive. The point to be made is that the provision of healthcare to uninsured Americans would be less expensive, and hence could be financed by lower switching costs.

45. National Center for Health Statistics (2007) estimated about 1.4 million deaths in 2004 just from the four leading medical causes of death alone (cancer, heart disease, strokes, and chronic respiratory ailments). Of course, more deaths resulted from other diseases. Furthermore, WrongDiagnosis (2008) reported the incidence rate for cancer only to be 1 out of 217 Americans (1.2 million Americans). Together these numbers would add up to about 1 percent of the US population. Moreover, there are no statistics regarding how many people contract undiagnosed terminal diseases in a given year. The inferences from these numbers are still highly speculative, because some uninsured Americans will obtain the selective medical attention needed to avert such diseases. These estimates are meant to be suggestive rather than definitively representative.

46. Stiglitz and Bilmes (2008) include roughly 4,000 more noncombat deaths in the death toll.

47. The direct financial burdens of the Iraq and Afghanistan campaigns would not impose the kind of burdens underscored in the literature on overstretch, which normally contemplates countries being stretched to the limit. However, when considering the full range of indirect costs on American society, this considerably raises the burden. Moreover, the greater international role dictated by the Bush Doctrine raised the burden to ever greater levels.

48. Stiglitz and Bilmes (2008, p. 117) have estimated that oil-price increases owing directly to the Iraq campaign have cost Americans close to half a trillion dollars.

49. Jack Snyder (1991) observes a historical tendency for expansionist policies to be driven by the ability of elites to generate perceptions that excessive expansion is necessary to effect cumulative gains and protect against cumulative losses.

50. Halper and Clarke (2004, p. 202) make use of the social-psychological category of frames to convey the method through which the Bush public relations campaign conditioned the mind-sets of Americans.

51. In the National Security Strategy of 2002, Bush called the war against terror "global" and maintained that in order to confront terrorists, we must "deny them sanctuary at every turn" (White House 2002a, pp. iv–v, 1). See also Smith 2007 (p. 207) and Halper and Clarke 2004 (p. 209).

52. Bush averred in the National Security Strategy of 2002 that "weak states . . . can pose as great a danger . . . as strong states" (White House 2002a, p. v).

53. In the National Security Strategy of 2002, Bush promoted a need to "strengthen alliances" and proclaimed that "in leading the campaign against terrorism, we are forging new, productive international relationships" (White House 2002a, pp. 1, 7).

54. Certainly, the Bush administration's own convictions about its theories suggested a growing element of blowback: elites became ever more convinced of their own rhetoric as the need for support increased and time progressed (see Snyder 1991, pp. 41–42).

55. For an especially insightful collection of essays on US unilateralism under Bush and its consequences, see Malone and Khong 2003.

56. The acrimony resulted not only because of a US posture of impunity in acting independently of allies and international bodies, but also because of a failure to at least consult allies and international organizations, which suggests a complete disregard of alliance and legal commitments (Halper and Clarke 2004, p. 229).

57. Michael Ignatieff (2003) cites the "moral authority" that international support lends to US foreign policy initiatives, effectively bolstering them through legitimacy. Since this legitimacy influences American public opinion, Bush found it increasingly harder to marshal his foreign policy without it. The legitimacy created greater x-efficiencies on the part of supporting nations that enhanced US influence. In this respect, legitimacy has indeed proved to be, as Charles Kegley and Gregory Raymond note, "the ultimate force multiplier" (2007, p. 121).

58. The European Union has continued pushing for a unified foreign policy at the same time that NATO has been pushing the development of a more European-based security function. Both of these threaten the role of the United States in the alliance, a role it cannot afford to forsake (Gardner 2005, p. 25).

59. Although European nations did state that they expected both countries to eventually join NATO.

60. While China has generally shared some of the goals of the United States regarding North Korea, there are also some points of divergence. Most important, tense relations on the peninsula would keep US attention focused there instead of on Taiwan (Kaplan 2008, pp. 69–72).

61. Since March 2005 the United States has pushed the Security Council to allow the International Criminal Court to prosecute war crimes in Sudan. This is a clear manifestation of the usefulness of the Court for US foreign policy. After the debacle in Somalia, the Court represents a means of relieving the United States of its risky roles as international policeman and judge in especially dangerous regional conflicts.

62. A number of US states have in fact proposed laws that would impose Kyoto quotas on their residents.

63. The authors are somewhat guarded in definitively proclaiming these factors as significant constraints, but the tone and logic they marshal appear to suggest that these factors should indeed be of concern to future administrations.

CHAPTER 5
In Lieu of Conclusions

THE ANALYSIS in this book has shown the power curse to be both pervasive and pernicious. Indeed, power illusion is difficult to prevent, because the process of power augmentation itself carries inherent elements that lead nations and their leaders into a false sense of security and influence. The cases analyzed have shown nations and their leaders falling into the power illusion trap across issues and across history. The breadth of case studies indicates the menacing and encompassing reach of the trap. Often leaders and their societies lack a sophisticated enough perspective to even arrive at the perception that they have indeed been victimized by the power curse. But the elements of the power curse and power illusion pertain to all nations intent on accumulating power. For very weak nations looking to arrive at some respectable threshold, even small augmentations of some power resources may leave them ever more debilitated in terms of net influence if they fall into the trap. Climbing out of weakness may be far more complicated than many believe. For aspiring powers, the road to primacy may indeed be filled with many land mines, obstacles that must be successfully negotiated if they are to achieve a level of influence that competes with dominant powers. For dominant powers, life in the elite circles of the global power structure may be far more difficult to maintain and far shorter-lived than such powers may suspect. In fact, the effects of the power curse and victimization from power illusion intensify as higher levels of power are reached, which is another reason for hegemonic decline. The greatest levels of power generate the most pernicious effects.

Compounding these threats is the dynamic nature of international politics in the modern world. While the threat of the power curse and the subsequent threat of power illusion remain ever-present, the dynamic nature of the international system will continue to obscure these threats as conceptualizations and sources of power change. Managing national security and influence is difficult enough even in a stagnant environment, but all the more so in the postindustrial world. The ever-expanding web of interdependence, globalization, democratization (in both its growth and its retreat), modernization, and technological change will continue to transform the very political foundations upon which power relations are determined and strategies of power augmentation are decided. Similarly, new threats from subnational groups such as terrorists will bring new actors with new sources of power into the game, further complicating strategies for managing foreign relations.

Policy Implications: Beating the Power Curse in a Dynamic World

In light of the ongoing challenges of the power curse and power illusion, as well as the compounding effects of the changes in today's dynamic international system, we need to address an important question: What strategies will best serve national leaders intent on maintaining national influence and security? Six such strategies are explored here. Indeed, the need for such strategies underscores why decisionmakers are victimized by the power curse, and ultimately by power illusion, over and over again. For greater clarification and historical application, these strategies will be linked to lessons learned from the case studies presented in this book.

1. Theories of power must be continually questioned and power audits must be continually undertaken, with significant sensitivity to the changing face of power in world politics. Such tasks will be extremely difficult, because they are inconsistent with common tendencies of human psychology. People are more paradigmatic (cognitively rigid) than exploratory. Theories or paradigms that people use to understand the world are fairly stable and compelling. Moreover, it is uncommon for people to frequently and empirically test their theories and critically scrutinize facts that support them (Jervis 1976). Hence the power curse will be especially difficult to confront, as history bears out. In Athens, hubris generated an insensitivity to the growing difficulty of managing an imperial network. Indeed, expansion stretched Athenian resources thinly, with the final breaking point being the Sicilian debacle. Self-reflection and accurate perceptions of changes in relative power fell prey to rigid theories of power based on naval supremacy. The rhetoric about Athenian supremacy remained the same while Athens's relative power position declined. But even this naval supremacy failed to combat the impact of shifting alliance patterns later in the war and the burden of a large empire throughout the century. In Vietnam, theories of security were heavily grounded in a Cold War orientation founded on the utility of large conventional forces and nuclear deterrence. The US administrations held rigidly to these models even though the war was progressing in ways that neutralized the conventional advantage of the United States. US decisionmakers were so distracted by these models that they wrongly equated success in conventional confrontations with winning the war. Similarly, the George W. Bush administration continued to bank on its military primacy to fight the battle against terrorism. The weapons and strategies proved ill-equipped to confront such an amorphous threat. Furthermore, the use of such weapons and strategies made the problem of terrorism worse. So too did the Bush administration bank on its nuclear and conventional supremacy as wedges that would deliver democracy and reduce the threat of weapons of mass destruction. And this too proved to be an illusory and ultimately counterproductive conviction.

The British state and Bank of England also proved deficient in conducting effective monetary power audits and reassessing their beliefs about monetary influence. The limited resources of the bank and its insular orientation made British finance far more vulnerable to international shocks than the monetary authorities perceived, especially as the international financial system grew larger. Fortunately, this risky environment was never tested, as both the actions of the Bank of France and good luck (few serious financial and political crises in the period) saved British finance from turbulence. Similarly, with respect to the silver situation, British authorities overrated the international power of India as a market for silver, and continued to do so even though conditions continued to deteriorate. They also continued to place unwarranted confidence in the strength of the Indian financial system and the ability of Indian monetary officials to guide India smoothly through the rough waters created by instability in the international silver market. This confidence also proved to be illusory, all the more so in the face of the ongoing deterioration.

2. *Leaders should think in terms of net rather than nominal power.* In accumulating power resources, leaders should be especially careful about assessing the costs of acquiring those resources, and factor those costs into their estimates of a nation's overall influence in international relations.[1] As with the first strategy, the case studies in this book suggest that leaders were significantly deficient with respect to this prescription as well. The Bush administration stands out as especially culpable. The objectives of the Bush Doctrine generated a process of self-feeding growth in US global engagement (much of it deriving from mission creep). The war against terror

and crusades against WMD and autocracy generated an international presence that proved economically and socially debilitating for the United States. And moreover, the doctrine generated significant seeds for future instability in the government budget, and in American society and the US economy as well. The American public has indeed paid a steep price for the Bush Doctrine, a price that has detracted a great deal from the nation's strength in virtually every aspect of American life. So too in the case of Athenian imperialism, the gains from empire were counterbalanced by a growing burden of imperial expansion, thus neutralizing the net gains in Athenian strength from direct acquisitions and imperial extraction. The imperial machine grew faster than did the resources that Athens could extract from its society to further that expansion. This process was destined to lead to a debilitating end, as indeed it did with Athens's defeat in the Peloponnesian War. So too in Vietnam, US decisionmakers paid a large price for the limited territorial gains they sought in the region. Trying to protect South Vietnam from insurgency and intrusion from the North, the US war effort sputtered along in a futile attempt to repel Communism. The burden on the economy was of course significant, as it ushered in a pernicious combination of slow growth and inflation (stagflation) and affected government finances for at least a decade. But even in terms of US international influence, the limited success of the US military campaign emboldened erstwhile Cold War foes (China and the Soviets) as well as raised the resolve of North Vietnam to stay the course in supporting the insurgency. All these outcomes debilitated the United States in its dealings with Communist nations in succeeding years.

3. Leaders should consider the manifold consequences of power-enhancing strategies. This prescription pertains principally to the problem of complexity. Indeed, power is neither exercised nor accumulated in a vacuum, as has been demonstrated throughout this book. Power-seeking behavior is always endogenous, and as such generates manifold consequences that feed back onto the original actions and ultimately alter the conditions within which these actions unfold. As with the first prescription, this one will also be challenging given common psychological tendencies. The cognitive costs of dealing with complexity are high, which explains why people are more paradigmatic than comprehensive in analyzing the world around them. This suggests the primacy of bounded rationality, based on limited information and simple models, in making decisions (Jervis 1976). As documented in the case studies, negative feedback can completely neutralize any immediate gains from power accumulation. Indeed, the manifold reactions to initial actions can even render those actions counterproductive and reduce influence. In the case of the United States under the Bush

Doctrine, its wars against terror, WMD, and autocracy ended up generating feedback processes that actually intensified the threats from all three phenomena. The unilateralism and impunity with which these goals were pursued also alienated erstwhile allies as well as nonaligned nations, such that the United States was increasingly forced to face such threats with limited multilateral support. As the United States increasingly took refuge in an insular approach to its problems, this multilateral support continued to deteriorate. The case of Vietnam showed similar problems facing the Johnson and Nixon administrations. Conventional war strategies proved completely counterproductive to the objective of abating the insurgency in the South. These strategies diverted enemy military initiatives into operations that were immune to the conventional strategies themselves, thus rendering the US war campaign anemic at best. But even here the conventional operations forced an occupation that undermined the very popular support that the United States needed to effectively arrest the growth of insurgency. Indeed, the occupation sowed the seeds of its own failure by producing an anti-imperialist sentiment among the Vietnamese people.

In the case of Athens, the process of empowerment through imperialism also generated widespread feedback that sowed the seeds of decline. Athens compromised much of the support that it had garnered as leader of the Greek forces against Persian incursions earlier in the century. As greater resources were required from the empire to feed Athens's imperial appetite, it continued to press its colonies and allies for greater sacrifices, sacrifices that ultimately turned those allies against itself and consequently left it exposed to the threat of a growing countercoalition during the Peloponnesian War. In the case of Britain and monetary relations in the nineteenth century, feedback also played a major role in limiting the effectiveness of solutions to the silver problem. Because of its own financial power and the size of the Indian silver market, Britain hesitated to facilitate a multilateral solution to the problem. As successive conferences failed, nations became increasingly tentative about contributing to a price-support regime for silver. As this support waned, the British were increasingly placed in an insular position, one that was insufficient to deliver a stable price for silver.

4. Leaders should judge power based on outcomes rather than resources. One of the stark lessons learned from the case studies is that decisionmakers appear to be especially tolerant of ongoing failures in attaining their most vital objectives. Much of this owes to the blinding effects of resource moral hazard: because decisionmakers in these cases were well endowed with significant material resources, setbacks did not generate the same sense of urgency and panic that might have arisen in the face of more modest stocks of resources. But this fourth prescription will also be difficult to institute because of informational asymmetries. It is far easier to count resources, especially hard resources, than interpret the precise meaning of outcomes. For example, in terms of personal savings, people find it far easier to assess their potential influence by counting their money than by assessing just how much people are conforming to their wishes. Indeed, one may have great influence without money, but a large bank account is far easier to quantify. But even here, problems of moral hazard appear compelling and pernicious. While a large bank account may ensure some level of influence, it can also significantly compromise such influence if feelings of invulnerability make people callous or insensitive to adverse outcomes. For example, the idea of "who needs friends when you have money" may leave a person with few people he or she can influence significantly in important ways; in other words, loyalty and affection can't be bought.

The Bush administration made few fundamental changes in its strategies to combat terrorism, WMD proliferation, and autocracy even in the face of outcomes suggesting that these strategies were not only failing, but also actually enhancing the threats in all three areas. Its strategies continued to bank on military strength and coercive diplomatic weight in world politics, despite the fact that these resources continually proved insufficient to deliver the goods. Belief systems among Bush and his leading advisers never deviated from a conviction that US primacy would ultimately dictate outcomes somewhere down the road. This tendency also plagued the war effort in Vietnam, where strategies remained oriented around big-war military operations. History, in this case, taught the United States all the wrong lessons, as such operations had never failed the nation in recent memory. These perceptions were bolstered all the more by the conventional superiority of the US military machine. Lessons from the outcomes also tapped into faulty historical applications: wars had never been determined by limited incursions and insurgent disturbances, but by the ultimate balance of conventional might and big battles. In a sense, everything that decision-makers were certain about ended up being wrong. This also manifested itself outside the theater of war as the United States continued to be victimized by its belief that deterrence could effectively produce containment. In the end, both the Soviets and China were far more involved in the war than the United States would have expected given its nuclear superiority over the Communist superpowers. In the case of Athens, growing rebelliousness among Delian states did little to reduce Athens's imperial appetite and sense of entitlement. Athens's own relative might became its greatest weakness. In their quest to secure a vast empire, Athenian leaders were little impressed even by Sparta's formidable military prowess, as the imperial question was seen as depending on naval supremacy. And there was little question that

Athens enjoyed absolute primacy on the seas relative to any other single city-state. But even in its setbacks in land battles during the Peloponnesian War, losses did little to dislodge Athenians from a comfort zone founded on ultimate economic and naval primacy in the Greek world.

In the case of Britain and monetary relations in the nineteenth century, insensitivity to outcomes, owing to a sense of financial primacy, was pervasive. Neither the British state nor the Bank of England ever undertook a direct and intended role as a manager of the international monetary system. In fact, the bank was more often the recipient of aid in crises than a lender of last resort. In this respect, Britain remained aloof toward the management of the international monetary system, something the Bank of France (which was relatively weaker and hence more vulnerable to shocks) could not afford to do. The British financial market was far more powerful relative to any others. Because of their faith in this financial primacy, bank and government officials remained fairly passive in the face of adverse developments in international finance. Surely, British markets would never have trouble drawing capital in need. So the prevailing belief was that Britain was fairly insulated from international crises. The silver problem also manifested such insensitivity to financial outcomes. It took many years for Britain to finally take action against the declining price of silver. This passivity drew much debate, but never panic. Indeed, the Indian market was the largest in the world, and hence was viewed as having the capacity to stabilize the price of silver if market conditions improved. Moreover, India was the financial ward of Britain, and Britain ultimately could influence sufficient capital flows to stabilize conditions in India. These perceptions of relative power even limited the sensitivity of Britain to failed attempts on the part of other nations to construct a multilateral regime that would stabilize the price of silver. This probably stands as Britain's most arrogant mistake with respect to the silver problem, as only such a collective effort promised to be robust enough to stabilize the market.

With respect to outcomes, the issue of interpretation also manifested itself across the case studies. And this suggests an especially difficult problem for confronting the power curse. As noted, people deal with cognitive complexity through paradigmatic thinking. They therefore tend to understand outcomes by filtering them through the preexisting theories that they use to make sense of the world around them—the perception and assessment of outcomes is theory-driven (Jervis 1976). But given that outcomes are filtered through the perceptual screen of such preexisting theories, it is often likely that the significance and the nature of the outcomes themselves are misinterpreted or misperceived. It is often the case that such cognitive rigidity distorts incoming information about occurrences in the world to conform to the preexisting beliefs and theories themselves. In this respect, people tend to be more rationalizers than rational (Jervis 1976). Evidence that might disconfirm such paradigms or preexisting theories may be distorted in ways that make it less salient as a source of falsification, or even distorted to the point of being transformed into perceptions of outcomes that actually confirm such paradigms or theories. There is ample evidence in the case studies that such cognitive rigidity distorted perceptions of outcomes in ways that sustained failing policies, thus weakening respective nations.

In the context of the cases, dominant paradigms and preexisting theories were strongly grounded in the relative power superiority of the nations in question. For the Bush administration, the occupation of nations perceived as bastions of terrorism and weapons of mass destruction (Iraq and Afghanistan) was equated with winning the war against the three evils (including autocracy). To buttress the invasions, coercive diplomacy was employed on a grand scale across the globe (Middle East, Asia, Europe) to achieve the same goals. In this case, even small victories remained cognitively salient in supporting beliefs that US economic and military primacy was the key weapon in combating the three evils. But this distorted the significance of adverse outcomes that delivered setbacks in more amorphous patterns. Even in the nations occupied, terrorism actually grew and substantive democracy was far from being realized. Coercive diplomacy and threats extracted some minor concessions on proliferation, but in reality they were far more de jure than de facto. But the realization of military occupation and promises to disarm trumped evidence that significant incursions were cutting against US goals regarding the three evils. Again, this was consistent with prevalent theories about success in international confrontations: that the real gains were accomplished on big battlefields and in the context of grand diplomacy. Smaller incursions were merely white noise, or minor leakage. But in this case, the incursions added up to be significant enough to "nick the US to death" with respect to its foreign policy objectives.

Vietnam showed precisely the same process. The United States was winning every major conventional battle against the North. Virtually all campaigns against key military targets, early in the war, were decisive and successful. The United States was delivering a trail of carnage throughout the theater of war: a sure sign of winning. But as in the case of Bush's wars, it was the totality, consistency, and indefatigable nature of smaller-scale resistance operations that ended up nicking the United States to death in Southeast Asia. And as with the Bush case, these incursions did not make salient impacts on decisionmakers' mind-sets, because no war had ever been lost with decisive confrontations in big-battle environments.

These rigid military lessons, as with the Bush case, significantly distorted the significance and real threat of the hidden war. In the case of Athens, Delian associations derived from alliance commitments against Persian invasions earlier in the century, and they were consummated in religious bonds among equals. This led Athens into a sense of guardianship that made it somewhat insensitive to the growing discontent on the part of the Delian members. If Athens demanded much from its Delian associates, surely it must have been entitled, given its commitment to defend them against military assaults from other city-states, and surely they should indeed contribute to their own defense. So outcomes that augured poorly for Athens in the long run were neatly conflated into beliefs that the empire was a secure source of strength for Athens. But even devastating defeats in land battles during the Peloponnesian War lost some of their sting in the mind-sets of prominent Athenians, because they were not perceived as reflective of the true application of Athens's power, which was on the seas. But once this sea power was ultimately lost toward the end of the war, Athens was defenseless in the face of the land superiority of Sparta and its allies. While Athenians prided themselves on their capacity to augur the future based on salient events, they appeared to be quite deficient in this case.

The British interpreted events in the international monetary system in similar ways. This led to several misperceptions that compounded deficiencies in the management of the international monetary system and the silver problem. The Bank of England continued to hold paltry gold reserves relative to the liabilities generated by international transactions. This was a potentially dangerous situation because of the limited capacity to export gold on short notice in case of a widespread international financial panic (fortunately, one never occurred in this period). But an arrogant sense of financial primacy in the London market made financiers and government officials interpret the significance of the gold holdings in a more cavalier fashion. So too with the limited financial crises of the period: outcomes that suggested that other central banks were more active in stabilizing international monetary relations made few inroads in dislodging a sense of financial security that led British officials to pursue a detached path in the international financial community. Similarly, deterioration in the price of silver was tolerated for a significant period, as such an outcome was not allowed to disconfirm perceptions of the health of Indian finance and the stability of the British market. All such outcomes were far less alarming given prevailing theories that distorted their true significance. Compounding these distortionary effects of British financial primacy was also a monetary orthodoxy grounded in a strong liberal orientation. This orientation dictated that adverse outcomes in markets were not necessarily secular and severely distortionary. Markets, in fact, would do much worse if they were tampered with. Hence, adverse signals in financial markets, whether they be crises or changes in the prices of precious metals, were often not harbingers of structural deterioration (and hence not severely threatening), but simply unfortunate temporary developments that with time would reequilibrate.

5. Leaders should emphasize diversity in power resources and flexibility in their use. In all the case studies there was a limited set of power resources used to obtain vital objectives on the part of the principal actors. In all cases, there was also a lack of flexibility in applying resources to the realization of these objectives. Often this was manifest in a deficiency in the use of soft-power options (discussed in the next strategy). But at a more general level, the cases demonstrated limited diversity and flexibility even within each of the respective contexts of hard and soft power themselves. In the case of the Bush Doctrine, coercive diplomacy and conventional force dominated the agenda for bringing about Bush's three sacred goals. But this rather restricted use of US power was in large part driven by political commitments that were difficult to disengage from or annul. Starting with such a strategy made responses to foreign problems path-dependent. Having started with tough and large-scale actions (threat and invasion), it was hard to retreat significantly from such brinkmanship, because this strategy represented an opening move in a game of "chicken." It was of course feared that backing away and taking refuge in a more restrained set of diplomatic options would have compromised the resolve of the United States in the perceptions of opponents. But Bush also made a domestic commitment to the American public to stay the course in a resolute war against the three evils facing the United States. Backing off this promise would have compromised Bush's domestic political standing. But the conventional military primacy of the United States somewhat suffocated alternative military and nonmilitary responses to terrorism, WMD, and nation building through the muscle-boundedness emanating from moral hazard.

A similar dynamic plagued Johnson and Nixon during the Vietnam War. The United States in this case also fell prey to conventional military primacy, which made it muscle-bound in its quest to destroy insurgency in the South and deter the North from supporting this insurgency. Johnson too, like Bush, committed himself to a resolute path during the period of escalation. This commitment also had international and domestic sources and implications. Resolute support for the South placated the American Right, but also served as a signal that was hoped to inspire the South to fight and the North to disengage from interference. Johnson too was at this point committed to a strong move in a game of chicken, and once played, this move limited his options down the road. Nixon, although in a less precarious position than Johnson with respect to the war, found it difficult not to inherit the gauntlet that Johnson had bequeathed, although Nixon found ways to disengage from a large-scale land war.

Athens showed a deplorable lack of imagination in managing the Delian League and expanding its presence in the Aegean. But much of this rigidity was driven by the self-feeding process of imperialism. As the burden of expansion grew, the methods of extracting resources from the league had to grow more severe. To simply attribute such a posture to common imperialistic tendencies in the ancient world is to neglect the fact that Sparta had a far different kind of relationship with its allies and colonies. But then again, Sparta did not exhibit Athens's appetite for empire. Britain and the Bank of England, too, demonstrated fairly rigid reactions to problems in international monetary relations in the nineteenth century. The British state developed few tools to oversee the bank and monetary relations even within Britain itself. The bank relied predominantly on the use of the discount rate to stimulate capital flows, while other central banks showed far greater perspicacity in developing diverse tools of central banking. This rigidity made both the bank and the British state poor candidates for dealing with international financial crises. Similarly, the British state seriously explored few options in abating the secular decline in the price of silver. Various options presented themselves in the international arena (conferences), yet these opportunities were left unexploited. Even within its own sphere (the empire and the isles), it made limited use of specifically British and colonial resources to confront the silver problem. Management of the Indian monetary system relied on the traditional staid and unimaginative procedures that prevailed before the silver problem. These proved to be of limited effectiveness. Little was done to restructure the institutions governing the system, or the system itself for that matter. Britain, in fact, made little use of the Bank of England in dealing with the problem even after a unilateral course was selected.

6. Soft power should form an important part of a nation's arsenal. Specifically within the context of the hard-soft power nexus, decision-makers continued to neglect important soft-power options in dealing with their problems. And in all of the cases, such options demonstrated the potential to be far more effective in dealing with many of the problems than the hard options that were eventually selected. In all of the cases, this neglect of soft power had enervating effects on the nations considered. One of the glaring lessons from the case studies, in fact, attests to the pervasiveness of a tendency for hard-power strategies to drown out soft-power strategies, even when the former appeared to be inferior or counterproductive. This, moreover, attests to the strength of power illusion. Actors maintained strategies that worked against their interests when superior options were available. In this respect, the effectiveness of the strategies they pursued was illusory. The Bush Doctrine itself is a multifaceted study in victimization from hard-power illusion. All of the harder strategies used to bring about Bush's three sacred goals ended up generating substantial counterproductive outcomes. Yet Bush stayed the course. In each of the objectives, soft power promised a means of addressing specific problems in a more constructive and effective way, yet these options were summarily dismissed or never considered in the first place. To make matters worse, the hard strategies that were used actually undermined already-existing soft-power resources and made the use of new soft resources either difficult or impossible. The strategies eliminated a plethora of support systems that might have facilitated the objectives by antagonizing both target nations as well as allies. This unfortunate outcome made the environments in which the problems existed all the more difficult to manage, and eliminated important networks of multilateral legitimacy and direct support that would have helped the United States address varied problems.

Major failures in Vietnam and Athenian imperialism owed significantly to the paucity of soft-power strategies as well. The US war effort against insurgency in Southeast Asia employed strategies that not only were poorly adapted to the direct task at hand, but also actually made the problem more difficult to solve. The failure to employ broad and vigorous pacification methods undermined the growth in support for the US effort among the South Vietnamese people, a fundamental precondition for abating insurgent sentiment in the South. This problem was compounded by the reluctance of the United States to encourage political reforms that might undercut the rebellious fervor among the people of the South. The large-war methods founded on large troop presence and the employment of conventional forces further alienated popular support not only in the South, but also among the American populace. Hence the methods undermined the soft domestic power necessary to carry on an effective war effort as well. In the end, the United States was essentially defeated by the use of its own hard power, more so than by the insurgents and their North Vietnamese allies. Similarly in the case of Athens, the neglect of soft power ultimately proved to be one of the most important reasons for its loss of the empire and the war, as well as its decline as an Aegean hegemon. Failure to develop a strong base of support among its Delian allies produced a festering malady that proved to be an ongoing burden for Athens. Adding to its empire, and employing the same methods of control and maintenance, compounded the problem. As long as Athens maintained the unilateral resources to deal with the burden, the entire system of colonial management and expansion could continue.

But this led to a vicious cycle of exploitation as further expansion necessitated a concomitant rise in extraction of resources, which continued to undermine Athenian soft power. The process itself was destined to culminate in crises for Athens as long as the Athenian appetite grew. The final straw came later in the Peloponnesian War, with Athens making a rash decision to expand beyond the Aegean during the Sicilian campaign. This set in motion a set of events that clearly manifested the paucity of Athenian soft power, which contributed to the empire's ultimate demise.

The British were similarly beset by a deplorable lack of appreciation for the merits of soft strategies in dealing with prevailing monetary challenges in the nineteenth century. The Bank of England did little in building networks of cooperation, even among its domestic banks, to help manage its own financial system. Certainly it was not going to do so at the international level to manage crises in the international financial system. But these soft strategies were ultimately the most effective in dealing with severe international crises. Moreover, the British state failed to encourage such cooperation among the Bank of England and central banks. As noted, it was lucky for the British that the system was not tested with severe crises in the late nineteenth century (either political or financial). The Bank of France proved to be much more committed as an international manager than the British state or Bank of England. It did develop networks of cooperation far more vigorously than the Bank of England in confronting financial shocks in the system during the century. The lessons about soft power appeared to be much more salient among the French than the English. And finally, in the context of the silver problem, the only real viable solution to the declining price of silver was a soft solution. The only method robust enough to stabilize the price of silver lay in a multilateral regime committed to remonetization. It is on this issue that British actions against their own interests were perhaps most contemptible, because Britain could have sealed the deal with minimal burdens on its own financial system and that of India as well. The British were therefore especially negligent in not solving the silver problem, because they held the key to consummating a regime with modest sacrifices on their own part. In both cases—managing international crises and managing the silver problem—soft-power strategies held the key to addressing vital British monetary goals, and time and time again Britain remained detached from such options, even though these options engendered limited sacrifices on Britain's part.

In sum, the problems of the power curse and power illusion will be difficult to solve, precisely because they manifest common psychological tendencies on the part of humans in dealing with their environments. But there are many such problems facing humans in general, and national leaders specifically, that are often dealt with successfully. In that people continue to successfully confront many such natural pitfalls, there is indeed hope that national leaders and decisionmakers can be equally committed and perspicacious in thinking outside of the conundrum and bringing their nations to greater strength and prosperity. The attainment of greater national power should in principle always be considered a good thing for the nation in question. But like any other good thing in principle, if it is pursued in excess or obtained in ways that are deleterious to the interests of a nation, then it may end up being more of a detriment than a blessing. Indeed, national leaders, like all of us, need to be careful about how they attain what they wish for.

More on Methodology

The five cases studies all reflect periods in which great powers succumbed in varying degrees to the effects of the power curse. Since these periods all exhibited a general deterioration in the power positions of the states and actors involved, the cases display inferential limitations owing to problems of insufficient variation in the dependent variable across cases (i.e., selection on the dependent variable as a result of cross-sectional limitations in variation; Keohane, King, and Verba 1994, pp. 129–149). However, the cases do show abundant instances of longitudinal variation of the relevant variables across time, thus enhancing the inferential value of the findings. In the case of Athens, there was a distinct change in its later power position in the Aegean and its relations with the Delian League compared to earlier in the fifth century B.C.E. As its need to expand increased, it found the task of sustaining a growing empire increasingly burdensome. The curse of overstretch increasingly cut into Athens's power position as it compromised its soft power in order to expand its empire and engage in military campaigns. Snapshots taken of Athens both in the early and late century showed a far different configuration of policies and consequent outcomes. In the case of British monetary leadership in the nineteenth century, variations within British policy and across central banks testified to the impact of the power curse as manifest in financial moral hazard. As the power of the Bank of England increased, the British state increasingly removed itself from the position of financial guarantor (especially in the banking reforms of 1825). Moreover, there were significant cross-sectional variations across central banks of the period. Central banks with far less financial power than the Bank of England displayed both policies and actions that were far less contaminated by financial moral hazard. In fact, they proved far more enlightened and perspicacious within their own financial systems and within the greater international system, the Bank of France especially.

With respect to the depreciation of silver, there was no significant variation in the power of Great Britain, nor a concomitant change in its international monetary policy. It remained fairly uncooperative throughout the late nineteenth century when silver both maintained its value and subsequently declined. However, as long as nations did cooperate and maintain open minting of silver, the price of silver (and hence the value of the rupee) did not deteriorate. This outcome lends stronger credence to the counterfactual that some multilateral regime to prop up the value of silver would indeed have solved the rupee problem, as underscored by all the leading British monetary commissions of the period. Hence a change in British monetary policy promised to pay significant dividends in solving the India problem. But in this specific case, a general disposition of complacency and overconfidence, bred by years of financial primacy, led to a course of action that undermined the stability of Indian finance, and concomitantly took its toll on the economic power of Britain.

Similarly, the Vietnam War also showed a fairly consistent pattern of US actions and policies in fighting insurgency. Moreover, the war unfolded over an abbreviated time period. However, there was some variation with respect to policies of pacification. While earlier military strategies systematically disregarded pacification (soft-power options) as a major component, the later war effort embraced them to a greater extent under the command of General Creighton Abrams, especially after he appointed William Colby as director of pacification efforts in Vietnam. And indeed the evidence marshaled by scholars who analyzed these pacificatior efforts suggests that they were a more effective strategy in abating insurgency. Yet the evidence also suggests that such efforts were too little and too late as a means of reversing a deteriorating political-military initiative.

In the case of Bush's foreign policy, the time frame (as with Vietnam) was also short, and it is difficult to locate major variation in the orientation of foreign policy over those eight years. The Bush Doctrine appeared to be compelling from the early days of the president's tenure, and of course 9/11 occurred early in Bush's term, thus reinforcing his policy orientation. However, there were some changes in outcomes that followed changes in policy. Bush's policy orientation was distinctly different from that of the Clinton administration. During the Bush years, instances of terrorism proliferated significantly after 9/11 as Bush embarked on an extensive hard crusade against terrorism. Also, foreign relations across the globe deteriorated, although a plethora of those relations were strained to begin with. The same can be said of US relations within international organizations and alliances. And, finally, one can certainly see a distinct deterioration in the three major goals of US foreign policy in this period (abating terrorism, limiting WMD, promoting democracy abroad), as Bush's policies made these goals all the more difficult to achieve and resulted in outcomes all the more distant from US hopes and expectations.

Notwithstanding the longitudinal variation of the principal variables within the cases, limits in cross-case or cross-sectional variation still present a problem. For the purpose of introducing cross-case variation, I present here a brief discussion of two control cases. These cases analyze actors—the Bank of France under the gold standard in the nineteenth century, and Britain during its counterinsurgency efforts in Malaya in the twentieth century—that were less powerful than actors they might be compared with in the primary cases, and show different outcomes in behavior relating to the processes of the power curse. These cases provide interesting methodological foils for the case of the Bank of England under the gold standard, and the case of the US war in Vietnam, respectively.[2]

The Bank of France and Monetary Leadership in the Nineteenth Century

The Bank of France represents an interesting foil against which to compare the Bank of England with respect to the processes comprising the financial power curse. It was significantly weaker than the Bank of England as a financial actor, and as we would expect based on the logic of the power curse, it exhibited far less moral hazard with respect to the management of its own domestic financial system and the greater international financial system. Differences in financial influence themselves were manifest in differing abilities to attract capital from both domestic and international markets. As noted, the Bank of England was unrivaled among central banks of the nineteenth century. Ultimately, it was the final resting point for international capital when it so chose, and such choice was manifest principally through changes in its discount rate. Such strength had perverse consequences for its management of both domestic and international finance. Both roles were undermined by an orientation and practices that limited its development of tools and perspicacity in central banking.

The Bank of France stood in strong contrast: it was a far better central banker both for France and ultimately for the international system. Unlike the Bank of England, the Bank of France had developed far more extensive central-banking tools and far more perspicacious practices in using such tools. But, as noted, this was generally the case with respect to other central banks in developed nations during this period; hence all weaker banks outperformed the Bank of England as central bankers. The Bank of France, domestically, was far more vigilant about monitoring and accommodating to the needs of French finance, in order to ultimately maintain a stable system. Above and beyond the tools, sensitivity, and perspicacity, the bank was far better at developing the financial networks and cooperation within French finance to enhance a superior central-banking arsenal and policies.

One of the main differences was in the propensity to manage reserves. Much of the Bank of England's moral hazard was manifest in stocking grossly insufficient central-banking (i.e., gold) reserves, which were a source of instability and risk in both domestic and international finance throughout the period. But this was a function of the pulling power of the bank, so such reserves could be sustained as long as the bank could attract capital when in need and hence defend convertibility. And while this thin film of gold never excessively compounded numerous and serious domestic and international financial meltdowns during the period, it was nonetheless a failure in responsible management of finance and national convertibility generated by moral hazard. Conversely, the Bank of France was hailed throughout the period as a repository of a "hoard of gold." The hoard itself represented a more pronounced commitment to maintaining financial stability and national convertibility. Since the Bank of France did not have the pulling power of the Bank of England, it required a larger store of gold in times when financial crises occurred or national convertibility was threatened. Its relative inferiority as a financial magnet made it far less cavalier than the Bank of England in managing the national gold stock. But the gold stock also reflected another more responsible orientation about domestic central banking. The Bank of France's discount rate, its major instrument for effecting gold flows, was kept within far more stable boundaries relative to the rate of the Bank of England, so as to promote more stable conditions in domestic capital markets. The Bank of England's more pronounced gyrations in its rate were necessary because it chose to manage its reserves through flows rather than through stocks, a consistent source of instability in both British as well as international finance throughout the period. A more inflexible discount-rate policy made the Bank of France relatively weaker in influencing gold flows; hence it required a larger gold stock to absorb shocks in domestic financial crises. But even in managing existing gold stocks, the Bank of France still outperformed the Bank of England in its more diverse and ingenious use of gold devices.

At the international level, it could be said that if indeed the classical gold standard had a leader, it was not the Bank of England but instead the Bank of France. Relative to the Bank of England, which produced a very poor record as an international financial leader, the Bank of France blazed a far more impressive trail in absorbing international financial shocks and preventing crises. Again, this was a function of its relative financial weakness. Because France was a second-tier financial power, crises in the first-tier financial system of Britain would spill into the country. More specifically, during international disturbances or crises, capital would ultimately be siphoned off to Britain. Hence any disturbance or crisis occurring in Britain would cause capital to flow from France to Britain in order to accommodate the greater demand for capital in the latter nation. While Britain's relative superiority in pulling capital allowed it the luxury of being more complacent about providing leadership for international finance (i.e., international financial moral hazard), France's inferior pulling power gave its central bank far greater incentive to intervene as a stabilizing agent in international markets. In fact, the Bank of France undertook far more stabilizing functions than did any other central banks of the period.

This role of international banker was manifest in a variety of functions, which themselves were reflective of both the commitment and the ingenuity of the Bank of France in absorbing international shocks and averting crises. It was the most animated lender of "first" resort to other central banks throughout the period. In this respect, it was a preemptive stabilizer, in that it sought to interdict financial disturbances when they were still limited in their fallout. Interestingly, this was also a function of its relative financial weakness, given that the Bank of France was not confident about its abilities to abate large-scale and widespread crises in their later stages. Also, the Bank of France was more often the provider of loans to the Bank of England than it was the recipient. In this sense, it served as a de facto central bank to the Bank of England: it was the latter's so-called second gold reserve. In general, it initiated more capital flows during periods of liquidity shortage than did any other central bank of the period. This engineering of capital flows took differing forms. Sometimes the transfers were purely bilateral. Other times, they involved a consortium of lenders organized by the Bank of France.[3] Still other times, the transfers were engineered through third parties (i.e., supplying capital to markets that served as sources for other troubled markets). The arrangements also involved different kinds of financial actors (public and private) and differing-sized consortia.

In sum, the Bank of France had far less financial power relative to the Bank of England, but as a result was far less cursed with respect to its role as a domestic and international central bank. While the power of the Bank of England led it to languish under a cavalier orientation clouded by financial moral hazard, the relative weakness of the Bank of France led it to behave far more beneficially with its own domestic financial system and within the greater international monetary system.

British Counterinsurgency in Malaya in the Twentieth Century

The British campaign against Communist insurgents in Malaya stands in strong contrast to the US experience in Vietnam. A preponderantly stronger United States failed to achieve what its much militarily weaker counterpart achieved in a roughly equal period of time. The British campaign against insurgency (the Malayan Emergency) began in 1948 when Malaya's Communist Party declared that it would use violence to achieve its political objectives, and ended in 1960 when newly independent Malaya declared that the war against Communist counterinsurgency was officially over. In keeping with the logic of the power curse, the relative military inferiority of Britain compared to the United States proved to be the crucial factor in its success, while the latter's failure to win a counterinsurgency war stemmed from its greater endowment of military strength. Britain's relatively inferior military standing ultimately encouraged it to organize a more effective counterinsurgency campaign relative to that of the great US military machine in Vietnam.

John Nagl (2002) identifies the early emergence of an "expeditionary" military culture in British strategy for dealing with colonial matters (certainly visible as early as the eighteenth century). This emanated from a long legacy of asymmetries in military capacity. Britain emerged as a naval power and preserved its international interests primarily through power over the seas. Land forces were always inferior and thus served an ancillary role to naval operations. Since Britain lacked the manpower to coercively impose British rule over colonial territories, strategies to secure colonies became oriented around small forces, extensive cooperation with local police authorities, and a general orientation of pacification. World Wars I and II weakened Britain's military capacity, and thus moved strategies ever more away from coercive operations and toward the prevailing model forged over the preceding two centuries. This model was enhanced all the more by the experiences that the British military acquired in fighting smaller guerrilla wars against the Japanese during World War II. The prevailing blueprint for military operations in colonial theaters thus came to feature the following goals and strategies: minimal use of force, understanding the people and politics in the theaters of engagement, effective intelligence gathering, winning the hearts and minds of indigenous populations, working closely with and through local constabularies, working within the constraints of indigenous public opinion, integrating political objectives with military objectives, extensive civil-military cooperation, and ingenuity and flexibility in field operations.

This blueprint was primed for activation when Malayan insurgency erupted in 1948. Interestingly, the shadow of World War II operations set the British response somewhat off course in the early part of the campaign. Officers who had just emerged from six years of a big war held to such operations, and pushed for larger-scale search and destroy tactics. But a number of factors shifted British operations back on track. First, the British government and high command realized that such methods were failing to abate Malayan insurrection.[4] Second, the British model of colonial military operations was never shelved, but instead conducted alongside larger-scale operations. After a bumpy start over the first several years, British counterinsurgency settled into the general framework of the model forged over the preceding centuries.[5]

The British demonstrated great flexibility in using military tactics (both small- and big-war), and these tactics were always well integrated. Military command structures were well integrated and included representatives from indigenous groups allied with the British (Federal War Council, Federal Executive Council, and Director of Operations Committee). This integrated command model was replicated at the local level with district and state executive committees. Field operations were oriented around an incremental approach to winning the war against insurgency. This made the British public more tolerant of a longer campaign, and also made setbacks seem all the less alarming (outcomes that significantly hamstrung the United States in Vietnam). The British, far more so than the Americans in Vietnam, proved especially perspicacious in adapting to the complexity of counterinsurgency initiatives by emphasizing the creation, testing, and implementation of innovative techniques. The "Ferret" force model of guerrilla warfare proved especially effective: small groups mimicked insurgency tactics, made use of local trackers and interpreters, and conscripted recruits from the local population. Both British soldiers and indigenous soldiers were provided with the requisite training to carry out such operations in specially designed "jungle warfare" schools.

The British emphasized the integration of political goals with military goals—a far better adaptation to the complexity of a counterinsurgency campaign than that demonstrated by the Americans in Vietnam. Unlike the latter, the British approached the Malayan insurgency more as a political than a military war, and were ultimately successful at building a political equilibrium (through the multiethnic Alliance Party) that undermined support for the insurgency. This political equilibrium was a component of a general political orientation that underscored the importance of pacification. Pacification initiatives were aggressively carried out at all levels of the political economy.[6] After large-scale battles, for example, it was a priority of the British to reestablish a favorable political equilibrium. This required the British to work closely with local populations in establishing effective security and political functions. But such fallout was limited by the smaller-war operations of the British; hence pacification was much easier to achieve as compared to the US experience in Vietnam. Especially crucial targets for the British pacification initiative were rural Chinese squatters. These squatters were an especially dangerous potential source of support for the Malayan insurgents. The British successfully co-opted these groups through a multitude of strategies, some of which involved allowing the groups to field their own security forces.

One of the glaring differences between the US experience in Vietnam and the British experience in Malaya was the far greater success of the latter in making political and security inroads into local communities. This was the key to undercutting insurgency, since insurgency found its main lifeline across rural villages. In this respect the British were more successful at cutting insurgents off from sources of supply and recruits. But such local inroads also carried another key for counterinsurgency: effective intelligence. Realizing the difficulty of fighting a dispersed and clandestine enemy without abundant and reliable information, the British undertook aggressive and innovative intelligence strategies that allowed them to conceal the identity of informants. Ultimately, for all these reasons, the British proved far superior to the Americans at winning the hearts and minds of the indigenous people, an absolutely necessary condition for winning a war against insurgents.

In the final analysis, the weaker British were far more successful than the stronger Americans during virtually all phases of counterinsurgency. This differential performance owed much to differing endowments of military power. In the end, the Americans perceived themselves as far too strong to have to adapt to a very unique war (they became victims of moral hazard in facing complexity), while the British, to their good fortune, were spared such a choice. Much of this difference was manifest in their reliance on softer solutions to the insurgency, given their inferior military endowments compared to the Americans, who fell victim to the hubris of their hard power.

Toward an Integrated Theory of Power: Cosmopolitik

The theoretical reasoning and case studies presented in this book suggest that the power curse and power illusion can be pervasive in the international system. And the fact that their effects can be enervating to national influence suggests that, with respect to paradigms of international politics, the joint set among the three main paradigms of international politics—realism, constructivism, and neoliberalism—need not be null. The search for intersecting sets among these three paradigms has been challenging, to say the least. There has appeared a general recalcitrance among the practitioners of the paradigms (especially the realists) toward attempts at reconciliation (Sterling-Folker 2002, p. 74; Copeland 2000). While constructivism and neoliberalism appear to overlap significantly in their embrace of institutions, the two paradigms have been traditionally seen from both sides as antithetical to realism (Barkin 2003, p. 325).[7] The findings in this book appear all the more compelling in that they have not only marshaled an intersecting set among the three paradigms, but also located this intersection at the very point of greatest conflict among the paradigms: power (Wendt 1999, p. 114).[8] In that some synthesis has been found on the issue thought to be least likely to bridge the theoretical gap, these findings could be considered "crucial" from a methodological point of view (Eckstein 1975; Gerring 2004, p. 347; King, Keohane, and Verba 1994, pp. 209–212).[9] Indeed, the ideas of soft power, the power curse, and power illusion open up possibilities for synthesizing the three paradigms. Such synthesis would be built on a mutual acknowledgment of the need for more sophisticated and complex understandings of the way that power in international relations manifests itself in the modern world.[10] This more cosmopolitan vision might itself inspire a new paradigm or vision of international politics: cosmopolitik.[11]

The crucial findings in this book suggest that, indeed, points of harmony can be established among the three competing paradigms of international relations in the realm of power seeking, and that these points represent a point of departure for greater theory building. These points of harmony can be built around four propositions that, although not constituting an integrated vision or theory of power, provide points of departure for building such a vision or theory.

Proposition 1: The optimization of both absolute and relative power can be a legitimate goal of statecraft. This proposition is consistent with both realism's prime directive of power optimization, and constructivist and neoliberal beliefs that individual capabilities can effectively coexist with collective harmony (i.e., individual strength is not inconsistent with group welfare if individuals conceive of their interests in terms of group utility). In this respect, all three paradigms can embrace the idea of power augmentation and optimization (Barkin 2003, p. 327). Being both absolutely and relatively strong can benefit individual nations in myriad ways without necessarily imposing adverse outcomes on the group. Moreover, if nations conceive of their fates as inextricably tied to the collective structures in which they operate, individual strength can enhance the goals of other nations.

There is nothing in constructivism or neoliberalism that proscribes power augmentation or even optimization. The more important question involving power is: Power for what purpose? Constructivists and neoliberals do not object to nations being powerful or influential. The thing that distinguishes constructivists from realists on this issue is that for the former, perceptions of what constitutes power are intersubjective and driven by cognitions about sources of influence in international relations. Indeed, these cognitions are created through socialization in the international arena. Realists see power as a more objective phenomenon, principally made up of hard sources (military, land, and other material assets). Neoliberals conceptualize power in a broader context of political economy, power resources not strictly limited to hard resources that have direct military applications. Indeed, nations may amass many economic resources and strategies of cooperation that enhance their international influence. For realists there is little distinction among power-seeking strategies that nations follow, something constructivists deny. Moreover, there is an objective hierarchy of national goals for realists that puts power augmentation at the very top. For constructivists and neoliberals, the hierarchy is subjective and does not place amassing hard resources in a venerated position in all cases. But constructivists and neoliberals indeed embrace the value of power augmentation and optimization, if it can be used in support of varied goals (and not just in the context of military capacity in an anarchic world).[12] The idea of soft power is a manifestation of a more constructivist and neoliberal take on the utility of power. Up until the idea of soft power, constructivists and neoliberals emphasized processes and phenomena that constrained nations: norms, rules, laws, institutions, and cognitions that drove nations to limit their aggressiveness and competitiveness (Wendt 1999, p. 114).[13] With the idea of soft power, constructivism and neoliberalism can embrace phenomena and processes that empower nations rather than restrain them. So in this case, realists, neoliberals, and constructivists could all agree that nations have an incentive to be powerful. But empowerment through the use of soft power is also consistent with a realist conception of power optimization, in that the diversification among hard- and soft-power resources is the best way to optimize power and consequently maximize security. Only through such a diversification can power truly be optimized.

Even if power is conceived as a zero-sum game, augmenting relative power need not delegitimate a constructivist or neoliberal vision of power. Indeed, the question "Power for what?" is most relevant in this context. Growing relatively more powerful than another need not be menacing to the latter if the stronger nation is acting consistently within constructivist or neoliberal behavioral boundaries (i.e., the nation is not growing stronger to dominate or exploit the weaker nation, which according to the power curse could be self-defeating for the aggressive nation).[14] In fact, it would be consistent with these boundaries that this greater strength could trickle down to weaker nations through benign hegemony or greater paternalism, such as through having stronger allies or receiving greater aid (Kindleberger 1986; Ikenberry and Kupchan 2004). But if indeed this power is used outside of the behavioral boundaries prescribed by neoliberal and constructivist institutions, nations are not naive and can defend themselves against such bald-faced aggression. In fact, this aggressive behavior, as the idea of the power curse has shown, has a built-in feedback mechanism that can significantly compromise the influence of nations acting with such impunity. Even the most animated realist would not condone self-destructive aggression.

Proposition 2: National power is endogenous. National power is not determined simply by the isolated actions of any given nation: it is not exogenous. Because the effectiveness of a nation's power can only be determined in the context of interactions with other nations, power itself is a social phenomenon. Power is defined by the social context in which it is developed and exercised: it is contingent, or endogenous. This social context is a complex system, because international relations themselves are complex (Jervis 1997). Power, therefore, is neither exogenous (i.e., given) nor linear. More weapons need not give a nation more security in the face of feedback effects (e.g., security dilemma). Because of complexity, it is possible for power to be a zero-, positive-, or negative-sum phenomenon, depending on the context within which that power arises and evolves. If an ally gains greater power, then power can be a positive-sum phenomenon. If an enemy gains greater power, then power can be zero-sum. If both nations in competition match each other's power, then power can be negative-sum as money is spent in order to gain parity. All three paradigms would embrace the idea of power as an endogenous phenomenon.

Proposition 3: Nations will maximize their security in an anarchic world. People understand that while no external impediments exist to prevent them from reaching mutually beneficial outcomes, there are also no external impediments guaranteeing that nations will not act in ways that are detrimental to the interests of other nations. Therefore, all nations bear the risk of being victims of large-scale violence, and consequently must take measures to protect themselves. In this respect, nations will wish to maximize their security. This is consistent with the realist assumption of anarchy, and that in the face of such anarchy, security must be maximized (Mearsheimer 2001, p. 30). But such protection must be administered in ways that prevent misperceptions about intentions so as to avoid security dilemmas or other deleterious feedback processes. In this respect, protection must be conceptualized within the context of the social structures averred by constructivists and neoliberals: protect oneself in a manner most conducive and sensitive to group interests, because in an interdependent world, individual safety is contingent upon collective safety (i.e., security is indivisible). This collective vision of security is a manifestation of the importance of soft power: a nation's power derives significantly from the attitudes and perceptions of other nations.

Neoliberals fundamentally assent to the realist proposition about the pervasiveness of anarchy and the quest for security. While neoliberals differ with realists with respect to issue hierarchy, they nonetheless assent to the realist emphasis on security as occupying a principal goal of nations. They differ, however, as to their visions of the level of vulnerability and threat that nations face in the modern international system (Keohane and Nye 1989). Constructivists concede that anarchy may in fact exist, but that perceptions of anarchy and the behavioral manifestations of these perceptions will differ according to the mind-sets of differing individuals; in other words, these perceptions and manisfestations will be socially constructed (Wendt 1992). Yet while security may be socially constructed, and hence seemingly conflict with realists' objective visions of security, Michael Williams (2003), in his work on the Schmittian foundations of the Copenhagen School's idea of securitization, suggests strong elements of compatibility between realist and constructivist visions of national security. In this respect, he shows that even constructed visions of security demonstrate consistent elements (extensive threat and extreme necessity) that render images and goals that merge toward common understandings of security in a realist vein (in this case, images of vital national interests develop through discursive legitimation and the practical ethics of discourse).

Above and beyond Williams's work, there is a compelling paradox in realism's ontology that suggests possibilities for further interfacing constructivist, neoliberal, and realist approaches to security. Ironically, realism's ontology of human behavior ultimately predicates conflict and competition upon an ability of humans to act collectively: people within the nation, and often nations themselves in the form of alliances, coalesce in order to protect themselves in an anarchic environment. Jennifer Sterling-Folker (2002) identifies this ontology as a manifestation of a pervasive Darwinian element in the realist logic. But such Darwinian logic would suggest that the associational or collective action on the part of actors would be selected in terms of the imperative of maximizing security. And certainly in this context, the in-group versus out-group argument that realists have marshaled in defense of the paradox—that in-group cooperation is present in perpetrating out-group competition—becomes problematic. From an evolutionary standpoint, selection proceeds both within groups and between groups in order to arrive at optimal capacities for survival (Sterling-Folker 2002). But even from a purely institutional context, the capacity for optimal group selection is conterminous with the dictates of security. In this respect, even a realist prime directive of maximizing security would involve extensive intergroup (international) cooperation. This has been articulated across numerous decades by some of the field's leading realists. For example, John Herz (1957), in discussing possibilities for the demise of the territorial state, argued that sovereignty had historically been determined by the imperatives of delivering maximum security to the actors involved. Some forty years later, Robert Jervis (2002), in a partial validation of Herz's argument, embraced the advent of security communities as the optimal response to security in the modern age. Indeed, the quest for security across all three paradigms interfaces well in this respect.

Proposition 4: Power optimization can only occur through the combination of both hard- and soft-power resources. Indeed, material power is required at some level for protection, but material capability alone is ill-equipped to optimize influence. The optimization of national influence requires both hard- and soft-power resources. Soft power is the antithesis of a menacing posture and therefore breaks down adversarial elements among other nations that might restrict a nation's influence in the community of nations. Moreover, the respect and affection garnered through prevailing social structures renders a nation's influence all the greater, as others then more willingly follow its lead. Since diversification facilitates a goal embraced by all three paradigms (power and security optimization), the inclusion of soft power need not conflict with realist logic. And certainly, neoliberals and constructivists alike have attested to the optimality of a diversified portfolio of power resources (Hall 1997; Keohane and Nye 1989; Nye 2002; Goldstein and Keohane 1993).

In this respect, empowerment through diversification represents a means through which constructivist and neoliberal elements (i.e., soft power) can actually empower rather than limit the power-seeking tendencies of nations. As noted, many of the elements of soft power that have heretofore been embraced by neoliberals and constructivists have largely been conceptualized as constraints. Indeed, norms, rules, principles, institutions, cooperation, and beliefs have been seen as phenomena that restrain nations from power-seeking behavior. In this respect, the phenomena have been envisioned as disempowering. Embracing the richness of soft power leads to an acknowledgment that such phenomena can actually be empowering. And hence, acknowledging such empowering qualities would bring constructivist and neoliberal conceptions of power into greater harmony with realist tenets involving the optimization of power.

In sum, a number of venerated tenets of realism need not conflict with some of the fundamental tenets of neoliberalism and constructivism with respect to the concept of power. The realist tenets about the optimization of power and influence, and the maximization of security, are consistent with objectives posited by constructivists and neoliberals. Indeed, in the interdependent and complex communities of today's international system, true optimization of the goals underscored by realists for individual nations can be principally accomplished only by the conceptualization of individual actions within frameworks that embrace elements of neoliberalism and constructivism. Not doing so can lead to consequences that debilitate rather than benefit nations. Hence, by embracing the interdependent and complex nature of international politics, realist visions of power can more easily interface with those of neoliberalism and constructivism. Indeed, such an acknowledgment may forge a foundation for a more integrated theory of international relations: cosmopolitik.

Notes

1. Karl Deutsch (1966, p. 155) underscored the importance of a "net" conception of power over four decades ago.

2. On introducing control cases to address problems of selecting on the dependent variable, see Skocpol 1979 (p. 140) and King, Keohane, and Verba 1994 (p. 129). Fuller studies of both cases have been undertaken in Gallarotti 2005 and Nagl 2002, the latter of which compares the British experience in Malaya to the US experience in Vietnam. My analysis derives from those sources and seeks to underscore relevant arguments in the case studies that involve variables pertaining to the power curse.

3. In forging networks of financial cooperation with other banks both inside and outside France, the Bank of France also demonstrated greater reliance on soft

financial power relative to the Bank of England. Consistent with the hard-soft manifestations of the power curse, it was a relative deficiency in hard power that made the Bank of France rely more on soft power in this case.

4. Interestingly, the US counterparts in Vietnam remained fairly obtuse to such information that big-war tactics were failing, much of which derived from differing perceptions of power. Perceptions of preponderant power led US elites to see failures more as temporary setbacks than harbingers of US vulnerability. British humility, on the other hand, led elites to be much more compelled by such information.

5. Generals Harold Briggs and Gerald Templer proved especially astute commanders of the counterinsurgency campaign (Nagl 2002, pp. 87–91).

6. Even early on in the campaign, the British (unlike the Americans in Vietnam) underscored the importance of addressing the political and economic conditions that bred and sustained the insurgency. In this respect, the British campaign was far more inclusive of soft-power solutions compared to the US campaign in Vietnam.

7. By presenting these paradigms as single entities, this analysis obfuscates the great diversity of visions within each paradigm, each of which is in fact a battleground. The following citations serve to clarify the competing strands within the respective paradigms more clearly. Wendt, in a personal correspondence, notes that attempts to integrate realism and constructivism come almost exclusively from the constructivist side; on attempts to synthesize realism and constructivism, see Wendt 1999, Barkin 2003, Williams 2003, Sterling-Folker 2002, Johnston 2008, Onuf 2008, and Hall 1997. Works that demonstrate a more realist orientation include Jervis 1970, Copeland 2000, and Walt 1987, although such works are somewhat more crypto-attempts at bridging the gap. Attempts to synthesize realism and neoliberalism include Fukuyama 2006 and Ikenberry and Kupchan 2004 (using terms such as "realistic Wilsonianism," "realist democratic," and "liberal realism"); on this synthesis, see also Niou and Ordeshook 1994. On the relation between realism and neoliberalism, see Keohane and Nye 1989, Baldwin 1993, and Niou and Ordeshook 1994. On comparisons of neoliberalism and constructivism, see Sterling-Folker 2000. On constructivism, see especially Onuf 1989, Wendt 1999, and Adler 2002.

8. In fact, various scholars have proclaimed that there is much more convergence among realists and constructivists on the centrality of power than has been traditionally acknowledged (Wendt 1999, p. 97; Barkin 2003, p. 327).

9. In that integrative properties appear in an area considered to be least fertile for theoretical synthesis, the idea of more general integration of the paradigms becomes all the more compelling.

10. As noted in Chapter 2, the international system has evolved in ways that have heightened the value of normative and cooperative behavior. In effect, these changes have raised the utility of soft strategies and have cut against the utility of the orthodox realist hard strategies.

11. The term relates to Ulrich Beck's "cosmopolitanism" (2005), which is meant to convey a broad view of the manifestations of power in a new global age. While the term "cosmopolitik" shares many of the theoretical and prescriptive issues marshaled in Beck's term, it nonetheless reflects significant differences in points of emphasis and theoretical-prescriptive concerns. I have chosen "cosmo-

politik" simply to connote a more modern and sophisticated view of power that better fits changes in the world system and the challenges of the power curse.

12. Even here there is no real difference among the paradigms in the idea of maximizing security. Constructivists and neoliberals merely disagree with realists on the precise strategies and power resources that will deliver that security. There is nothing in constructivism and neoliberalism that proposes to compromise a nation's safety.

13. Exceptions to this have come in the work on empowerment of ideas and norms through moral authority and principled beliefs. See Hall 1997 and Goldstein and Keohane 1993.

14. In this context, the interrelation of norms and power structures would be most visible, hence marking a compelling tribute to the coexistence of a realist and nonrealist vision of international change (Barkin 2003, p. 337).

References

Adler, Emanuel. 2002. "Constructivism and International Relations." In Walter Carlsnaes, Thomas Risse, and Beth A. Simmons, eds., *Handbook of International Relations,* pp. 177–191. London: Sage.

Allawi, Ali A. 2007. *The Occupation of Iraq: Winning the War, Losing the Peace.* New Haven: Yale University Press.

Alt, James E., Randall L. Calvert, and Brian D. Humes. 1988. "Reputation and Hegemonic Stability: A Game Theoretic Analysis." *American Political Science Review* 82 (June):445–466.

Alterman, Jon B. 2004. "Not in My Back Yard: Iraq's Neighbors' Interests." In Alexander T. J. Lennon and Camille Eiss, eds., *Reshaping Rogue States,* pp. 357–371. Cambridge: Massachusetts Institute of Technology Press.

Andreades, A. 1909. *History of the Bank of England.* Translated by Christabel Meredith. London: P. S. King.

Ansari, Ali M. 2004. "Continuous Regime Change from Within." In Alexander T. J. Lennon and Camille Eiss, eds., *Reshaping Rogue States,* pp. 265–282. Cambridge: Massachusetts Institute of Technology Press.

Arreguin-Toft, Ivan. 2005. *How the Weak Win Wars: A Theory of Asymmetric Conflict.* Cambridge: Cambridge University Press.

Assunção, Lucas. 2003. "Turning Its Back to the World? The United States and Climate Change Policy." In David Malone and Yuen Foong Khong, eds., *Unilateralism and U.S. Foreign Policy,* pp. 297–317. Boulder: Lynne Rienner.

Axelrod, Robert. 1984. *The Evolution of Cooperation.* New York: Basic.

Bagchi, Amiya Kumar. 1989. *The Presidency Banks and the Indian Economy, 1876–1914.* Calcutta: Oxford University Press.

Bagehot, Walter. [1873] 1921. *Lombard Street: A Description of the Money Market.* New York: Dutton.

Baldwin, David A. 1989. *The Paradoxes of Power.* New York: Blackwell.

———, ed. 1993. *Neorealism and Neoliberalism: The Contemporary Debate.* New York: Columbia University Press.

———. 2002. "Power and International Relations." In Walter Carlsnaes, Thomas Risse, and Beth A. Simmons, eds., *Handbook of International Relations,* pp. 177–191. London: Sage.

Barkin, J. Samuel. 2003. "Realist Constructivism." *International Studies Review* 5:325–342.

Barnett, Michael, and Raymond Duvall. 2005. "Power in International Politics." *International Organization* 59 (Winter):39–75.

Barnett, Roger W. 2003. *Asymmetrical Warfare: Today's Challenges to U.S. Military Power.* Washington, D.C.: Brassey's.

Bartlett, C. J. 1969. "Statecraft, Power, and Influence." In C. J. Bartlett, ed., *Britain Pre-Eminent: Studies of British World Influence in the Nineteenth Century,* pp. 172–193. London: Macmillan.

Beck, Ulrich. 2005. *Power in the Global Age: A New Global Political Economy.* Malden: Polity.

Berenskoetter, Felix. 2007. "Thinking About Power." In Felix Berenskoetter and M. J. Williams, eds., *Power in World Politics,* pp. 1–22. London: Routledge.

Berenskoetter, Felix, and M. J. Williams, eds. 2007. *Power in World Politics.* London: Routledge.

Betts, Richard K. 2002. "The Soft Underbelly of American Primacy: Tactical Advantages of Terror." *Political Science Quarterly* 117:19–36.

Blinken, Anthony J. 2003. "Winning the War of Ideas." In Alexander T. J. Lennon, ed., *The Battle for Hearts and Minds: Using Soft Power to Undermine Terrorist Networks,* pp. 282–298. Cambridge: Massachusetts Institute of Technology Press.

Block, Fred. 1977. *The Origins of International Economic Disorder.* Berkeley: University of California Press.

Bordo, Michael D., and Hugh Rockoff. 1996. "The Gold Standard as a 'Good-housekeeping Seal of Approval.'" *Journal of Economic History* 56 (June): 389–428.

Boserup, Anders, and Andrew Mack. 1975. *War Without Weapons: Non-Violence in National Defense.* New York: Shocken.

Brooks, Stephen G., and William C. Wohlforth. 2008. *World out of Balance: International Relations and the Challenge of International Primacy.* Princeton: Princeton University Press.

Brzezinski, Zbigniew. 2004. *The Choice: Global Domination or Global Leadership.* New York: Basic.

———. 2007. *Second Chance: Three Presidents and the Crisis of American Superpower.* New York: Perseus.

Calleo, David. 2003. "Power, Wealth, and Wisdom." *National Interest,* Summer: 5–15.

Cerny, Philip G. Forthcoming. "Reconfiguring Power in a Globalizing World." In Stuart Clegg and Mark Haugaard, eds., *Handbook of Power.* London: Sage.

Christensen, Thomas J. 2005. "Worse Than a Monolith: Disorganization and Rivalry Within Asian Communist Alliances and U.S. Containment Challenges, 1949–69." *Asian Security* 1 (January):80–127.

Clarke, Kevin A., and David Malone Primo. 2007. "Modernizing Political Science: A Model-Based Approach." *Perspectives on Politics* 5 (December): 741–753.

Clodfelter, Mark. 1989. *The Limits of Air Power: The American Bombing of North Vietnam.* New York: Free Press.

Connor, W. Robert. 1984. *Thucydides.* Princeton, NJ: Princeton University Press.

Copeland, Dale C. 2000. "The Constructivist Challenge to Structural Realism." *International Security* 25 (Autumn):187–212.

Cox, Michael. 2007. "Is the United States in Decline—Again?" *Internatinoal Affairs* 83:643–653.

Cox, Robert W. 1980. "The Crisis of World Order and the Problem of International Organization in the 1980s." *International Journal* 35 (Spring): 370–395.

———. 1987. *Production, Power, and World Order: Social Forces in the Making of History.* New York: Columbia University Press.

Crane, Gregory. 1998. *Thucydides and the Ancient Simplicity.* Berkeley: University of California Press.

Crenshaw, Martha. 2003. "Coercive Diplomacy and the Response to Terrorism." In Robert J. Art and Patrick M. Cronin, eds., *The United States and Coercive Diplomacy,* pp. 305–358. Washington, D.C.: US Institute of Peace Press.

Dahl, Robert A. 1957. "The Concept of Power." *Behavioral Science* 2:201–215.

De Cecco, Marcello. 1974. *Money and Empire: The International Gold Standard, 1890–1914.* Totowa: Rowman and Littlefield.

"Defending and Advancing Freedom: A Symposium." 2005. *Commentary* 120 (November):21–68.

Deutsch, Karl W. 1966. *The Nerves of Government.* New York: Free Press.

de Wijk, Rob. 2003. "The Limits of Military Power." In Alexander T. J. Lennon, ed., *The Battle for the Hearts and Minds: Using Soft Power to Undermine Terrorist Networks,* pp. 3–28. Cambridge: Massachusetts Institute of Technology Press.

Digeser, Peter. 1992. "The Fourth Face of Power." *Journal of Politics* 54 (November):977–1007.

Doyle, Michael W. 1997. *Ways of War and Peace*. New York: Norton.

Eckstein, Harry. 1975. "Case Study and Theory in Political Science." In Fred Greenstein and Nelson Polsby, eds., *Handbook of Political Science*, vol. 7, *Political Science: Scope and Theory*, pp. 79–133. Reading: Addison-Wesley.

Ellis, Jason D. 2004. "The Best Defense: Counterproliferation and U.S. National Security." In Alexander T. J. Lennon and Camille Eiss, eds., *Reshaping Rogue States*, pp. 50–72. Cambridge: Massachusetts Institute of Technology Press.

Erlich, Carl S. 1996. *The Philistines in Transition*. Leiden: Brill.

Ewans, Martin. 2005. *Conflict in Afghanistan: Studies in Asymmetric Warfare*. London: Routledge.

Fallows, James. 1979. "Muscle-Bound Superpower." *Atlantic Monthly*, October: 59–78.

Feis, Herbert. 1930. *Europe, the World's Banker*. New Haven: Yale University Press.

Ferguson, Niall. 2003. "Power." *Foreign Policy*, January–February:18–27.

Fetter, Frank. 1965. *Development of British Monetary Orthodoxy, 1797–1875*. Cambridge: Harvard University Press.

Finkelstein, Israel, and Neil Asher Silberman. 2006. *David and Solomon*. New York: Free Press.

Forde, Steven. 2000. "Power and Morality in Thucydides." In Lowell S. Gustafson, ed., *Thucydides' Theory of International Relations*, pp. 151–173. Baton Rouge: Louisiana State University Press.

Fraser, Matthew. 2003. *Weapons of Mass Distraction: Soft Power and American Empire*. New York: St. Martin's.

French, A. 1964. *The Growth of the Athenian Economy*. London: Routledge and Kegan Paul.

Fukuyama, Francis. 2006. *America at the Crossroads*. New Haven: Yale University Press.

Galbraith, John Kenneth. 1960. "The 'Turbulent Frontier' as a Factor in British Expansion." *Comparative Studies in Society and History* 2 (January): 150–168.

Gallagher, John, and Ronald Robinson. 1953. "The Imperialism of Free Trade." *Economic History Review* 6:1–15.

Gallarotti, Giulio M. 1989. "Legitimacy as a Capital Asset of the State." *Public Choice* 63 (October):43–61.

———. 1991. "The Limits of International Organization: Systematic Failure in the Management of International Relations." *International Organization* 45 (Spring):183–220.

———. 1993. "The Scramble for Gold: Monetary Regime Transformation in the 1870s." In Michael Bordo and Forrest Capie, eds., *Monetary Regimes in Transition*, pp. 15–67. Cambridge: Cambridge University Press.

———. 1995a. *The Anatomy of an International Monetary Regime: The Classical Gold Standard, 1880–1914*. New York: Oxford University Press.

———. 1995b. "It Pays to Be Green: The Managerial Incentive Structure and Environmentally Sound Strategies." *Columbia Journal of World Business* 30 (Winter):38–57.

———. 2000. "The Advent of the Prosperous Society: The Rise of the Guardian State and Structural Change in the World Economy." *Review of International Political Economy* 7 (Spring):1–52.

———. 2004. "Nice Guys Finish First: American Unilateralism and Power Illusion." In Graham F. Walker, ed., *Independence in an Age of Empires: Multilateralism and Unilateralism in the Post 9/11 World*, pp. 225–236. Halifax: Center for Foreign Policy Studies, Dalhousie University.

———. 2005 "Hegemons of a Lesser God: The Bank of France and Monetary Leadership Under the Classical Gold Standard." *Review of International Political Economy* 12 (October):624–646.

Gallarotti, Giulio M., and Arik Y. Preis. 1999. "Politics, International Justice, and the United States: Toward a Permanent International Criminal Court." *UCLA Journal of International Law and Foreign Affairs* 4:1–54.

Gardner, Hal. 2005. *American Global Strategy and the "War on Terrorism."* Aldershot: Ashgate.

Gardner, Lloyd. 2002. "The Last Casualty: Richard Nixon and the End of the Vietnam War, 1969–75." In Marilyn B. Young and Robert Buzzanco, eds., *A Companion to the Vietnam War*, pp. 229–259. Oxford: Blackwell.

Garst, Daniel. 1989. "Thucydides and Neorealism." *International Studies Quarterly* 33 (March):3–27.

George, Alexander L., and Andrew Bennett. 2005. *Case Studies and Theory Development in the Social Sciences*. Cambridge: Massachusetts Institute of Technology Press.

George, Alexander L., and Timothy J. McKeown. 1985. "Case Studies and Theories of Organizational Decision Making." *Advances in Information Processing and Organization* 2:21–58.

Gerring, John. 2004. "What Is a Case Study and What Is It Good For?" *American Political Science Review* 98 (May):341–354.

Gerschenkron, Alexander. 1962. *Economic Backwardness in Historical Perspective*. Cambridge: Harvard University Press.

Gilpin, Robert. 1975. *U.S. Power and the Multinational Corporation: The Political Economy of Foreign Direct Investment*. New York: Basic.

———. 1981. *War and Change in World Politics*. New York: Cambridge University Press.

———. 1996. "Economic Evolution of National Systems." *International Studies Quarterly* 40 (September):411–431.

Gleick, James. 1988. *Chaos Theory*. New York: Penguin.

Goldstein, Judith, and Robert O. Keohane. 1993. "Ideas and Foreign Policy: An Analytic Framework." In Judith Goldstein and Robert O. Keohane, eds., *Ideas and Foreign Policy: Beliefs, Institutions, and Political Change*. Ithaca: Cornell University Press.

Gould, Stephen Jay. 1989. *Wonderful Life*. New York: Norton.

Gray, John. 1962. *Archaeology of the Old Testament World*. London: Thomas Nelson.

Great Britain. 1888. *Report of the Gold and Silver Commission*. Reprinted in Ralph Robey, ed., *The Monetary Problem, Gold and Silver: Final Report of the Royal Commission, 1888*. New York: Columbia University Press, 1936.

———. 1893. *Report of the Herschell Committee*. In *British Parliamentary Papers: Monetary Policy Currency*, vol. 7, pp. 9–51. Shannon: Irish University Press.

———. 1899. *Report of the Fowler Committee*. In *British Parliamentary Papers: Monetary Policy Currency*, vol. 7, pp. 461–489. Shannon: Irish University Press.

Guoliang, Gu. 2004. "Redefine Cooperative Security Not Preemption." In Alexander T. J. Lennon and Camille Eiss, eds., *Reshaping Rogue States*, pp. 73–85. Cambridge: Massachusetts Institute of Technology Press.

Hall, Rodney Bruce. 1997. "Moral Authority as a Power Resource." *International Organization* 51 (Autumn):591–622.

Halper, Stephen, and Jonathan Clarke. 2004. *America Alone: The Neoconservatives and the Global Order*. New York: Cambridge University Press.

Halperin, Morton. 1974. *Bureaucratic Politics and Foreign Policy*. Washington, D.C.: Brookings Institution.

Haskel, Barbara G. 1980. "Access to Society: A Neglected Dimension of Power." *International Organization* 34 (Winter):89–120.

Heisbourg, François. 2004. "A Work in Progress: The Bush Doctrine and Its Consequences." In Alexander T. J. Lennon and Camille Eiss, eds., *Reshaping Rogue States*, pp. 3–18. Cambridge: Massachusetts Institute of Technology Press.

Herz, John. 1957. "Rise and Demise of the Territorial State." *World Politics* 9 (April):473–493.

Higgins, Andrew. 2004. "At Expense of U.S., Nations of Europe Are Drawing Closer." *Wall Street Journal*, December 23:A1, A6.

Hilsman, Roger. 1967. *To Move a Nation*. New York: Doubleday.

Hoffman, Stanley. 1968. *Gulliver's Troubles, or Setting of American Foreign Policy*. New York: McGraw Hill.

Hunt, Richard A. 1995. *Pacification: The American Struggle for Vietnam's Hearts and Minds*. Boulder: Westview.

Huntington, Samuel P. 1971. *Political Order in Changing Societies.* New Haven: Yale University Press.

———. 1993. "Why International Primacy Matters." *International Security* 17 (Spring):68–83.

Ignatieff, Michael. 2003. "Canada in the Age of Terror-Multilateralism Meets a Moment of Truth." In Graham F. Walker, ed., *Independence in an Age of Empires: Multilateralism and Unilateralism in the Post 9/11 World,* pp. 31–40. Halifax: Center for Foreign Policy Studies, Dalhousie University.

Ikenberry, G. John. 2001. "Getting Hegemony Right." *National Interest* 63 (Spring):17–24.

Ikenberry, G. John, and Charles A. Kupchan. 2004. "Liberal Realism: The Foundations of a Democratic Foreign Policy." *National Interest,* Fall: 38–49.

Inglehart, Ronald, Miquel Basanez, and Alejandro Moreno. 1998. *Human Values and Beliefs: A Cross-Cultural Handbook.* Ann Arbor: University of Michigan Press.

Inglehart, Ronald, and Pippa Norris. 2003. "The True Clash of Civilizations." *Foreign Policy,* March–April:62–70.

Isser, Stanley. 2003. *The Sword of Goliath: David in Heroic Literature.* Atlanta: Society of Biblical Literature.

Jervis, Robert. 1970. *The Logic of Images in International Relations.* Princeton: Princeton University Press.

———. 1976. *Perception and Misperception in International Politics.* Princeton: Princeton University Press.

———. 1978. "Cooperation Under the Security Dilemma." *World Politics* 30 (January):167–214.

———. 1988. "The Political Effects of Nuclear Weapons: A Comment." *International Security* 13 (Autumn):80–90.

———. 1993. "International Primacy: Is the Game Worth the Candle?" *International Security* 17 (Spring):52–67.

———. 1997. *System Effects: Complexity in Political and Social Life.* Princeton: Princeton University Press.

———. 2002. "Theories of War in an Era of Leading-Peace Power." *American Political Science Review* 96 (March):1–14.

———. 2003a. "The Compulsive Empire." *Foreign Policy,* July–August: 82–87.

———. 2003b. "Understanding the Bush Doctrine." *Political Science Quarterly,* Fall:365–388.

———. 2005. "Why the Bush Doctrine Cannot Be Sustained." *Political Science Quarterly,* Fall:351–377.

Johnson, Chalmers. 2004. *The Sorrows of Empire: Militarism, Secrecy, and the End of the Republic.* New York: Metropolitan.

———. 2006. *Nemesis: The Last Days of the American Republic*. New York: Metropolitan.

Johnston, Alastair Iain. 2008. *Social States: China in International Institutions, 1980–2000*. Princeton: Princeton University Press.

Kagan, Donald. 1969. *The Outbreak of the Peloponnesian War.* Ithaca: Cornell University Press.

———. 1991. *Pericles of Athens and the Birth of Democracy.* New York: Free Press.

———. 2003. *The Peloponnesian War.* New York: Viking.

Kagan, Robert. 2003. *Of Paradise and Power: America and Europe in the New World Order.* New York: Knopf.

Kagan, Robert, and William Kristol. 2000. "The Present Danger." *National Interest,* Spring:57–69.

Kaplan, Fred. 2008. *Day Dream Believers: How a Few Grand Ideas Wrecked American Power.* Hoboken, NJ: John Wiley and Sons.

Kaplan, Morton A. 1957. *System and Process in International Politics.* New York: Wiley.

Kaufman, Edward. 2003. "A Broadcast Strategy to Win Media Wars." In Alexander T. J. Lennon, ed., *The Battle for Hearts and Minds: Using Soft Power to Undermine Terrorist Networks,* pp. 299–313. Cambridge: Massachusetts Institute of Technology Press.

Kegley, Charles W., Jr., and Gregory A. Raymond. 2007. *After Iraq: The Imperiled American Imperium.* New York: Oxford University Press.

Kellert, Stephen. 1993. *In the Wake of Chaos: Unpredictable Order in Dynamical Systems.* Chicago: University of Chicago Press.

Kennedy, Paul. 1987. *The Rise and Fall of the Great Powers.* New York: Random.

Keohane, Robert O. 1984. *After Hegemony: Cooperation and Discord in the World Political Economy.* Princeton: Princeton University Press.

Keohane, Robert O., and Joseph S. Nye, Jr. 1989. *Power and Interdependence.* Glenview, Ill.: Scott Foresman.

Keynes, John Maynard. [1913] 1971. *Indian Currency and Finance.* In *The Collected Writings of John Maynard Keynes,* vol. 1. London: Macmillan.

Kindleberger, Charles P. 1984. *A Financial History of Western Europe.* London: Allen and Unwin.

———. 1986. *The World in Depression, 1929–1939.* Berkeley: University of California Press.

King, Gary, Robert O. Keohane, and Sidney Verba. 1994. *Designing Social Inquiry: Scientific Inference in Qualitative Research.* Princeton: Princeton University Press.

King. W. T. C. 1936. *History of the London Discount Market.* London: Routledge.

Kissinger, Henry. 2003. *Ending the Vietnam War.* New York: Simon and Schuster.

Komer, Robert W. 1986. *Bureaucracy at War: U.S. Performance in the Vietnam Conflict.* Boulder: Westview.

Krasner, Stephen D., ed., 1983. *International Regimes.* Ithaca: Cornell University Press.

Krisch, Nico. 2003. "Weak as Constraint, Strong as Tool: The Place of International Law in U.S. Foreign Policy." In David Malone and Yuen Foong Khong, eds., *Unilateralism and U.S. Foreign Policy,* pp. 41–70. Boulder: Lynne Rienner.

Kristol, Irving. 1995. *Neoconservatism: The Autobiography of an Idea.* New York: Free Press.

Kupchan, Clifford. 2004. "Real Democratik." *National Interest,* Fall:26–37.

Lake, David. 1983. "International Economic Structures and Foreign Policy." *World Politics* 35 (July):517–543.

Lambakis, Steven, James Kiras, and Kristen Kolet. 2002. *Understanding "Asymmetric" Threats to the United States.* Fairfax: National Institute for Public Policy.

Lankov, Sergei. 2007. "How to Topple Kim Jong Il." *Foreign Policy,* March–April:70–74.

Lasswell, Harold D., and Abraham Kaplan. 1950. *Power and Society: A Framework for Political Inquiry.* New Haven: Yale University Press.

Leibenstein, Harvey. 1966. "Allocative vs. X-Efficiency." *American Economic Review* 56 (June):392–415.

Lennon, Alexander T. J., ed. 2003. *The Battle for Hearts and Minds: Using Soft Power to Undermine Terrorist Networks.* Cambridge: Massachusetts Institute of Technology Press.

Lennon, Alexander T. J., and Camille Eiss, eds. 2004. *Reshaping Rogue States.* Cambridge: Massachusetts Institute of Technology Press.

Lewin, Roger. 1992. *Complexity: Life at the Edge of Chaos.* New York: Macmillan.

Lind, Michael. 1999. *Vietnam, the Necessary War: A Reinterpretation of America's Most Disastrous Military Conflict.* New York: Free Press.

Lindert, Peter. 1969. *Key Currencies and Gold, 1900–1913.* Studies in International Finance no. 24. Princeton: Princeton University Press.

Lukes, Steven. 2007. "Power and the Battle for Hearts and Minds: On the Bluntness of Soft Power." In Felix Berenskoetter and M. J. Williams, eds., *Power in World Politics,* pp. 83–97. London: Routledge.

Macdonald, Douglas J. 1992. *Adventures in Chaos: American Intervention for Reform in the Third World.* Cambridge: Harvard University Press.

Mack, Andrew. 1975. "Why Big Nations Lose Small Wars: The Politics of Asymmetric Conflict." *World Politics* 27 (January):175–200.

Mahbubani, Kishore. 2003. "The United Nations and the United States: An Indispensable Partnership." In David Malone and Yuen Foong Khong, eds., *Unilateralism and U.S. Foreign Policy,* pp. 139–152. Boulder: Lynne Rienner.

Malone, David. 2003. "A Decade of U.S. Unilateralism." In David Malone and Yuen Foong Khong, eds., *Unilateralism and U.S. Foreign Policy,* pp. 19–38. Boulder: Lynne Rienner.

Malone, David, and Yuen Foong Khong, eds. 2003. *Unilateralism and U.S. Foreign Policy.* Boulder: Lynne Rienner.

Maoz, Zeev. 1989. "Power, Capabilities, and Paradoxical Conflict Outcomes." *World Politics* 41 (January):239–266.

McGregor, Malcolm F. 1987. *The Athenians and Their Empire.* Vancouver: University of British Columbia Press.

McKinnon, John D. 2008. "Bush's Vision of NATO Takes Root." *Wall Street Journal,* April 3:A7.

McKinnon, John D., and Stephen Power. 2008. "Bush to Call for Greenhouse-Gas Curbs." *Wall Street Journal,* April 16:A1, A16.

McNamara, Robert S. 1995. *In Retrospect: The Tragedy and Lessons of Vietnam.* New York: Times Books.

McNeil, William H. 1982. *The Pursuit of Power: Technology, Armed Force, and Society Since A.D. 1000.* Chicago: University of Chicago Press.

Meade, Walter Russell. 2004. "America's Sticky Power." *Foreign Policy,* March–April:46–53.

Mearsheimer, John. J. 2001. *The Tragedy of Great Power Politics.* New York: Norton.

Milner, Helen V. 1988. *Resisting Protectionism: Global Industries and the Politics of International Trade.* Princeton: Princeton University Press.

Monten, Jonathan. 2007. "Primacy and Grand Strategic Beliefs in US Unilateralism." *Global Governance,* January–March:119–139.

Mueller, John. 1988. "The Irrelevance of Nuclear Weapons: Stability in the Postwar World." *International Security* 13 (Autumn):55–79.

Muravchik, Joshua. 2000. "American Power—For What? A Symposium." *Commentary,* January:40–41.

Nagl, John A. 2002. *Counterinsurgency Lessons from Malaya and Vietnam: Learning to Eat Soup with a Knife.* Westport: Praeger.

National Center for Health Statistics. 2007. "Deaths: Leading Causes." http://www.cdc.gov/nchs/fastats/lcod.htm.

Newhouse, John. 2003. "The Threats America Faces." *World Policy Journal* 19 (Summer):21–37.

Niou, Emerson M. S., and Peter C. Ordeshook. 1994. "'Less Filling, Tastes Great': The Realist-Neoliberal Debate." *World Politics* 46 (January):209–234.

Nolte, Georg. 2003. "The United States and the International Criminal Court." In David Malone and Yuen Foong Khong, eds., *Unilateralism and U.S. Foreign Policy,* pp. 71–94. Boulder: Lynne Rienner.

Nordhaus, William D. 2002. "The Economic Consequences of a War with Iraq." Available at http://www.econ.yale.edu/~nordhaus/iraq.pdf.

Nuscheler, Franz. 2001. *Multilateralism vs. Unilateralism.* Bonn: Development and Peace Foundation.

Nye, Joseph S., Jr. 1990a. *Bound to Lead: The Changing Nature of American Power.* New York: Basic.

———. 1990b. "Soft Power." *Foreign Policy,* Fall:53–71.

———. 2002. *The Paradoxes of American Power: Why the World's Only Superpower Can't Go It Alone.* New York: Oxford University Press.

———. 2003. "The Velvet Hegemon: How Soft Power Can Help Defeat Terrorism." *Foreign Policy,* May–June: 74–75.

———. 2004a. *Power in the Global Information Age: From Realism to Globalization.* London: Routledge.

———. 2004b. *Soft Power: The Means to Success in World Politics.* New York: PublicAffairs.

———. 2007. "Notes for a Soft-Power Research Agenda." In Felix Berenskoetter and M. J. Williams, eds., *Power in World Politics,* pp. 162–172. London: Routledge.

Onuf, Nicholas G. 1989. *World of Our Making: Rules and Rule in Social Theory and International Relations.* Columbia: University of South Carolina Press.

———. 2008. "Structure? What Structure?" Conference paper, Aberystwyth University, September 15–17.

Osgood, Robert E., and Robert W. Tucker. 1967. *Force, Order, and Justice.* Baltimore, MD: Johns Hopkins University Press.

"The Other Struggle in the Gulf." 2007. *The Economist,* September 8:16.

Pape, Robert A., Jr. 1990. "Coercive Air Power in the Vietnam War." *International Security* 15 (Autumn):103–146.

Patron, Maurice. 1910. *The Bank of France in Its Relation to National and International Credit.* 61st Congress, 2nd sess. Washington, D.C.: National Monetary Commission.

Pentagon Papers. 1971–1972. Vols. 3–4. Boston: Beacon.

Pew Research Center. 2003. "Views of a Changing World 2003." http://people-press.org/reports/display.php3?reportid=185.

Piven, Francis Fox. 2004. *The War at Home.* New York: New Press.

Platt, D. C. M. 1968. *Finance, Trade, and Politics in British Foreign Policy, 1815–1914.* Oxford, UK: Oxford University Press.

Polanyi, Karl. 1957. *The Great Transformation.* Boston: Beacon.

Prestowitz, Clyde. 2003. *Rogue Nation: American Unilateralism and the Failure of Good Intentions.* New York: Basic.

Ray, James Lee. 1995. *Democracy and International Politics: An Evaluation of the Democratic Peace Proposition.* Columbia: University of South Carolina Press.

Rice, Condoleezza. 2000. "Promoting the National Interest." *Foreign Affairs,* January–February:45–62.

Rofe, Alexander. 1987. "The Battle of David and Goliath: Folklore, Theology, Eschatology." In Jacob Neusner, Baruch A. Levine, and Ernest S. Frerichs, eds., *Judaic Perspectives on Ancient Israel,* pp. 117–151. Philadelphia: Fortress.

Romilly, Jacqueline de. 1963. *Thucydides and Athenian Imperialism.* New York: Barnes and Noble.

Root, Hilton L. 2008. *The Alliance Curse: How America Lost the Third World.* Washington, D.C.: Brookings Institution.

Rosecrance, Richard. 1999. *The Rise of the Virtual State: Wealth and Power in the Coming Century.* New York: Basic.

Rosenthal, Monroe, and Isaac Mozeson. 1990. *Wars of the Jews.* New York: Hippocrene.

Rotberg, Robert I. 2003. "The New Nature of Nation-State Failure." In Alexander T. J. Lennon and Camille Eiss, eds., *Reshaping Rogue States,* pp. 79–93. Cambridge: Massachusetts Institute of Technology Press.

Roy, Tirthankar. 2000. *The Economic History of India, 1857–1947.* Oxford: Oxford University Press.

Rubin, Barry. 2004. "Lessons from Iran." In Alexander T. J. Lennon and Camille Eiss, eds., *Reshaping Rogue States,* pp. 141–153. Cambridge: Massachusetts Institute of Technology Press.

Ruelle, David. 1991. *Chance and Chaos.* Princeton: Princeton University Press.

Ruggie, John Gerard. 1983. "International Regimes, Transactions, and Change: Embedded Liberalism in the Postwar Economic Order." In Stephen D. Krasner, ed., *International Regimes,* pp. 195–232. Ithaca: Cornell University Press.

Russett, Bruce, and John R. Oneal. 2001. *Triangulating Peace: Democracy, Interdependence, and International Organization.* New York: Norton.

Saul, S. B. 1960. *Studies in British Oversees Trade, 1870–1914.* Liverpool: Liverpool University Press.

Schmidt, Brian C. 2007. "Realist Conceptions of Power." In Felix Berenskoetter and M. J. Williams, eds., *Power in World Politics,* pp. 43–63. London: Routledge.

Shambaugh, David. 2004. "China and the Korean Penninsula: Playing for the Long Term." In Alexander T. J. Lennon and Camille Eiss, eds., *Reshaping*

Rogue States, pp. 171–186. Cambridge: Massachusetts Institute of Technology Press.

Sharp, Grant. 1978. *Strategy for Defeat: Vietnam in Retrospect*. San Rafael: Presido.

Simons, William E. 1971. "The Vietnam Intervention, 1964–65." In Alexander L. George, David K. Hall, and William E. Simons, *The Limits of Coercive Diplomacy: Laos, Cuba, Vietnam*. Boston: Little, Brown.

Skocpol, Theda. 1979. *States and Social Revolutions*. Cambridge: Cambridge University Press.

Smith, Tony. 2007. *A Pact with the Devil*. New York: Routledge.

Snidal, Duncan. 1985. "The Limits of Hegemonic Stability Theory." *International Organization* 39 (Spring):579–614.

Snyder, Jack. 1991. *The Myth of Empires: Domestic Politics and International Ambition*. Ithaca: Cornell University Press.

Snyder, Jack, and Robert Jervis. 1993. *Coping with Complexity in the International System*. Boulder: Westview.

Sorley, Lewis. 1999. *A Better War: The Unexamined Victories and Final Tragedy of America's Last Years in Vietnam*. New York: Harcourt Brace.

Southgate, Donald. 1969. "Imperial Britain." In C. J. Bartlett, ed., *Britian Preeminent: Studies of British World Influence in the Nineteenth Century*, pp. 152–171. London: Macmillan.

Souza, Philip de. 2002. *The Peloponnesian War, 431 B.C.–404 B.C.* New York: Routledge.

Sterling-Folker, Jennifer. 2000. "Competing Paradigms or Birds of a Feather? Constructivism and Neoliberal Institutionalism Compared." *International Studies Quarterly* 44 (March):97–119.

———. 2002. "Realism and the Constructivist Challenge." *International Studies Review* 4:73–100.

Stiglitz, Joseph, and Linda Bilmes. 2008. *The Three Trillion Dollar War*. New York: Norton.

"Terrorism Index." 2007. *Foreign Policy*, September–October:60–67.

Thakur, Ramesh. 2003. "UN Peacekeeping Operations and U.S. Unilateralism and Multilateralism." In David Malone and Yuen Foong Khong, eds., *Unilateralism and U.S. Foreign Policy*, pp. 153–180. Boulder: Lynne Rienner.

Thies, Wallace. J. 1980. *When Governments Collide*. Berkeley: University of California Press.

Thomas, Jim. 2008. "Sustainable Security: Developing a Security Strategy for the Long Haul." http://www.cnas.org/en/cms/?1924.

Thucydides. 1985. *History of the Peloponnesian War*. Translated by Rex Warner. New York: Penguin.

US Department of Defense. 2007. "Active Duty Military Personnel by Rank/ Grade." http://siadapp.dmdc.osd.mil/personnel/military/rg0708.pdf.

"US Military Index." 2008. *Foreign Policy,* March–April:71–77.

US Senate. 1910. *Interviews on the Banking and Currency Systems of England, Scotland, France, Germany, Switzerland, and Italy.* 61st Congress, 2nd sess. Washington, D.C.: National Monetary Commission.

von Hippel, Karin. 2003. "Democracy by Force: A Renewed Commitment to Nation Building." In Alexander T. J. Lennon and Camille Eiss, eds., *Reshaping Rogue States,* pp. 108–129. Cambridge: Massachusetts Institute of Technology Press.

Waldrop, M. Mitchell. 1992. *The Emerging Science at the End of Order and Chaos.* New York: Simon and Schuster.

Walt, Stephen M. 1987. *The Origins of Alliances.* Ithaca: Cornell University Press.

———. 1999. "Musclebound: The Limits of U.S. Power." *Bulletin of the Atomic Scientists,* March–April:1–5. http://www.thebulletin.org/article.php?art_ofn=ma99walt.

Waltz, Kenneth. 1979. *Theory of International Politics.* Reading: Addison Wesley.

Wendt, Alexander. 1992. "Anarchy Is What States Make of It: The Social Construction of Power Politics." *International Organization* 46 (Spring):391–425.

———. 1999. *Social Theory of International Politics.* Cambridge: Cambridge University Press.

White House. 2002a. *National Security Strategy of the United States.* Washington, D.C., September.

———. 2002b. *National Strategy to Combat Weapons of Mass Destruction.* Washington, D.C., December.

———. 2006. *National Security Strategy of the United States.* Washington, D.C., September.

Wilcoxon, George Dent. 1979. *Athens Ascendant.* Ames: Iowa State University Press.

Wilkins, Myra. 2003. "Conduits for Long-Term Investment in the Gold Standard Era." In Marc Flandreau, Carl-Ludwig Holtfrerich, and Harold James, eds., *International Financial History in the Twentieth Century: System and Anarchy,* pp. 51–76. Cambridge: German Historical Institute and Cambridge University Press.

Williams, Mary Frances. 1998. *Ethics in Thucydides: The Ancient Simplicity.* Lanham: University Press of America.

Williams, Michael C. 2003. "Words, Images, Enemies: Securitization and International Politics." *International Studies Quarterly* 47:511–531.

Wirtz, James J., and James A. Russell. 2003. "U.S. Policy on Preventive War and Preemption." *Nonproliferation Review* 10 (Spring):113–123.

Wolfers, Arnold. 1981. *Discord and Collaboration.* Baltimore: Johns Hopkins University Press.

Wood, Elmer. 1939. *English Theories of Central Banking Control, 1819–1858.* Cambridge: Harvard University Press.

"The World's Most Dangerous Place." 2008. *The Economist,* January 5:7.

Wright, Robin. 2008. "Since 2001, a Dramatic Increase in Suicide Bombings." *Washington Post,* April 18:A18.

WrongDiagnosis. 2008. "Prevalence and Incidence of Cancer." http://www.wrongdiagnosis.com/c/cancer/prevalence.htm#incidence_intro.

Yarmolinsky, Adam, and Gregory D. Foster. 1983. *Paradoxes of Power: The Military Establishment in the Eighties.* Bloomington: Indiana University Press.

Ziegler, Phillip. 1988. *The Sixth Great Power: A History of One of the Greatest of All Banking Families, the House of Barings, 1762–1929.* New York: Alfred A. Knopf.

Index

Abrams, General Creighton, 80, 84, 167
Afghanistan, 101, 103, 112, 124, 126, 128–130, 133, 136, 137, 141–144, 148–151, 160
Africa, 127
Alcibiades, 46, 90
Allawi, Ali, 103
Alliance curse, 77, 95
Anarchy, 176–177
Ansari, Ali, 121
Anti-Ballistic Missile Treaty (ABMT), 135, 139
Al-Qaida, 114, 118, 148
Asymmetric war and threats, 79, 82, 109, 115, 117–119, 140, 149
Athenian imperialism, 17, 37–48, 154, 156–159, 161–165, 166; Peloponnesian War, 40, 45–48, 89, 156, 157, 158–159, 161, 164–165
Axis of evil, 106, 143
Azziz al-Rantissi, Abdel, 103

Baathists, 193,104
Bagehot, Walter, 56, 92, 93
Baldwin, David, 34
Balkans, 101
Bank of England, 48, 50, 52–59, 67, 91–93, 159, 161, 163, 165, 168–171, 180
Bank of France, 54, 55, 57, 58, 91, 92, 155, 159, 165, 167, 168–171, 179–180
Barings, 58
Barnett, Michael, 36
Bechtel, 124
Beck, Ulrich, 3, 180
Berenskoetter, Felix, 1
Berlin Wall, 122
Betts, Richard, 105, 114, 115, 149
Bhutto, Benazir, 113
Bilmes, Linda, 130, 132, 150, 151
bin Laden, Osama, 114
Biological Weapons Convention (BWC), 119, 135, 140
Bland Act of 1878, 65
Block, Fred, 17
Blowback, 151
Bounded rationalisty. *See* Decisionmaking
Briggs, General Harold, 179
British finance, 48–72, 155, 157–158, 159, 161, 163, 170; managing

the nineteenth-century gold standard, 48–59, 155, 159, 161, 165; silver depreciation in the nineteenth and twentieth centuries, 59–72, 155, 157, 159, 161, 163, 165, 167
Brooks, Stephen, 146, 147
Brzezinski, Zbigniew, 105, 122, 149
Bush, George W., 99–102, 107–114, 116, 119, 124, 126, 127, 132–134, 136, 138–140, 142, 143, 146–148, 151, 152, 155, 158, 160, 162, 164, 167; Bush Doctrine, 7, 13, 99–152, 155–156, 162, 164, 167–168

Canning, George 51
Case study method, 4–6, 37, 92, 101, 102, 166–168, 174, 179; crucial cases, 5, 7, 37, 101, 174, 180; process tracing, 5; selecting on the dependent variable, 6, 166–168, 179; structured-focused comparison, 5
Center for a New American Security, 150
Chechnya, 140
Chemical Weapons Convention, 119
China, 101, 110, 111, 117, 125, 126, 140, 143, 146, 149, 152, 156, 158, 173
Clarke, Jonathan, 113, 132, 149, 151
Clarke, Kevin, 4
Cleisthenes, 39
Cleon, 90
Clinton, Bill, 107
Colby, William, 64, 167
Cold peace, 112
Cold War, 112, 123, 125, 155
Commitment trap, 77, 95
Commonwealth of Independent States (CIS), 119
Complexity in international politics, 10–15, 25, 32, 34, 72–88, 94–97, 102–114, 148, 156–157, 172–173, 176, 179; feedback, 10, 11, 18, 25, 32, 75–77, 79, 80, 83–87, 94, 95, 103–106, 108, 112, 142, 156–157, 176
Comprehensive Nuclear Test Ban Treaty (CTBT), 119, 135
Constructivism, 7, 174–179, 180
Containment, 125
Convention on Small Arms, 140
Copenhagen School, 177
Cosmopolitanism, 180
Cosmopolitik, 174–179, 180
Crenshaw, Martha, 149
Czech Republic, 137

Dahl, Robert, 1, 11
David and Goliath, 10, 13–15, 18, 19, 20–22, 24, 33–36; battle in the valley of Elah, 10, 15, 21, 36; Book of Samuel, 10, 15, 18, 20, 21, 33–36; King Saul, 18, 21, 34, 35
De-Baathification, 103, 104
De Cecco, Marcello, 94
Decisionmaking 33, 154–166; bounded rationality, 156
Delian League. *See* Athenian imperialism
Democratic peace, 30
Democratic transition, 100, 102–109, 111–114, 117, 119–124, 127, 128, 132, 135–137, 141–143, 145, 148, 154–156, 158, 159, 162, 167
Deprivation costs, 130, 131

Deutsch, Karl, 34, 179
de Wijk, Rob, 116
Doha Round, of GATT, 101
Domino theory, 123, 133
Duvall, Raymond 3

Egypt, 111, 115
European Union, 113

Feedback. *See* Complexity in international politics
Ferret force model, of guerrilla warfare, 172
Foreign Policy magazine, 150
France, 140

Galbraith, John, 16
Gallarotti, Giulio, 179
Gardner, Hal, 125
Georgia, 110, 137
Germany, 140, 150
Gilpin, Robert, 16, 19, 27, 33
Globalization, 3, 23, 30, 115, 117, 121, 123, 154
Gold standard (classical), 48–72, 168–171
Goliath. *See* David and Goliath
Guardian state, 30, 31
Gulf War, 110, 131, 149

Haiti, 143, 144
Halliburton, 12
Halper, Stephen, 113, 132, 149, 151
Hamas, 103, 108, 118, 127, 147
Haskel, Barbara, 36
Hegemony. *See* Primacy
Heisbourg, François, 149
Herz, John, 178
Hezbollah, 108, 109, 118, 127, 147
Hoffman, Stanley, 94
Hu Jintao, 149
Hunt, Richard, 84
Hussein, Saddam, 103, 104, 110, 148

Ignatieff, Michael, 152
India, 101, 117, 138, 146, 159; Indian finance pre-1914, 59–72, 93, 94, 155, 161, 165, 167
Indonesia, 127
Institutionalization of hegemony, 139
International Criminal Court (ICC), 134, 140, 141, 144, 145, 152
International relations: current state of, 2, 3, 28–31, 153, 154, 173–180; theories of, 7, 174–179, 180
Iran, 101, 109, 110, 112, 121, 126, 132, 136, 138, 140, 143
Iran-Contra affair, 127
Iran-Iraq War, 118
Iraq, 103–105, 108, 110, 111, 124, 126–133, 136, 137, 141–144, 148–151, 160; Iraq tax, 127; Iraq syndrome, 109
Israel, 103, 108, 110, 125, 140

Japan, 125, 138, 150, 171
Jervis, Robert, 7, 10, 11, 16, 29, 31, 94, 105, 148–150, 178
Johnson, Chalmers, 125, 128
Johnson, Lyndon, 73, 77, 79, 94–96, 157, 162
Jordan, 121

Kagan, Robert, 175
Kaplan, Abraham, 1
Kaplan, Fred, 101

Kegley, Charles, 115, 152
Kennedy, Paul, 16, 35, 122
Keohane, Robert, 28, 31
Keynes, John Maynard, 66, 69, 70, 91, 92, 94
Khomeini, Ayatollah, 121
Kim Dae Jung, 108
Kim Jong Il, 107, 108, 122, 134, 143, 149
King Saul. *See* David and Goliath
Kiras, James, 114, 149
Kissinger, Henry, 82, 96, 149
Kolet, Kristen, 114, 149
Komer, Robert, 85, 94, 96
Kosovo, 112, 124, 136, 141, 143, 149, 150
Kurds, 103
Kuwait, 110
Kyoto Protocol, 134, 139, 145, 146, 152

Lambakis, Steven, 114, 149
Land Mines Treaty, 135
Lankov, Sergei, 122
Lasswell, Harold, 1
Latin America, 101, 125, 127
Law of the Sea, 134, 140
Lebanon, 108, 115, 121, 127
Leibenstein, Harvey, 12
Liberal imperialism, 100, 106, 107, 120
Liberal realism, 180
Liberia, 142
Lidderdale, William, 58
Liverpool, Lord, 51
Libya, 121

Malaya: British counterinsurgency in, 85, 168, 171–173, 179
McCone, John, 95
Macdonald, Douglas, 95
McNamara, Robert, 73, 75, 82
McNeil, William, 36
Mearsheimer, John, 20, 26, 33
Medvedev, Dmitry, 149
Meji Restoration, 150
Melian dialogue, 90
Meta-power, 137, 139
Microsoft, 113
Middle East project, 111
Mission creep. *See* Overstretch
Moral hazard, 17, 19–22, 25, 32, 34, 35, 41, 43, 48–59, 64, 79, 84, 91, 92, 95, 113–122, 142, 146, 158, 162, 166, 169
Mueller, John, 29
Musharraf, Pervez, 112

Nagl, John, 96, 97, 171, 179
National Center for Health Services, 151
National Security Strategy of 2002, 134, 147, 148, 150, 151
NATO. *See* North Atlantic Treaty Organization
NATO-Russia Council. *See* North Atlantic Treaty Organization
Neoconservatism, 100, 111, 143
Neoliberal institutionalism, 7, 28, 174–179, 180
Newhouse, John, 150
9/11. *See* September 11, 2001
Nixon, Richard, 86, 96, 157, 162–163
Nordhaus, William, 131, 150
North Atlantic Treaty Organization (NATO), 73, 87, 88, 112, 128, 135–138, 140–142, 152;

Bucharest summit (April 2008), 136; NATO-Russia Council, 140
North Korea, 101, 107, 108, 110, 111, 122, 126, 127, 133, 134, 136–141, 143, 149, 152; North-South relations, 12
Nuclear Non-Proliferation Treaty (NPT), 119
Nunn-Lugar Cooperative Threat Program, 119
Nye, Joseph, 26, 28, 30, 31, 36, 91, 92, 150

Obama, Barack, 150
OPEC. *See* Organization of Petroleum Exporting Countries
Operation Plan 5030, 107
Operation Rolling Thunder. *See* Vietnam
Opportunity costs/switching costs, 130, 131
Organic democratization, 121
Organization of Petroleum Exporting Countries, 132
Over-learning from history, 110
Overstretch, 16–19, 32, 35, 37–48, 122–134, 142, 156, 166; mission creep, 16, 17, 44, 123, 128, 129, 155

Pacification, 8, 103, 105, 116, 117, 120, 171–173. *See also* Vietnam
Pakistan, 101, 110, 113, 115, 117, 150
Palestine, 110, 117, 141–143
Pape, Robert, 74, 75, 95
Paradox of peace, 138
Paris peace talks, 86
Peisistratus, 39, 43, 44
Peloponnesian War. *See* Athenian imperialism
Pentagon Papers, 75, 94
Pericles, 38, 44, 90
Perini, 124
Pew Research Center, 106, 110, 141, 142, 148
Philippines, 142
Poland, 137
Political gap, 121
Power: hard power, 4, 7, 11, 13, 17, 24, 26–33, 38, 40, 45, 48, 49, 58, 59, 77, 78, 81, 94, 100–103, 106, 112, 114–118, 120, 122, 134, 157, 162–165, 175, 178–179, 180; optimization of, 9, 174–175, 178; paradoxes of, 3, 7, 9; soft power, 4, 7, 11, 13, 17, 24, 26–33, 38, 40, 45, 48, 49, 58, 59, 64, 79–88, 101–103, 106, 109, 112, 114–120, 122, 134, 142, 147, 150, 162–168, 174–180
Primacy, 7, 9, 16, 19, 20, 34, 100, 101, 114, 115, 123, 134, 142, 147, 153–155, 158, 159, 161, 162; financial primacy, 48–59, 64, 147, 158, 159, 161–162; hegemonic decline, 4, 16, 18, 20, 153, 164
Primo, David, 4
Prisoner's Dilemma, 63
Putin, Vladimir, 112

Rational failure, 128
Raymond, Gregory, 115, 152
Reagan, Ronald, 100, 128
Realism, 7, 9, 10, 26, 27, 36, 174–179, 180, 181
Reichsbank, 51, 54, 55

"Roadmap for Peace in the Middle East," 103
Rogue regimes, 121
Roh Moo Hyun, 108
Roll-back theory, 100
Root, Hilton, 95
Russia, 101, 110–112, 117, 128, 136–138, 140, 149, 156, 158

Saudi Arabia, 111, 115, 117, 121, 131
Schmidt, Brian, 36
Scowcroft, Brent, 148
Securitization, 177
Security Council. *See* United Nations
Security dilemma, 176
September 11, 2001 (9/11), 99, 112, 114, 115, 126, 128, 134, 135, 167
Shah of Iran, 121
Shanghai Cooperative Organization, 140
Sharp, Admiral Grant, 94, 95
Sherman Act of 1892, 65
Shiites, 103, 104, 110
Silver depreciation, in the nineteenth and twentieth centuries. *See* British finance
Siniora, Fouad, 108
Six-party talks, 107, 137, 138, 149
Smith, Tony, 100
Snyder, Jack, 16, 17, 35, 88, 151
Solon, 39, 88
Somalia, 149, 52
Sorley, Lewis, 84, 95
Southgate, Donald, 62
South Korea, 108, 111, 117, 122, 139
Sterling-Folker, Jennifer, 177
Stiglitz, Joseph, 130, 132, 150, 151
Sudan, 152
Sunnis, 103
Switching costs. *See* Opportunity costs/switching costs
Synthetic neurosis, 132, 133
Syria, 109, 115, 121, 126, 127, 143

Taiwan, 125, 126, 139, 152
Taylor, General Maxwell, 73
Templar, General Gerald, 180
Terrorism, 2, 29, 99, 100, 102–109, 112–120, 122, 124, 126–128, 132, 135–137, 140, 143, 148, 150, 151, 154–157, 158, 160, 162, 167–168; index poll of 2007, 148, 149, 150
Thomas, Jim, 116, 126
Thucydides, 45–48, 89, 90
Turkey, 111

Ukraine, 137
United Healthcare, 150
United Nations, 134, 135, 137, 138, 141–143; Security Council, 135, 137, 138, 141, 142, 149, 152; Security Council Resolution 688, 141; Charter Article 51, 138
US Air Force, 126
US Army, 126
US foreign policy, 99–152
US Marine Corps, 126
US Navy, 126
U Thant, 87

Vicious cycle of unilateralism, 22–25, 32, 59–72, 134–146, 157
Vietnam War, 72–88, 103, 105, 109, 114, 148, 149, 155–160, 162–163, 164, 167, 171, 172, 173, 180; Operation Rolling Thunder, 74, 94, 95; pacification, 83, 85, 164, 167; Vietnam syndrome, 109

Walt, Stephen, 127, 147
Waltz, Kenneth, 26, 31, 33, 34
Weapons of mass destruction (WDM), 2, 99, 102–109, 111, 112–114, 118–120, 122–124, 127, 128, 132, 134–137, 141–143, 149, 150, 154–157, 158, 160, 162, 168
Wendt, Alexander, 180
Westmoreland, William, 80
Williams, Michael, 177
Wohlforth, William, 146, 147
Wolfers, Arnold, 102
World politics. *See* International relations
WMD. *See* Weapons of mass destruction

X-efficiencies and X-inefficiencies, 12, 18, 79, 82, 85, 116, 119, 152

Yassin, Shaikh Ahmad, 103

About the Book

CAN INCREASING POWER in international politics be a bad thing for nations? In this provocative book, Giulio Gallarotti argues that the answer is clearly yes—as demonstrated by a series of examples that span geography, history, and issues.

Gallarotti systematically develops the idea of the power curse and its concomitant, the power illusion. Establishing that the process by which nations augment power can produce adverse consequences, he goes further to show how, to the extent that they fail to correct for the negative effects of power, governments choose foreign policy strategies that are ultimately self-defeating. He cogently supports his theory in discussions of ancient Greece, nineteenth-century Britain, and the United States during both the Vietnam War and the George W. Bush administration.

Giulio M. Gallarotti is professor of government at Wesleyan University. He is author of *The Anatomy of an International Monetary Regime: The Classical Gold Standard, 1880–1914*.